STUCK IN NEUTRAL

PRINCETON STUDIES IN AMERICAN POLITICS:
HISTORICAL, INTERNATIONAL, AND
COMPARATIVE PERSPECTIVES

SERIES EDITORS

Ira Katznelson, Martin Shefter, Theda Skocpol

A list of titles in this series appears at the back of the book

STUCK IN NEUTRAL

BUSINESS AND THE POLITICS OF
HUMAN CAPITAL
INVESTMENT POLICY

Cathie Jo Martin

PRINCETON UNIVERSITY PRESS

PRINCETON, NEW JERSEY

LIBRARY OF CONGRESS CATALOGING-IN-PUBLICATION DATA

MARTIN, CATHIE J.

STUCK IN NEUTRAL : BUSINESS AND THE POLITICS OF HUMAN
CAPITAL INVESTMENT POLICY / CATHIE JO MARTIN.

P.   CM. -- (PRINCETON STUDIES IN AMERICAN POLITICS)

INCLUDES BIBLIOGRAPHICAL REFERENCES AND INDEX.

ISBN 0-691-00960-0 (CL : ALK. PAPER). — ISBN 0-691-00961-9 (PB : ALK. PAPER)

1. SOCIAL RESPONSIBILITY OF BUSINESS—UNITED STATES. 2. HUMAN
CAPITAL—UNITED STATES. 3. UNITED STATES—SOCIAL POLICY.

I. TITLE. II. SERIES.

HD60.5.U5M37 1999

658.4'08—dc21   99-22805

THIS BOOK HAS BEEN COMPOSED IN SABON

THE PAPER USED IN THIS PUBLICATION MEETS THE
MINIMUM REQUIREMENTS OF ANSI/NISO Z39.48-1992 (R1997)
(*PERMANENCE OF PAPER*)
HTTP: //PUP.PRINCETON.EDU

PRINTED IN THE UNITED STATES OF AMERICA

1   3   5   7   9   10   8   6   4   2

1   3   5   7   9   10   8   6   4   2
(Pbk.)

FOR MY TRUE LOVES

James Robert Milkey

"LET ME COUNT THE WAYS"

Julian Martin Milkey and
Jonathan Robert Milkey

"NO MORE TYPING!"

CONTENTS

ACKNOWLEDGMENTS

I WISH to give a special thanks to the hundreds of business managers and public-sector employees who helped me to make sense of the issues addressed in this book. Empirical research is always something of an Alice in Wonderland experience, and I thank you for letting me into your world.

The Robert Wood Johnson and Russell Sage Foundations gave generously to this project; I wish to thank Lewis Sandy and Eric Wanner in particular. Malcolm Litchfield at Princeton University Press has been a wonderful editor on every front. I also wish to thank the series editors, Theda Skocpol, Ira Katznelson, and Marty Shefter, for their enthusiasm.

Many colleagues helped me to figure out what this book is about. I wish to thank John Ferejohn, Chris Rossell, Ceci Rouse, Bob Shapiro, and Duane Swank for assistance in the statistical investigation. I am also very grateful to Jim Alt, Stuart Altman, Suzanne Berger, Linda Bergthold, Dennis Berkey, Bob Blendon, John Brigham, Larry Brown, Walter Dean Burnham, John Campbell, Peter Monk Christiansen, Bill Crotty, John Campbell, John Gerring, Marie Gottschalk, Peter Hall, Rich Harris, Christine Herrington, Chris Heye, Jennifer Hochshield, Larry Jacobs, Tim Knudsen, Marty Levin, Mike Lipsky, Ira Magaziner, Ted Marmor, Andy Martin, Eileen McDonough, Sid Milkis, Mark Mizruchi, Jim Morone, Victor Nee, Ben Page, Sofia Perez, Mark Peterson, Paul Pierson, David Plotke, Dennis Quinn, Marc Roberts, Dave Robertson, Harvey Sapolsky, Joe Schwartz, Mark Silverstein, Jim Shoch, Ben Ross Sneider, Sven Steinmo, John Stephens, Peter Swenson, Rosemary Taylor, Steve Teles, Kathy Thelen, David Vogel, Kent Weaver, Margaret Weir, Graham Wilson, Søren Winter, Alan Wolfe, and Nick Ziegler. Thanks for their research assistance go to Michael Beebe, Kimberley Webb, and Kate White.

My family will be happy to know that this book is finally finished. My mother, Mary MacKenzie, deserves a major tribute for her help in copyediting. Thanks for their enduring support and encouragement also go to Bob and Patty Martin; Mary, Jim, Mike, Joe, and Christina Kozlowski; Robin, John, Katy, Patty, Jay, and Carly Hanley; Jim, Sidney, and Lindsey Martin; Julie and John Sheerman; Evelyn and Gordon Fitch; Ruth and Bob Milkey; Joanne, Michael, and Camille Ertel; and John, Lindley, Thomas, and Dean Milkey.

Thanks also to my friends who let me sleep in their guest rooms and provided other support in innumerable ways: Kari Moe and Bob Giloth, Nora Dudwick, Cathy Boone and Peter Trubowitz, Carol Conaway,

Sarah Robinson and Sal D'Agastino, Becky Webb, Jimmy Gray Pope and Nancy Marks, Gary Humes and Kaitlan Bruin, Dave Booth and Annie Tobin, Steve and Jerrie Wasserman, Tom Blanton and Ann Lewis, Dave Zimansky, Wes and Janice Loegering, Janice Mallman, Janice and Mark Kettler, Guy Molyneux, Joanne John, the Brewer family, Florence Cohen, Jørgen Ole, and Marianne Børch.

Finally, I come to the dear members of my own little family. My husband, Jim, has been with this project from beginning to end and deserves extravagant expressions of gratitude and love, as well as the Nobel Peace Prize. My sons, Jules and Jack, came late into the project, did everything they could to delay publication, but have made me incredibly happy.

Tables are revised from Cathie Jo Martin, "Nature or Nurture?" *American Political Science Review* 89, no. 4 (1995): 898–913.

ABBREVIATIONS

APPWP	Association of Private Pension and Welfare Plans
AFDC	Aid to Families with Dependent Children
AMA	American Management Association
CARE	Concerned Alliance of Responsible Employers
CBO	Congressional Budget Office
CED	Committee for Economic Development
CFO	Chief financial officer
CARE	Concerned Alliance of Responsible Employers
ERIC	ERISA Industry Committee
ERISA	Employee Retirement Income Security Act
FMLA	Family and Medical Leave Act
FUTA	Federal Unemployment Tax Act
HAC	Health Action Council of Northeast Ohio
HIAA	Health Insurance Association of America
HMO	Health maintenance organization
HR	Human resources
JOBS	Job Opportunities in the Business Sector
MSA	Medical savings account
NAB	National Alliance of Business
NAEYC	National Association for the Education of Young Children
NAFTA	North American Free Trade Agreement
NAM	National Association of Manufacturers
NAW	National Association of Wholesaler-Distributors
NCF	National Civic Federation
NFIB	National Federation of Independent Business
NLC	National Leadership Coalition
NWLB	National War Labor Board
OECD	Organisation for Economic Co-operation and Development
POS	Point of service
PPI	Prospective Pricing Initiative
PPO	Preferred provider organization
TRAC	Tax Reform Action Coalition
WBGH	Washington Business Group on Health
WLDF	Women's Legal Defense Fund

STUCK IN NEUTRAL

INTRODUCTION

L IKE ALL classic antagonisms—oil and water, day and night, Tracy and Hepburn—business and social policy have little in common at first glance. American managers are known for their suspicion of excessive government intervention. Lockean liberalism permeates our nation's collective political thought and has kept a host of social democratic inventions off the books. The Rube Goldberg quirks of our political system give managers good reason to doubt the efficacy of political interventions. Our weak labor movement has dampened employers' incentives to support social initiatives for shopfloor peace.[1]

Yet managers have periodically shown an interest in social initiatives to enhance workers' productivity, to ameliorate labor unrest, or to augment demand for their products.[2] Today some American managers are drawn to social policies to increase investment in human capital, programs (in training, health care, and child care) considered to increase productivity by improving workers' skills, knowledge, or health.[3] Proponents claim that these policies contribute to economic growth; thus growth and equity can be achieved simultaneously.[4] As Jerry Murphy of the Siemens Corporation puts it, "Doing the right thing and the bottom line go hand in hand." Jim O'Connell of Ceridan explains this support for social policies: "Companies not only have a conscience, but in addition there's a profitability motive. . . and a feeling that companies are pursuing competitiveness."[5]

Opinion polls demonstrate that employers are interested in policies to increase human capital investment. Training initiatives to prepare workers for highly skilled jobs have attracted substantial corporate support. Sixty-four percent of a National Association of Manufacturers study were

[1] Louis Hartz, *The Liberal Tradition in America* (New York: Harcourt, Brace, 1955); David Vogel, "Why Businessmen Distrust Their State," *British Journal of Political Science* 8, no. 1 (1978): 45–78; Mike Davis, *Prisoners of the American Dream* (New York: Verso, 1986).

[2] James Weinstein, *The Corporate Ideal in the Liberal State: 1900–1918* (Boston: Beacon Press, 1968); Sanford Jacoby, *Modern Manors* (Princeton: Princeton University Press, 1997); Jill Quadagno, *The Transformation of Old Age Security* (Chicago: University of Chicago Press, 1988).

[3] Gary Becker, *Human Capital* (New York: Columbia University Press, 1964), 1.

[4] Martin Neil Baily, Gary Burtless, and Robert Litan, *Growth with Equity* (Washington, D.C.: Brookings Institution, 1993); Otis Graham, *Losing Time* (Cambridge: Harvard University Press, 1992), chap. 4.

[5] Interview with Jerry Murphy, May 29, 1996; interview with Jim O'Connell, May 20, 1996.

interested in "a national, business-run remedial education program."[6] Comprehensive overhaul of the health system enjoyed much business support before the legislative misfortunes of the Clinton health plan. A 1991 Harris poll found two-thirds of its corporate sample at least somewhat accepting of a mandated standard benefits plan.[7] One month after the Family and Medical Leave Act was signed into law, a Towers Perrin study found almost 80 percent of employers reporting positive views of these programs. In a 1992 survey only one-third of NAM members agreed with the statement, "There is no case for increased government activism in support of business. . . . government should simply get out of businesses' way."[8]

U.S. business attitudes and behaviors toward policies to increase human capital investment are puzzling in several, somewhat contradictory respects. First, given the well-documented reasons for "businessmen to distrust their state," why do managers ever support such government initiatives?[9] For example, why did employers express such solid support for Clinton's employment and training policies, Goals 2000 and School-to-Work, and continue to defend the training package even when it came under attack by the Republican Right after the 1994 election?

Second, when employers claim to have strong financial interests in a policy designed to increase human capital investment, why do they sometimes fail to lobby vigorously for its legislation? Given the early hoopla about big-business support for national health reform, why did large employers disappear so suddenly from the political arena? Given the widely noted political power of big business in America, why could these companies not succeed in forcing legislators to deliver an acceptable health-financing bill?

Third, what accounts for the enormous gap between public policy and private company benefits, and why are employers, at times, reluctant to endorse initiatives that mirror norms in private provision? For example, the Family and Medical Leave Act ratified what three-fourths of large employers already had in place, yet the major umbrella business groups doggedly opposed it for seven years, shifting to a position of neutrality only when it became apparent that the act would pass.

Finally, why has there been such great variation in employers' responses to social issues that one would expect to elicit similar reactions? The poli-

---

[6] Towers Perrin produced for the National Association of Manufacturers, "Today's Dilemma: Tomorrow's Competitive Edge," obtained from Towers Perrin, November 1991, 30.

[7] "Leaders Look at Health Care," *Business and Health* 9, no. 2 (1991): 8–9.

[8] Towers Perrin, "Family and Medical Leave Programs," May 1993; Susan Dentzer and John Bare, "They're Just Plain Angry," *U.S. News and World Report,* July 20, 1992, 48.

[9] Vogel, "Why Businessmen Distrust State."

cies are not completely comparable, but all are linked to economic growth albeit in somewhat different ways. Unambiguous ideological aversion should result in more consistent corporate responses to social initiatives.

This book takes us into the world of corporate deliberation to investigate employers' attitudes toward human capital investment policies. We find in our journey that the puzzling variations in attitudes can be understood only with attention to the institutional mechanisms that help managers to formulate their interests. Managers are more likely to support these policies when their organizations bring them into contact with the noncorporate world of policy analysis, where they are likely to encounter more positive views of government action than they do in exclusively corporate circles.

Organizational forms for thinking about public policy vary across firms and business networks. Some firms have developed government affairs departments to cope with expanding regulation; ironically, these organizational units have become a beachhead within the firm for the spread of attitudes friendly toward public-policy solutions. Some firms participate in groups to strategize about their relations with government; these have become forums for learning about policy ideas that challenge more traditional corporate views. Thus explaining employer preferences requires taking stock of the institutional resources for gathering and processing information about public policy.

Why should we care about how managers determine their preferences for public policy? I suggest that this seemingly academic exercise has important implications for the range of social policy solutions that are politically feasible in America.

Social policy initiatives have reached a stalemate today. Whether one viewed the election of 1994 as "morning in America" or the morning after, the Democratic vision of social renewal now seems all but moribund. Although the ambitious Republican Contract with America also ultimately disappointed its authors in many particulars, the GOP's Magna Carta dramatically recast the terms of the social debate. Conventional wisdom might chalk up the current stalemate in social policy to blanket business opposition, but this simplistic account is belied by a series of disconnects: between the private opinions of large employers and the public direction of social legislation, between the private rhetoric of corporate responsibility and the public philosophy of the Republican Contract, between company social provision and national public policy.

An institutional analysis of employers' preference formation helps us to understand why American managers often stop short of endorsing public policies that they seem to favor in opinion polls and that are accepted by their peers in many Western European countries. The patterns of corporate deliberation investigated in this book give insight into a central feature of business interest representation—stalemate. Despite the popular view of big business as the Goliath of American politics, the large employers most likely to support human capital investment policies are weakly organized in most areas of policy. Although large corporations often dominate regulatory politics directly connected to their core production activities, they are less well equipped to act on shared social concerns. Lacking a forum for expressing collective interests, these companies are stuck in neutral, unable to generate positions in debates about broad collective, social goods.

The Business Debate over Human Capital Investment Policy

Investment in human capital has received increased attention among managers in recent years for several reasons. First, information technology has enhanced the importance of human capital because this new technology requires highly trained workers to rapidly shift tasks; indeed, some argue that knowledge is now the greatest component of competitive advantage.[10] Technological life-spans have been decreasing rapidly since the microprocessor revolution, and this premature aging of products and processes keeps would-be competitors scrambling to stay forever young. In an era when products and production processes are changing quickly, when consumer tastes cry out for variety (operationalized as limited production runs), and when computer technologies favor the jack-of-all-trades over the assembly-line automaton, workers must possess the mental agility to adapt to their ever-changing tasks.

Second, globalization and international trade have made the U.S. economy more vulnerable to imports; in fact, it hardly makes sense to speak of a national economy when a big part of the GDP consists of imports and exports.[11] We have historically enjoyed a comparative advantage on the basis of our highly skilled, well-educated workforce, and we need to maintain this advantage to compete in upper-end product markets. At the same time globalization has increased managers' exposure to foreign human capital practices, making them aware of the comparative advantages of other systems. Many managers believe that their companies' foreign competitors enjoy unfair trade advantages due to European and Japanese governments' social and economic programs. For example, Brad Butler (CEO of Proctor and Gamble) was struck by the profound differences in skills offered by his company's U.S. and Japanese workers and

---

[10] Robert Reich, *The Next American Frontier* (New York: Time Books, 1983), 236.

[11] U.S. Bureau of the Census, *Statistical Abstract of the United States, 1995* (Washington, D.C.: U.S. Government Printing Office, 1995), 451.

convinced the Committee for Economic Development to initiate a major study of training and education.[12] For CEOs such as Butler, the experience of manufacturing abroad brought with it an increased awareness of the comparative advantages of other social systems.

Third, corporate America has been a major provider of social benefits, filling in the vacuum of a limited government welfare state, but these are increasingly costly. Where other countries have public health insurance, training programs, child allowances, and pensions, we have a patchwork system of benefits largely provided through our jobs.[13] Employers pay for about one-third of the nation's health coverage and administer plans that cover a majority of Americans.[14] Companies spent $50.6 billion training their workers in 1994.[15] These privately provided benefits add enormously to labor costs: benefits represented 18.7 percent of payroll in 1951 but were up to 38 percent by 1990.[16]

Multinational trade and the pressures for lower wage rates are making it more difficult for many companies to provide social benefits today. In 1989 the average hourly wage was $17.58 in Germany and $2.32 in Mexico.[17] For manufacturing that relies on highly skilled employees the higher costs of labor may be offset by a better-trained workforce, but the economic pressure to relocate elsewhere is still very real. Increased openness also tends to reduce public social spending; consequently, in this zero-sum context business and other groups have greater difficulty agreeing to collective positions on public policy.[18]

Although economists and managers of many theoretical persuasions worry about adequate investment in human capital, support for government policies to increase investment is by no means universal. Such policies have generated debate among both economists and managers. Although united in their desire to stay competitive and profitable in international markets, employers are divided over the road to growth and

[12] Interview with Scott Fosler, former CED staff person, November 1995. See also Kevin Phillips, *Staying on Top* (New York: Random House, 1984); Michael Dertuzous, Robert Solow, and Richard Lester, *Made in America* (Cambridge: MIT Press, 1989).

[13] Beth Stevens, "Labor Unions, Employee Benefits, and the Privatization of the American Welfare State," *Journal of Policy History* 2, no. 3 (1990): 233–60

[14] Katherine Levit, Helen Lazenby, Suzanne Letsch, and Cathy Cowan, "National Health Care Spending," *Health Affairs* 10, no. 1 (1989): 117–30.

[15] "Industry Report," *Training*, October 1994, 30.

[16] Beth Stevens, *Complementing the Welfare State* (Geneva: International Labor Organisation, 1986), 24; Joseph Piacentini and Jill Foley, *EBRI Databook on Employee Benefits* (Washington, D.C.: EBRI, 1992), 29.

[17] Robert Walters and David Blake, *The Politics of Global Economic Relations* (Englewood Cliffs, N.J.: Prentice-Hall, 1992), 129.

[18] Claus Offe, *Contradictions of the Welfare State* (Cambridge: MIT Press, 1984).

the role of social policy in this process. Many agree that world competition and rapid technological change are challenging all countries to alter their systems of social provision, as the national regulatory structures suited for the 1950s and 1960s seem inappropriate to the new rules of battle in the global, postindustrial economy.[19] Yet managers, like economists, disagree about how to revamp social supports to achieve efficiency and competitiveness.

Business advocates of a high-performance workplace (to borrow President Clinton's term) believe that government policies are necessary to increase investment in human capital. These managers generally do not want broad new programs of the New Deal vintage, preferring regulations that work through existing private markets and do not interfere with their own private programs. They believe that training contributes to productivity in developing workers' skills, important today because the return on investment in skills is roughly twice that of the return on research and development.[20] Health care makes a contribution to productivity by improving the mental functioning and physical capacities of both current and future workers.[21] Policies designed to control the enormous costs of health care are also relevant to competitiveness. Whereas the United States spent 13.4 percent of GDP on health care in 1993, the United Kingdom spent 6.6 percent and Germany 8.5 percent.[22] Programs to help workers reconcile their working lives with their responsibilities to families contribute to the cognitive development of future workers, cut down on retraining costs, and improve the productivity of working parents by reducing the absenteeism and stress connected to problematic

[19] Organisation for Economic Co-operation and Development, *New Orientations for Social Policy*, Social Policy Studies no. 12 (Washington, D.C.: OECD Publications and Information Centre, 1994); Torben Iversen, *Contested Economic Institutions* (New York: Cambridge University Press, 1999).

[20] Lester Thurow, *The Future of Capitalism* (New York: William Morrow, 1996), 77; Commission on the Skills of the American Workforce, *America's Choice: High Skills or Low Wages* (Washington, D.C.: National Center on Education and the Economy, 1990); Office of Technology Assessment, *Worker Training* (Washington, D.C.: U.S. Government Printing Office, 1990); Lisa M. Lynch, "Payoffs to Alternative Training Strategies at Work," in *Working under Different Rules,* ed. Richard Freeman (New York: Russell Sage Foundation, 1994), 63–95; Ray Marshall and Marc Tucker, *Thinking for a Living* (New York: Basic Books, 1992).

[21] Rebecca Blank, "Does a Larger Social Safety Net Mean Less Economic Flexibility?" in Freeman, *Working under Different Rules,* 161–62; R. Bertera, "The Effects of Workplace Health Promotion on Absenteeism and Employment Costs in a Large Industrial Population," *American Journal of Public Health* 80, no. 9 (1990): 1101–5.

[22] David Wilsford, "States Facing Interests," *Journal of Health Politics, Policy, and Law* 20, no. 3 (1995): 574; Carl Schramm, "Living on the Short Side of the Long Run," *Health Affairs* 9, no. 1 (1990): 162–65.

child care.[23] In addition, proponents argue that these social policies, especially when found in cooperative systems of labor-management relations, increase productivity by enhancing workers' satisfaction with their jobs.[24] Robert Reich stresses the urgency of investment in human capital: "Either the United States adjusts to the new realities of international competition and shifts its human capital resources to higher-valued productivity, or it consigns itself to a gradually declining standard of living, relative to the rest of the industrialized world."[25]

In addition, other reasons not directly linked to investment in human capital may motivate business's interest in public policies. Companies that provide benefits would like government to force their competitors also to offer them; much of the corporate debate about national health reform, for example, fixed on ending cost shifting. Some big corporate spenders (often with fast commitments to their unions) would like the government to bail them out by assuming some of the costs of social provision. Again, some automobile and steel companies sought national health reform to escape their commitments to early-retired unionized workers. Finally, some firms believe that a coherent government policy could rationalize the current system of social delivery and encourage greater provision of a collective benefit. Thus many companies seek a comprehensive employment and training policy to expand private investment in this critical area.

Other business managers prefer that government take a laissez-faire approach, worrying that social policies will only hamper competitiveness and economic growth. These managers may well recognize the importance of investing in human capital, but may believe that government will generate the wrong programs and regulations or believe that only the market can allocate resources correctly to this end. Some advocates of limited intervention by the government believe that the best course of action for both countries and firms is to cut social spending in order to lower labor costs, to reduce budget deficits, to free up investment capital, and to scale back joblessness. Other managers believe that social provision to enhance investment in human capital is necessary, but is best provided within the company without any role for government.

[23] Ellen Galinsky, James Bond, and Dana Friedman, *The Changing Workforce* (New York: Families and Work Institute, 1993); Committee for Economic Development, *Why Child Care Matters: Preparing Young Children for a More Productive America* (New York: Committee for Economic Development, 1993); Dana Friedman, *Linking Work-Family Issues to the Bottom Line* (New York: Conference Board, 1991); Allen Kraut, "Organizational Research on Work and Family Issues," in *Work, Families, and Organizations*, ed. Sheldon Zedeck (San Francisco: Jossey-Bass, 1992), 208–35.

[24] Thomas Kochan, Harry Katz, and Robert McKersie, *The Transformation of American Industrial Relations* (New York: Basic Books, 1986).

[25] Reich, *The Next American Frontier,* 267.

An Institutional Model of Business Preference Formation

The central question of this book is to ask how managers come to support government policies to foster human capital investment, in the form of public programs, subsidies, or regulations mandating private action. Corporate attitudes differ between policies and across time; therefore, one wants to know what brings some employers to decide that human capital needs require government remedies. This entails understanding how corporate players develop policy preferences and resolve to pursue those preferences in the political arena.

(It is important to reiterate that business advocates do *not* promote all social spending, but only those policies that induce investment in human capital such as training, health, and work-family programs. Similarly, this book does *not* investigate corporate opinion about all social programs, but confines its research to the same subset of the social-welfare universe. In addition, it is *not* my ambition to provide an answer to the economic disagreements, but rather to explain how the political and organizational features of business representation in America shape corporate input on economic and social questions.)

An easy first response to this question is the story already told: fierce competition in global markets has changed the interests of some employers, especially in large, export-oriented, unionized manufacturing enterprises. Managers have turned to government for broader human capital investment policies in order to improve worker productivity, level the playing field, and end cost shifting.

Although changing economic conditions explain changing preferences among some managers, they do not tell us the whole story. Some but not all employers have expressed an interest in policies to promote a high-performance workplace, and economic characteristics alone cannot predict the distribution of their preferences. Interests can be difficult to pigeonhole: firms have conflicting goals, and widespread concern about a problem does not translate into agreement about its causes and effects. Managers cannot be sure that their actions will achieve the intended outcomes. Business managers must be brought to view high-performance workplace arguments as consistent with their interests; promoters of these policies must link them to important managerial concerns such as profitability and productivity.[26]

---

[26] This is true of private provision as well, for example, a Work/Family Directions study found that companies that connected work-family issues to worker productivity were significantly more likely to provide family leave. Hal Morgan and Frances Milliken, "Keys to Action: Understanding Differences in Organizations' Responsiveness to Work-and-Family Issues," *Human Resource Management* 31, no. 3 (1992): 238, 243.

The book's central argument is that managers' preferences are deeply influenced by the organizational facilities for processing policy within their firms or business networks. To understand how firms gravitate toward such ideas as the high-performance workplace, one must examine the organizational structures that expose them to these ideas. I have coined the term *corporate policy capacity* to describe the institutional resources dedicated to gathering, processing, and disseminating technical arguments about social initiatives. Three kinds of institutional resources included in corporate policy capacity increase the likelihood that managers will adopt new ways of viewing public policy, such as programs to develop a high-performance workplace.

First, experts on policy within the firm or within the business policy network are likely to enhance managers' acceptance of human capital investment policies. These private policy professionals, largely concentrated in human-resource and government affairs departments, interpret problems to their peers and change their companies' attitudes toward public policy.

Second, a company's participation in deliberative groups exposes managers to a wide range of policy ideas. Groups provide forums to explore issues in depth, and activists use these groups to draw attention to their issues and to convert managers to their perspective.

Third, the ability to link the human capital investment perspective to other business concerns will increase a policy's acceptance; thus policy legacies from earlier public and private experiences in an issue area matter to current patterns of support. Spin doctors in the business community must present solutions in a way that does not scare off corporate backers. When presented with public-policy initiatives, managers must be persuaded that short-term, individual interventions are no longer viable and that a problem needs a collective, governmental response. Thus some benefits managers believed that national health reform was acceptable only because market reforms had proven unsuccessful.

This emphasis on organizational resources of the firm or the business policy network is not to say that money is unimportant; money matters enormously to policy debates. Small businesses and insurers raised millions of dollars to fight national health reform. But business managers themselves are often targets of these information campaigns by think tanks across the political spectrum. The Work in America Institute offers different advice than does the Heritage Foundation, but both aim to shape the corporate mind. Business associations not only lobby but deliberate. Although we usually measure business strength in terms of money and raw economic power, ideas and organizational resources devoted to promoting those ideas vastly influence how managers think about political issues.

Some readers might object to the connection made between the high-performance workplace view and policy expertise, because it could be read as suggesting that some managers ascribe to a laissez-faire perspective purely out of ideology or inertia, while others endorse the high-performance workplace view for substantive reasons. Let me emphasize that it is not my intention to disparage one side as simply ignorant and to commend the other as the guardians of scientific fact. Rather, this is a story of competing theories and an explanation of how new paradigms gain adherents. Laissez-faire thinking usually enjoys a "policy monopoly" in the business world, although at intervals this prevailing theory is challenged by alternative perspectives.[27] To understand how the challenging makes inroads into the dominant perspective's domain, one must identify the sources of information and channels of influence.

The book uses two sets of case comparisons to evaluate corporate policy capacity: a firm-level study of companies' preferences for national health reform and a policy-level comparison of corporate involvement with training, health, and work-family acts. First, I investigated the impact of corporate policy capacity on decision making in a study of a company's positions on national health reform. At the firm level a company's exposure to high-performance workplace policy arguments should influence its expressed political preferences.

I found that two of the institutional measures of corporate policy capacity were statistically significant in determining company positions on national health reform. Firms with government affairs offices in Washington, D.C., and those that participated in political groups that exposed them to a range of ideas about health-financing problems were more likely to believe that the health system needed systemic reform and to back employer mandates. Respondents were often confused about health reform before their groups studied the issue, but exposure to outside expert opinion brought them to accept a broader role for government in this area. Thus, how companies viewed their interests (and whether they bought into the human capital investment model) depended in large part on how they got their information.

Second, I explored how differences in corporate policy capacity shape the involvement of issue-specific business networks in three areas of investment in human capital: training, health, and work-family policies. Employers entered into the recent legislative campaigns over human-capital investment in very different ways. Despite the appearance of enormous corporate interest in health reform during the prelegislative period, managers quickly distanced themselves from the Clinton plan during the con-

---

[27] See also Frank Baumgartner and Bryan Jones, *Agendas and Instability in American Politics* (Chicago: University of Chicago Press, 1993).

gressional markup period. Although the Family and Medical Leave Act only ratified what many large firms were already doing, few managers publicly endorsed this initiative. In comparison the training initiatives of the Clinton administration were widely backed by large employers.

The institutional features of the business networks organized around health, work-family, and training policies were important factors in this variation. Corporate advocates brought much greater organizational resources to training than to the other two areas.[28] Thus, the *private experts* on training and health policy had more resources within the firm than work-family experts. Company training and health benefits are administered by traditional human-resource departments that often enjoy close ties to government affairs units, whereas company work-family benefits have largely been handled by newly established departments run by outsiders to the company. The issues were connected to different ideas or *policy legacies*. Training prospered in its link to education reform; work-family policy was hurt by its ties to the women's movement. The *group profiles* of three business policy networks were quite unequal in strength. A political commitment to training evolved among businesses long ago when Lyndon Johnson encouraged the formation of a corporatist-type employer association, the National Alliance of Business. No similar central groups organized managers in the realms of health and of work-family.

A National Profile of Business Deliberation

If institutional structures matter to how managers think about their interests at the micro level, they also give insight into cross-national comparisons. Individual behaviors add up to national patterns, and this exercise of investigating (and empirically demonstrating) how institutional structures shape individual deliberations gives us an improved understanding of the distinctions between American employers and their foreign peers.

Despite subnational deviations (the exceptions that prove the rule), the general institutional profile of American business makes it difficult for employers to generate collective positions on social issues. The voice of business in America is fragmented—many groups claim to speak for employers. Each industrial sector has its own trade association and often more than one. These sectoral groups are not brought together under the

---

[28] As I suggest in chapter 1, training policy remains limited from a cross-national perspective, reflecting, in part, the lack of a centralized collective bargaining tradition that has brought the social partners together in other countries to negotiate a broad training framework.

auspices of an economy-wide peak association, as in many other nations, but operate as independent agents.

This weakness in political organization means that American managers have a more difficult time finding common ground than their counterparts elsewhere.[29] Although fragmented business interests at times may take collective action to oppose undesired outcomes and to avoid a harm, it is more difficult for them to achieve sufficient coordination to secure collective goods.[30] Managers need organizational cover to take risky positions—they need to believe that their peers will commit to a social course and that they will not be punished for following it. Although a single peak association might be able to force its members to come to agreement, a structure of multiple umbrella organizations gives members the option of "exit" if they do not agree with a majoritarian position on policy.[31] Fearful of alienating members, associations resort to a least-common-denominator politics: expressing broad, inoffensive principles and but seldom taking the lead on politically contentious ventures. Thus, despite its reputation for political power, big business is so politically fragmented that its representative associations usually engage in only the most limited of political activities. As one respondent put it, "I can't tell you how many times I've sat in a room where all but one person supported a position; and if that one person objected, we didn't do it." Carol Tucker Foreman of Foreman and Heidepriem complained, "The rule of trade association politics is they must be bound by the least efficient, [least] effective member. If I'm the best company in my field, I may have more in common with consumers and environmentalists, for example, than with the guy in my industry who is the least efficient."[32]

Profiles of small-business groups offer a sharp contrast to the behavior of umbrella organizations. Despite the myth of big-business domination of public policy, these small-business associations are much better organized and more influential in debates over policy. In the old days, when the well-heeled Washington lobbyists met with strategically placed committee chairs, the medley of small-business interests who lacked charismatic CEOs or any other defining feature were often ignored. Yet the explosion of computer technologies in politics has turned former liabilities into assets for the crowd of small employers. Now small-business groups offer a readily organized mass base that can pressure government at strategic moments. Although in the 1960s small-business associations had limited

---

[29] Graham Wilson, *Business and Politics* (Chatham, N.J.: Chatham House, 1990).

[30] Thanks to the anonymous reviewer for highlighting this point. See also Thomas Schelling, *Micromotives and Macrobehavior* (New York: Norton, 1978).

[31] Albert O. Hirschman, *Exit, Voice, and Loyalty* (Cambridge: Harvard University Press, 1978).

[32] Kirk Victor, "Step Under My Umbrella," *National Journal,* April 23, 1988, 1063.

power, by the 1980s the National Federation of Independent Business and other groups had emerged as important trade associations. The vacuum caused by the weak organization of large employers has enabled a shift in the balance of business power in Washington.

Implications for Public Policy

This institutional profile of employer representation sets parameters for the types of policies that American managers support. The frailty of political groups representing large employers and the corresponding strength of small business give corporate politics a systematic bias toward the latter's political agenda. However, divisions over policy do not reduce to big versus small, for owners of small businesses are a diverse group. Many small companies oppose government policies for human capital investment, but small entrepreneurial firms with a highly trained workforce often support them. Some large companies (such as Pepsico and General Mills) that pay their low-skilled workers close to the minimum wage share small employers' concerns about the costs of policies to promote human capital investment. But the major small-business associations in Washington are quite conservative in general and especially hostile toward social initiatives that increase payroll taxes.

In part due to this balance of corporate power, recent legislation to promote human capital investment has not fared well. The United States now spends 15 percent of the GNP on medical care, yet health reform was the spectacular policy defeat of the 1990s. Until recently the United States had no mandated paternal leave and the shortest mandated maternity leave among industrial nations. An emasculated parental leave bill passed only after seven years, ultimately excluded small firms, and covered less than half of American workers.[33] Recent initiatives to promote training passed Congress but were quite limited. Thus, whereas the United States spent 0.54 percent of GDP on total public labor market programs in 1995–96, Denmark spent 6.62 percent, Ireland 4.3 percent, and Germany 3.8 percent.[34]

The story told here suggests an interesting twist to the legislative fortunes of the high-performance workplace initiatives. Many managers would like government policies to promote human capital investment; yet

[33] Francoise Core and Vassiliki Koutsogeorgopoulou, "Parental Leave: What and Where?" *OECD Observer*, August–September 1995, 15–20; "FMLA Found to Be Neither Expensive Nor Overused," *Personnel Journal* 75, no. 3 (1996): 19–20.

[34] Organisation for Economic Co-operation and Development, *Employment Outlook* (Paris: OECD, July 1997), table K, "Public Expenditures and Participant Inflows in Labour Market Programmes in OECD Countries," 184–90.

policymakers are unlikely to get much help from these potential legislative allies. Organizational weakness is the constraint against action. The relative organizational strength of the opponents (largely small business) and relative weakness of proponents (largely big business) diminish the expression of the private sector's backing for these social policies. The part of the business community most likely to support social policies is least likely to present its views effectively in the legislative process. Far from being too strong to permit the enactment of social initiatives, large employers have been too weak organizationally to act toward their expressed collective concerns.[35]

Of course other factors may have influenced the outcomes in these battles over policy. Concerns about budget deficits dominated discussions of all new government initiatives in the 1980s and 1990s and greatly constrained the options available to policymakers.[36] The initiatives discussed in this book were all proposed or supported by Bill Clinton, and the president's involvement complicates the story. Managers expressed limited support for the president and skepticism about the administration's capacity to manage its legislative agenda.[37] Health reform was cursed with a complicated plan and mismanagement by the administration and could probably have died for any number of reasons.

Despite the importance of other explanatory variables, it is important to consider the contribution of business politics to debates over policy. Although many managers viewed President Clinton with mistrust, they were drawn to the logic underlying his policies. Business inputs have an interactive effect with other influences on policymaking: rather like Nixon's opening China, business backing can lend a legitimacy to human capital investment initiatives, as happened with the training proposals. Corporate endorsements can provide cover to the initiatives, protecting them from a hostile press and making them more presentable to Republican audiences. When business managers help to fashion proposals, they can give their blessing from the outset and restrain later political attacks. Policy legislated with the strong backing of a broad spectrum of business

[35] See also Wolfgang Streeck, *Social Institutions and Economic Performance* (Newbury Park, Calif.: Sage, 1992), 77.

[36] Eugene Steurele, *The Tax Decade* (Washington, D.C.: Urban Institute, 1992); Paul Pierson, "The Deficit and the Politics of Domestic Reform," in *Social Divide,* ed. Margaret Weir (Washington, D.C.: Brookings Institution; New York: Russell Sage Foundation, 1998), 126–78.

[37] For example in March 1993 only 35 percent of managers supported Clinton, as opposed to 53 percent of the general public. "Business View of the New Administration," memorandum to Nightly Business Report Reuters Editors, from T. Keating Holland Yankelovich Partners, April 15, 1993, Roper Library, "Yankelovich Partners/Nightly Business Report 1993" file.

is generally subject to a different kind of political processing. Thus the large employers' support (or lack thereof) for policies promoting human capital investment can have an important impact on legislative outcomes.

I do not offer this story in the spirit of advocacy; this is not an argument for a political strategy of mobilizing business (or for any other kind of political tactic). But my analysis should help us to anticipate the consequences of such endeavors. In fact, activists supporting welfare state initiatives might agree with Robert Reich that Democratic efforts to court business and moderate Republicans will ultimately discourage the party's core constituents.[38]

Implications for the Political Economy

The political limitations of employers who are drawn to the logic of the high-performance workplace are bound to have an impact on economic development, but one's beliefs about the impact depends on one's view of the contending economic arguments. (It is beyond the purview of this book to assess the claims of the high-performance workplace advocates or of those who prefer a more hands-off approach by government.)

For those who desire a laissez-faire, noninterventionist stance by government, the political weakness of large employers is a blessing. Training, health, and work-family benefits will be provided in the marketplace if demand exists, and in any case provision is best left to the private sector. Followers of this laissez-faire wisdom point enthusiastically to strengths in the economic system today as evidence that government policies to push investment in human capital are unnecessary to economic health. Corporate profits have surged from 8 percent of national income in 1990 to 11 percent.[39] Unemployment has fallen below 6 percent, the lowest rate in twenty-four years, and much lower than the double-digit unemployment rates in many countries of the European Community.[40] American firms seem to have a commanding presence in international markets, and the United States continues to lead in productivity. In May 1997 *Business Week* described ours as the "wonder economy."[41]

---

[38] Robert Reich, "Up from Bipartisanship," *American Prospect*, May–June 1997, 26–32.

[39] "Deciphering the Profits Puzzle," *Business Week*, September 29, 1997, 26.

[40] Aaron Bernstein, "Sharing Prosperity," *Business Week*, September 1, 1997, 64; Commission of the European Communities, *Growth, Competitiveness, Employment: The Challenges and Ways Forward in the 21st Century*, Supplement 6/93 (Upland, Pa.: DIANE Publisher, 1995), 11, 40.

[41] "New Thinking about the New Economy," *Business Week*, May 19, 1997, 150.

In sharp contrast, advocates of the high-performance workplace view with alarm the difficulties of enacting human capital investment policies, fearing that without a national framework, the country will undertrain employees and fail to overhaul the health system. Those making high-performance workplace arguments worry that insufficient investment in human capital will depress workers' living standards. Corporate well-being has had little impact on workers, and real wages have been flat or negative since the early 1970s, so much so that the business press actually rejoiced over the *increase* in real wages in 1997—a modest 1.4 percent and the biggest rise in two decades.[42] Education and skills are an important determinant of income; thus the bifurcation of employment into high-skilled jobs and low-skilled jobs has produced a parallel bifurcation in income. Nearly a quarter of Americans were in the poor and near-poor category in the mid-1980s, as opposed to only 12.6 percent of Germans and 10.5 percent of Swedes.[43] There has also been a growth in the percentage of marginal workers in part-time or temporary jobs, positions usually without benefits or employment security.

High-performance workplace advocates also worry about the ramifications for economic competitiveness and fear that an underinvestment in human resources may make American firms in high-skilled, knowledge-intensive manufacturing sectors less competitive. Productivity growth continues to be languid, increasing only 1 percent a year over the past five years (although there has been some debate over whether the government is calculating this rate properly).[44] The United States leads in aggregate productivity, but Japan has higher productivity in key export sectors such as machinery, electrical engineering, and transport equipment.[45] While productivity grew only 1.1 percent in the United States from 1979 to 1989, it grew 2.8 percent in Japan, 2 percent in Italy, and 2 percent in France during that period.[46]

The political weaknesses of large employers may also hasten the decline of the large paternalistic firm. Many managers viewed reforming social policy as a last-ditch effort to save the private system of employee benefits. If public policy fails to bring health costs under control and to end cost

[42] "When Wage Gains Are Good News," *Business Week,* September 1, 1997, 104.

[43] Eileen Appelbaum and Ronald Schettkat, "Employment and Industrial Restructuring in the United States and West Germany," in *Beyond Keynesianism,* ed. Egon Matzner and Wolfgang Streeck (Brookfield, Vt.: Edward Elgar, 1991), 137; Lawrence Mishel and Jared Bernstein, *The State of Working America, 1992–93* (New York: M. E. Sharpe, 1993), 432.

[44] Stephen Oliner and William Wascher, "Is a Productivity Revolution Under Way in the United States?" *Challenge* 38, no. 6 (1995): 18–30.

[45] McKinsey Global Institute, *Manufacturing Productivity* (Washington, D.C.: McKinsey, 1993), 1–6.

[46] Mishel and Bernstein, *State of Working America,* 422.

shifting, firms are likely to continue to cut back their benefits. Downsizing and outsourcing are the logical directions for a once paternalistic firm that must cope with the new competitive climate and receives limited help from government.

The book is organized in the following fashion. Chapter 1 presents the theoretical argument and its relevance to social science (therefore, the lay reader wishing to skip over the literature review may proceed directly to page 33). Chapter 2 surveys historical battles over social policy. Chapter 3 begins the case studies with a firm-level comparison of business support for employer mandates in health. Chapter 4 describes the business networks organized around training and work-family policies. Chapters 5 through 7 explore how variations in the corporate policy capacity of business networks organized around training, health, and work-family issues have affected the legislative fortunes of major legislation in these areas. Chapter 8 considers the impact of the power struggle among businesses on the future political economy.

ONE

BUSINESS AND THE POLITICS OF

HUMAN CAPITAL INVESTMENT

SOCIAL-WELFARE interventions in the United States are commonly thought of as minimalist efforts to protect the destitute from the ills of abject poverty. Social programs are for the nation something like private charity for families: discretionary spending that often declines when we ourselves hit hard times. But this view neglects a subset of social policies designed to encourage investment in human capital. These policies (directed toward training, health care, and helping employees reconcile work and family) are designed to help workers cope with technological change and improve productivity.

The central problem of this book is to investigate when, why, and to what end business managers decide to support human capital investment policies. Thus the focus is on companies' endorsements of *public policy* solutions rather than on their *private social benefits*. Because corporate attitudes differ among firms and across policies, the critical question is, when do managers come to support public policy to increase investment in human capital? How do companies choose between competing economic visions? When do managers believe that these policies will contribute to economic growth?

A premise of my investigation is that business managers favor a social policy when they believe it to be in their interests. Corporate leaders with a social agenda have not abandoned the profit motive; indeed, they are just as eager for economic prosperity as their peers. They simply have the view that government can play a role in creating conditions favorable for economic growth. Specifically, they believe that selective social policies can be an asset rather than a liability to productivity and competitiveness. Thus it is important to understand the factors influencing how managers perceive their interests and options.

The book's primary thesis is that managers are more likely to support policies enhancing investments in human capital when their organizations bring them into contact with the noncorporate world of policy analysis, where they are likely to encounter more positive views of government policy than they do in exclusively corporate circles. Centrist and liberal academics, think tanks, and foundations envision a connection between government policies to foster human capital investment and economic growth that is quite different from the traditional corporate distrust of state intervention described by Vogel and others.[1] Although we usually think of corporate boardrooms and policy think tanks as worlds apart, there is considerable cross-fertilization between the two. Thus the ideas offered by the world of public policy may provide a counterweight to the ideological predispositions with which managers often intuitively greet social concerns.

Three organizational features of business augment this exchange of ideas with the broader policy world; I have labeled these features corporate policy capacity. First, a functional role for policy experts within the firm (for example, in government affairs and human-resource departments) creates a beachhead for these alternative ideas about policy. Second, a firm's participation in deliberative business groups often focuses attention on social concerns, expands contacts with government policymakers, and fosters an interest in policies for human capital investment. Finally a firm's past experiences with private and public policies, or policy legacies, shape managers' responses to social initiatives. If companies have historically recognized a role for government in an area, they are more likely to accept new social proposals. Policy legacies, like life lessons, can also be negative: failed experiments with private market interventions can push managers toward public solutions.

This chapter develops the concept of corporate policy capacity as an analytic tool for explaining the formation of preferences and political action, and locates this concept in the academic literature. I also describe the two case studies (a firm-level study and a comparison of business networks at the policy level) that provide the empirical basis for my conclusions.

First, the firm-level study determined the causal factors shaping company positions on national health reform. The dependent variable or object of explanation in this quantitative study was a company's preference for employer mandates in health. The sample consisted of randomly selected Fortune 200 companies. I met with these firms in 1993 and had follow-up contacts until the spring of 1995. Because my goal was to explore how corporate policy capacity within the firm shapes its preferences, the independent variables included measures of corporate policy capacity and a multitude of economic characteristics said to influence firms' decision making.

The second study was a comparison of managers' preferences and legislative involvement at the policy level in three areas of human capital investment: training, health, and work-family issues. The unit of analysis was the "business policy network," defined as the relatively stable universe of managers who engage in the public discourse over policy prob-

---

[1] David Vogel, *Kindred Strangers* (Princeton: Princeton University Press, 1996).

lems and their solutions.[2] This study sought to identify the conditions under which managers, having indicated individually that they support a policy, reach consensus within their policy networks and offer concrete support for their position. The dependent variable was the tangible expression of collective business support, defined as the official positions of groups claiming to speak for the business community on the issue.

To answer these questions, I investigated corporate engagement with the health, training, and work-family initiatives of Clinton's first term, cases where firms claimed publicly to have a clear economic interest in the policy but where business support during the legislative process varied enormously. I posited that the articulation of a group preference for a policy depended on political dynamics within the business networks and, consequently, examined how the institutional features of the business network in a policy area influenced agenda building and legislative engagement with that policy. My key independent variables were the institutional characteristics of the business policy networks.

Business and Theories of the Welfare State

Before turning to the central argument of the book, let us examine the scholarly literature on the welfare state and on preference formation to address two issues: why it makes sense to look at business's role in the development of social policy, and how an institutional analysis adds to our understanding of business preferences. Neither the literature on social policy nor that on business interests accounts adequately for corporate attitudes toward public policies for human capital investment, because neither considers situations in which corporate interests can be interpreted in various ways. Business preferences (with important exceptions) are

---

[2] The concept of policy community or policy network (as was initially developed largely by British political scientists) refers to the relatively stable group of public- and private-sector actors who share interests in an issue and who repeatedly interact to develop policy in this area (Grant Jordan, "Policy Communities: The British and European Policy Style," *Policies Studies Journal* 11, no. 4 [1983]: 603–15). The policy network idea differs from the early iron triangle concept in recognizing that state and societal actors influence one another and that the boundaries are more permeable than the earlier concept suggests (Hugh Heclo, "Issue Networks and the Executive Establishment," in *The New American Political System,* ed. Anthony King [Washington, D.C.: American Enterprise Institute, 1978], 88). I define *business policy network* as the relatively stable group of business managers who share interests in a policy problem and who seek to develop public or private policy solutions. Just as social-movement theory suggests that one should be able to predict levels of social activism by looking at the institutional characteristics of the movement, I believe that one should be able to predict business activism and expression of preference by analyzing the institutional characteristics of these business policy networks.

often ignored altogether in discussions of welfare state development, yet managers are often partners in social initiatives. In the following section, I attempt not to refute existing theories of the welfare state, but rather to flesh out the role of business.

First, working-class power analyses suggest that welfare states alter the balance of power between capital and labor. Countries with higher degrees of union organization and working-class participation in government through left parties have higher rates of welfare spending, less inequality of wealth, and less industrial conflict over labor's share of production.[3]

Although the model that relies on working-class power to explain cross-national differences in the welfare state captures many essential truths, some instances, in which business adversaries become allies to social initiatives, fall outside of its scope. A strong working class is only one force in favor of the welfare state; thus, control of the government by social democratic parties may not accurately predict the level of social benefits. The historical legacies of early bourgeois innovations influenced the implementation of social democratic policies after World War II.[4] Even when labor leads innovations in the welfare state, cross-class coalitions may be essential to legislative success. Labor activism may motivate managers to organize to quell unrest, but the ultimate ramification of this organization may be enhanced business acceptance of social interventions.[5]

Second, state-centered institutionalists hold that state actors take the lead in developing social policies in accordance with their own goals, beliefs, and bureaucratic interests; employers only interfere with these efforts. Thus countries in which bureaucrats have greater autonomy from business and a higher level of administrative capacity are likely to produce more universal and comprehensive welfare initiatives.[6] This approach

[3] Walter, Korpi, "Social Policy and Distributional Conflict in the Capitalist Democracies," *West European Politics* 3 (October 1980): 296–315; John Stephens, *The Transition from Capitalism to Socialism* (London: Macmillan, 1979). Stephens believes that business can be well organized as well, but it is imperative that labor is stronger.

[4] Michael Shalev, "Class Politics and the Western Welfare State," in *Evaluating the Welfare State,* ed. Shimon Spiro and Ephraim Yuchtman-Yaar (New York: Academic Press, 1983), 27–50; Gosta Esping-Andersen and Walter Korpi, "Social Policy as Class Politics in Post-war Capitalism: Scandinavia, Austria, and Germany," in *Order and Conflict in Contemporary Capitalism,* ed. John Goldthorpe (New York: Oxford University Press, 1984), 179–208.

[5] Peter Swenson, "Bringing Capital Back In, or Social Democracy Reconsidered," *World Politics* 43 (1991): 513–44; Francis Castles, *The Social Democratic Image of Society* (London: Routledge and Kegan Paul, 1978), 29.

[6] Hugh Heclo, *Modern Social Politics in Britain and Sweden* (New Haven: Yale University Press, 1974); Theda Skocpol and Ed Amenta, "Did Capitalists Shape Social Security?"

offers insights into the timing and form of policy innovations, and its emphasis on the role of ideas is a much-needed corrective to the materialist view often found in class analyses. Yet state entrepreneurship need not exclude participation by business; its dismissal of the corporate role is unnecessary to the major insights of the theory. Government actors may strategically cultivate private-sector allies in order to build support for their initiatives.[7]

Third, corporate liberal theory does investigate business support for social initiatives and identifies the economic functions served by social policies in capitalist systems. Social policies may address collective concerns of the *nation*, including economic growth and national security.[8] Business managers as a *class* may share a collective interest in social programs to curb labor militancy.[9] Individual *firms* may support regulations that impose costs on their competitors or government programs to assume excessive costs.[10] Managers may trade support of social reforms for action on other policies or seek to frame policies in their own terms.[11] Firms also offer expertise as private-sector innovators in social services.[12] At times they may join political coalitions in favor of public social spending and regulations.

Corporate liberal scholars have added much to our understanding of *why* managers support social initiatives; but lacking a model of microlevel deliberation, they tell us little about *when* and *how* managers decide that

American Sociological Review 50 (1985): 572–75; Margaret Weir, Ann Shola Orloff, and Theda Skocpol, *The Politics of Social Policy in the United States* (Princeton: Princeton University Press, 1988); Ellen Immergut, "Institutions, Veto Points, and Policy Results: A Comparative Analysis of Health Care," *Journal of Public Policy* 10, no. 4 (1990): 391–416; Sven Steinmo and Jon Watts, "It's the Institutions, Stupid!" *Journal of Health Politics, Policy, and Law* 20, no. 2 (1995): 329–72.

   [7] Cathie Jo Martin, *Shifting the Burden* (Chicago: University of Chicago Press, 1991); Grant McConnell, *Private Power and American Democracy* (New York: Knopf, 1966), 162; Jack Walker, "The Origins and Maintenance of Interest Groups in America," *American Political Science Review* 77 (1983): 390–406; Mark Peterson, "Interest Mobilization and the Presidency," in *The Politics of Interests,* ed. Mark Petracca (Boulder, Colo.: Westview Press, 1992); Donald Brand, "Corporatism, the NRA, and the Oil Industry," *Political Science Quarterly* 98, no. 1 (1983): 100–102.

   [8] John Myles, *Old Age and the Welfare State* (Lawrence: University Press of Kansas, 1989), 29, 12–13; William Graebner, *A History of Retirement* (New Haven: Yale University Press, 1980); Samuel Bowles and Herbert Gintis, *Schooling in Capitalist America* (New York: Basic Books, 1976), 193; Quadagno, *Transformation.*

   [9] Francis Fox Piven and Richard Cloward, *Regulating the Poor* (New York: Pantheon Books, 1977).

   [10] Colin Gordon, "New Deal, Old Deck: Business and the Origins of Social Security," *Politics and Society* 19, no. 2 (1991): 165.

   [11] J. Craig Jenkins and Barbara G. Brents, "Social Protest, Hegemonic Competition, and Social Reform," *American Sociological Review* 54 (1989): 891–909.

   [12] Edward Berkowitz and Kim McQuaid, *Creating the Welfare State* (New York: Praeger, 1988).

policies are in their interests. At a fundamental level business interests may be located in the patterns of industrialization or industrial structure, but assuming that corporate interests can be inferred from these suggests an inappropriate economic determinism. This literature generally agrees with Offe's claim that business interests are easily known, yet managers often disagree about the social needs for economic growth.[13] Employers may also suffer conflict between goals, wanting, for example, social benefits to increase workers' stability but fearing higher wage costs. We must understand how business interests are constructed and the role of the state, labor, and corporate associations in this process.

Fourth, corporatist scholars highlight the importance of business organizations to the fate of proposed economic and social policies. According to this view, the centralized, encompassing, unitary employers' associations found in many West European countries, labeled corporatist groups, are better able to generate class positions on political issues than the pluralist groups found in the United States. Business and labor organized into corporatist associations are more likely to engage in consensual negotiations with actors from government and labor.[14]

Despite important contributions, corporatist reflections on business's involvement with social initiatives suffers from several limitations. The theory says more about employers' collective action than about preference formation. Scholars usually do not consider their insights relevant to the U.S., as many assume that only in its purest form can corporatist organization positively affect policy outcomes.[15] The emphasis on national characteristics in most corporatist comparisons is ill suited to address subnational variation and to compare institutional processes at lower levels of decision making. Yet European integration may be challenging the autonomy of national peak associations (and social democratic leanings) of

[13] Claus Offe, "Two Logics of Collective Action," in *Disorganized Capitalism* (Cambridge: MIT Press, 1985), 183–84; Alain Liepietz, *Mirages and Miracles* (New York: Verso, 1987).

[14] Wolfgang Streeck and Philippe Schmitter, "Country, Market, State--and Associations?" in *Private Interest Government* (Beverly Hills, Calif.: Sage, 1985), 18–19; Peter Katzenstein, *Small States in World Markets* (Ithica, NY.: Cornell University Press, 1985); Colin Crouch, *Industrial Relations and European State Traditions* (New York: Oxford University Press, 1993). David Soskice, "Wage Determination: the Changing Role of Institutions in Advanced Industrialized Countries," *Oxford Review of Economic Policy* 6, no. 4 (1990):36–61; Arend Lijphart and Markus Crepaz, "Corporatism and Consensus Democracy in Eighteen Countries," *British Journal of Political Science* 21 (April 1991): 235–56; Kathleen Thelen *Union of Parts (Ithica, NY: Cornell University Press 1991).*

[15] Les Calmfors and John Drillfill, "Bargaining Structure, Corporatism and Macroeconomic Performance," *Economic Policy* 6 (April 1988): 12–61; Andrew Henley and Euclid Tsakalotos, "Corporatism and the European Labour Market after 1992," *British Journal of Industrial Relations* 30, no. 4 (December 1992): 567–86; But see also Sofia Perez, "From De-centralization to Re-organization," *Comparative Politics* forthcoming.

even the most corporatist countries.[16] Changes in the organization of work and a diversification of labor have prompted a decentralization of collective bargaining; many question whether this has also eroded the power of national groups.[17]

Finally, a recent strand of neocorporatist writing, the literature on varieties of capitalism, investigates the broad connections between social-welfare regimes, firms' strategies for economic competition, national models of production, and directions in the political economy. In addition to deriving economic advantage from physical and factor components, firms can enhance their competitive positions with institutional arrangements that encourage information exchange and consensus. Policies as varied as social-welfare schemes, systems of financing, and unemployment policies may encourage labor and management to develop close economic cooperation, increase long-term investment in skills, and enhance productivity. This cooperation may enable firms to move into market niches not otherwise available to them. Individual firms' strategies (shaped as they are by national systems of regulation) add up to national models of production.[18]

---

[16] On policy networks see Stephen Wilks and Maurice Wright, *Comparative Government-Industry Relations,* (Oxford: Clarendon Press 1987); William Coleman and Henry Jacek, *Regionalism, Business Interests and Public Policy* (Beverly Hills: Sage 1989); Jeffrey Hart, "The Effects of State-Societal Arrangements on International Competitiveness," *British Journal of Political Science* 22: 255–300; John Campbell, J. Rogers Hollingsworth, and Leon Lindberg, ed., *Governance of the American Economy* (New York: Cambridge University Press, 1991). On the debate over European integration and corporatism see Wolfgang Streeck and Philippe Schmitter, "From National Corporatism to Transnational Pluralism," *Politics and Society* 19, no. 2 (June 1991): 133–64; Herbert Kitschelt, Peter Lange, Gary Marks, and John Stephens, "Introduction," in *Continuity and Change in Contemporary Capitalism* (New York: Cambridge University Press 1999), 1–8; Liesbet Hooghe and Gary Marks, "The Making of a Polity," in *Continuity and Change,* 70–97; Peter Hall, "The Political Economy of Europe in an Era of Interdependence," in *Continuity and Change*; George Ross, *Jacques Delors and European Integration* (Oxford: Oxford University Press, 1995); Wayne Sandholtz and John Zysman, "1992: Recasting the European Bargaining," *World Politics* 42, no. 1 (October 1989): 95–128.

[17] Colin Crouch, "Trade Unions in the Exposed Sector," in Renato Brunetta and Carlo Dell'Aringa, eds., *Labor Relations and Economic Performance* (New York: NYU Press, 1990): 68–91; Jonas Pontusson and Peter Swenson, "Labor Markets, Production Strategies, and Wage Bargaining Institutions," *Comparative Political Studies,* 29, no. 2 (1996): 223–50; but see Michael Wallerstein, Miriam Golden, and Peter Lange, "Unions, Employers' Associations, and Wage-setting Institutions in Northern and Central Europe, 1950-1992," *Industrial and Labor Relations Review* 50, no. 3 (April 1997).

[18] See Peter Hall, "The Political Economy of Adjustment in Germany," in *Okonomische Leistungsfahigkeit und institutionelle Innovation,* ed. Frider Naschold, David Soskice, Bob Hancke, ad Ulrich Jurgens (WZB-Jahrbuch, 1997), 297–98; Philip Manow, "Welfare State Building and Coordinated Capitalism in Japan and Germany," paper presented at the conference "Varieties of Welfare Capitalism," Cologne, June 1998; Estevez-Abe, "The Welfare-Growth Nexus in the Japanese Political Economy," paper presented at the Annual Meeting of the American Political Science Association, San Francisco, August 29–September 1, 1996; Isabela Mares, "Is Unemployment Insurable?" *Journal of Public Policy* 17, no. 3 (1997):

This research makes an important contribution in recognizing the wide range of institutional factors that contribute to economic development, but suffers from problems similar to those of the corporate liberal tradition. The somewhat stylized discussion of the contribution of welfare state regimes to varieties of capitalism is rather deterministic. Within national models of production is much diversity. Sectors vary enormously in competitive strategies (depending, for example, on the necessary skill levels of workers), and even individual firms within sectors may choose vastly different routes to productivity. In fact, managers are aware of the drawbacks of various models of production and of the connection between government policies and economic strategies; consequently, managers struggle to change the policy context. Yet the theory does not provide us with a political model to evaluate these struggles between competing factions. My work attempts to fill this gap with a model to evaluate the political competition between factions of business over the social policies affecting future economic trajectories.

Economic and Institutional Theories of Political Action

If the welfare state literature largely fails to explain when managers support social initiatives, perhaps we should turn to theories of political action. As Hirshman points out, the scholarly debate gravitates to two views of human motivation, "the passions and the interests."[19] Those believing politics to be a matter of interests attribute motivation to economic forces; those interested in the politics of passion look to sociological or institutional forces. (I include under the appendage of "institutionalist" historical institutionalist, organizational analysis, some interest group, and social movement theorists.)

The economic approach has a short, easy explanation for political preference: it rests in the readily apparent economic interests of the individual. Managers should have stable preferences oriented toward achieving profitability and grounded in the material circumstances of their firms and industries. Although managers generally resist social regulations along with other claims on profits, companies may be supportive of or at least less hostile to social policies that hold special benefit for them, for example, that improve their market position vis-a-vis their competitors.

299–327; Stewart Wood, "Employer Preferences and Public Policy," paper present at the Annual Meeting of the American Political Science Assocation, Washington, D.C., August 28–31, 1997); Pepper Culpepper, "Individual Choice, Collective Action, and the Problem of Training Reform," in *The German Skills Machine,* ed. Culpepper and David Finegold (New York: Berghahn Books, 1999).

[19] Albert O. Hirschman, *The Passions and the Interests* (Princeton: Princeton University Press, 1977).

Thus an economic approach often infers company political positions from the economic structure of the industry in which the firm is located.[20] An economic model also assumes that problems of collective action are less serious for business than for labor, because managers have fairly concentrated interests in their area of economic production and can more easily gratify self-interests. A large firm may assume the costs of political action without side benefits, if it expects to receive so much from the collective outcome that it is willing to bear the entire costs itself. Industrial sectors with a few large firms are more likely to organize politically than those with many small companies.[21]

Institutional views make very different assumptions about preferences from economic models, taking neither preference nor political action for granted. They assume that motivations for political action are complex and may include material gains, solidary benefits such as friendship, and purposive rewards connected to the explicit cause of the group.[22] Recognizing that not all objective problems are expressed as political grievances, they argue that interests cannot simply be recognized but must be interpreted. Decision making almost always occurs under conditions of bounded rationality in which full information is not available.[23] Ideas are key to forming political preferences because ideological "frames" help people to

[20] Michael Porter, *Competitive Strategy: Techniques for Analyzing Industries and Competitors* (New York: Free Press, 1980); Alfred Chandler, *Strategy and Structure* (Cambridge: MIT Press, 1962); James Kurth, "The Political Consequences of the Product Cycle," *Industrial Organization* 33, no. 1 (1979): 1–34; Peter Gourevitch, *Politics in Hard Times* (Ithaca, N.Y.: Cornell University Press, 1986); Jeff Frieden, "Sectoral Conflict in U.S. Foreign Economic Policy, 1914–1940," *International Organization* 42, no. 1 (1988): 59–90; Ronald Rogowski, *Commerce and Coalitions* (Princeton: Princeton University Press, 1989); Lester Salamon and John Siegfried, "Economic Power and Political Influence," *American Political Science Review* 71 (1974): 1026–43.

[21] The economic approach assumes that decisions to engage in collective political action are made by rational individuals who calculate the costs and benefits of such action. Satisfying individual concerns is easier than organizing for broad collective concerns, because nonparticipants in collective struggles can enjoy the benefits of collective action without paying the costs and have reason to opt out of the group effort. Collective goods are nondivisible goods where the benefits are not allocated according to the costs. Producer interests are more likely to organize than consumer interests. Mancur Olson, *The Logic of Collective Action* (Cambridge: Harvard University Press, 1971); George Stigler, "The Theory of Economic Regulation," in *Chicago Studies in Political Economy,* ed. Stigler (Chicago: University of Chicago Press, 1971).

[22] Robert Salisbury, "An Exchange Theory of Interest Groups," *Midwest Journal of Political Science* 13 (February 1969): 1–32; James Q. Wilson, *Political Organizations* (New York: Basic Books, 1973); Jeff Berry, *Lobbying for the People* (Princeton: Princeton University Press, 1977); Allan Cigler and Burdett Loomis, *Interest Group Politics* (Washington, D.C.: Congressional Quarterly Press, 1986).

[23] James Davies, "Toward a Theory of Revolution," *American Sociological Review* 27 (1962): 5–19; R. M. Cyert and James March, *A Behavioral Theory of the Firm* (Englewood Cliffs, N.J.: Prentice-Hall, 1963); Paul DiMaggio and Walter Powell, eds., *The New Institu-*

perceive, to interpret, and to label the events happening around them.[24] Ideas shape perceptions of legitimacy and contribute to the formation of political identities, since bringing individuals to recognize collective interests depends on the reconstruction of a social, cultural, or political identity.[25] Multiple interests, intermediate goals, and uncertain causal relations force managers to think about which policies will best achieve profitability.[26] Institutionalists also challenge the economic assumption that preferences are a function of the individual and look instead to the forces transcending individuals that shape political preferences.

Institutionalists of all ilk converge in identifying three organizational characteristics that matter to preferences and to political action. First, institutional scholars analyze the internal resources and background (especially cognitive and organizational) of those within the movement or department. Social movement theorists identify the preexisting organizations from which members in a new movement are drawn; historical institutionalists explore the educational background of government bureaucrats.[27] Second, they examine the historical legacies or path-dependencies

---

tionalism in Organizational Analysis (Chicago: University of Chicago Press, 1991), Introduction.

[24] Erving Goffman, Frame Analysis (Cambridge: Harvard University Press, 1974); Peter Hall, ed., The Political Power of Economic Ideas (Princeton: Princeton University Press, 1989), 100; David Snow, E. Burke Rochford Jr., Steven Worden, and Robert Benford, "Frame Alignment Processes, Micromobilization, and Movement Participation," American Sociological Review 51 (1986): 464–81; Harry Eckstein, "A Culturalist Theory of Political Change," American Political Science Review 82 (1988): 790–91; J. G. A. Pocock, Politics, Language, and Time (Chicago: University of Chicago Press, 1989), 22, 25, 18; Celeste Condit, Decoding Abortion Rhetoric (Urbana: University of Illinois Press, 1990), 11.

[25] James Scott, Weapons of the Weak (New Haven: Yale University Press, 1985); Patricia Gurin, "Women's Gender Consciousness," Public Opinion Quarterly 49 (1985): 143–63; Alain Tourraine, "An Introduction to the Study of Social Movements," Social Research 52, no. 4 (1985): 749–88.

[26] Grahame Thompson, "The Firm as a 'Dispersed' Social Agency," Economy and Society 11, no. 3 (1982): 233; David Plotke, "The Political Mobilization of Business, 1974–1980: Do Classes Have Interests?" in Petracca, The Politics of Interests, 175–98; Neil Fligstein, The Transformation of Corporate Control (Cambridge: Harvard University Press, 1990), 1–2.

[27] Theda Skocpol, "Bringing the State Back In," in Bringing the State Back In, ed. Peter Evans, Dietrich Rueschemeyer, and Skocpol (New York: Cambridge University Press, 1985); Peter Irons, The New Deal Lawyers (Princeton: Princeton University Press, 1982); Terry Moe, "Interests, Institutions, and Positive Theory," in Studies in American Political Development 2 (New Haven: Yale University Press, 1987), 277; Doug McAdam, Political Process and the Development of Black Insurgency (Chicago: University of Chicago Press, 1982); Bert Klandersman, "The Formation and Mobilization of Consensus," in International Social Movement Research, ed. Bert Klandersman, Hanspeter Kriesi, and Sidney Tarrow (Greenwich, Conn.: JAI Press, 1988), 173–76; W. Richard Scott and John Meyer, "The Rise of Training Programs in Firms and Agencies," in Institutional Environments and Organizations, ed. Richard Scott and John Meyer (Thousand Oaks, Calif.: Sage, 1994), 228–54.

shaping participants' thinking. To this end they may look to the resolution of conflicts in organizational fields that begin path-dependent trajectories or to the prior policies that influence the form of new policy solutions.[28] Third, institutionalists assess the groups available to disseminating information, increasing trust that others will participate, creating patterns of coercion in which some participants pressure others to take action, and thereby nurturing collective action. Groups channel information, broaden political identities, and increase trust that others will join in potentially risky action.[29]

There has been (with notable exceptions) a bifurcation in the literature between those who study business and those who examine other political actors, with much of the business research largely accepting the assumptions of the economic approach and neglecting important questions about preference formation and political mobilization. Much of the business research ignores preferences altogether and focuses instead on the degree of corporate power, with some believing business to dominate and others viewing corporate actors as similar to other interest groups.[30] Debates also rage over the source of influence (direct instrumental power versus structural power) and the mechanisms for influence (political action committee [PAC] contributions versus grassroots lobbying).[31]

Those scholars of business who study preferences generally ground them in material circumstance. For example, industrial sector analysis makes an important contribution in illustrating that "business" is seldom able to speak with one voice and that firms' economic and political posi-

---

[28] Peter Hall, "Policy Paradigms, Social Learning, and the State," *Comparative Politics* 25, no. 3 (1993): 275–96; DiMaggio and Powell, *New Institutionalism,* "Introduction"; Margaret Weir, *Politics and Jobs* (Princeton: Princeton University Press, 1992); Paul Pierson, *Dismantling the Welfare State?* (New York: Cambridge University Press, 1944).

[29] Roger Friedland and A. F. Robertson, *Beyond the Marketplace* (New York: de Gruyter, 1990); Jane Mansbridge, "A Deliberative Theory of Interest Representation," in Petracca, *The Politics of Interests,* 32–57; Doug McAdam, "Micromobilization Contexts and Recruitment to Activism," *International Social Movement Research,* vol. 1 (Greenwich, Conn.: JAI Press, 1988), 128–36; Edward Laumann and David Knoke, *The Organizational State* (Madison: University of Wisconsin Press, 1987), 8–14; E. E. Schattschneider, *The Semi-Sovereign People* (New York: Holt, Rinehart, and Winston, 1960); Robert Putnam, *Making Democracy Work* (Princeton: Princeton University Press, 1993).

[30] David Jacobs, "Corporate Economic Power and the State," *American Journal of Sociology* 93 (1988): 852–81; for a rebuttal see Dennis Quinn, "Corporate Taxation and Corporate Economic Power," *American Journal of Sociology* 94 (1989): 1419–26.

[31] Ralph Miliband, *The State in Capitalist Society* (New York: Basic Books, 1969); Charles Lindblom, *Politics and Markets* (New York: Basic Books, 1977); Dan Clawson, Allan Neustadt, and Denise Scott, *Money Talks* (New York: Basic Books, 1992); David Vogel, *Fluctuating Fortunes* (New York: Basic Books, 1989); Sar Levitan and Martha Cooper, *Business Lobbies* (Baltimore: Johns Hopkins University Press, 1984); Michael Useem, *The Inner Circle* (New York: Oxford University Press, 1984).

tions vary according to the structures of their industries.[32] But these so-phisticated analyses shed little light on situations where firms have con-flicting goals, managers cannot be sure which actions will achieve the intended outcomes, and material circumstances are changing or could command a range of political preferences.[33]

Ideological arguments about business preferences avoid economic re-ductionism, yet these generally fail to illuminate situations where manag-ers are confronted with competing ideological choices. Vogel makes an important contribution in grounding managers' aversion to state power in a laissez-faire ideological tradition, in the limited role of government in industrial development, and in the absence of administrative discretion available to bureaucrats.[34] Yet his fairly static view of ideology cannot explain periods in which managers are more open to government inter-ventions. Quinn offers a more fluid understanding of ideology, arguing that preferences for macroeconomic growth strategies respond to image politics.[35] Osterman has found that companies who endorse the high-per-formance workplace ideas are more likely to provide social benefits within the firm.[36] Plotke suggests that neither ideology nor material concerns entirely explains corporate political action.[37]

Business school scholars writing in the strategic-choice tradition recog-nize that institutional variation leads firms with similar economic circum-stances to pursue different competitive and political strategies. Because companies operate under conditions of bounded rationality, organization mechanisms to process information greatly matter to strategic choice and choices of strategies create path dependencies affecting future delibera-tions.[38] But while introducing the concept of constructed interests into the study of firm deliberation, this literature insufficiently investigates the sources of information and the influence of actors outside the firm that guide strategic choice.

Business historians and French regulation theorists share with the stra-tegic-choice literature the emphasis on ideas as an organizing principle: strategic choices at the firm level can add up to national competitive strat-

---

[32] Kurth, "Political Consequences." Gourevitch considers other factors as well (Goure-vitch, *Politics in Hard Times*). See also Thomas Ferguson, "From Normalcy to New Deal," *International Organization* 38, no. 1 (1984): 41–94; Salamon and Siegfried, "Economic Power," 1026–43.

[33] Thompson, "Firm as Dispersed," 233.

[34] Vogel, *Kindred Strangers.*

[35] Dennis Quinn, "The End of the End of Ideology," unpublished paper.

[36] Paul Osterman, "Work/Family Programs and the Employment Relationship," *Admin-istrative Science Quarterly* 40 (1995): 681–700.

[37] Plotke, "Political Mobilization of Business."

[38] John Child, "Organization Structure, Environment, and Performance: The Role of Strategic Choice," *Sociology* 6 (1972): 1–22; Raymond Miles and Charles Snow, *Organiza-*

egies at the macro level. Every era offers alternative paths for economic development and ways to organize production; consequently, managers (guided by economic ideas) must sort out their interests. Thus capitalist development emerges as a product of contestation among contending business factions, which may be thought of as something akin to social movements. Legal and other institutions contribute to how actors articulate their interests.[39] My work shares these assumptions, but attempts to sort out the important institutional influences and to offer an empirically testable model applicable to different levels of analysis.

Finally, some analysts view business preferences and political action from an institutional perspective; yet these largely neglect social issues and/or have not attempted models of preference formation applicable to various levels of analysis. Harris and others have investigated the importance of government affairs departments to corporate deliberation.[40] Corporatist investigations, as discussed above, are explicitly institutional and have been quite helpful in emphasizing the uniqueness of U.S. managers from the vantage of cross-national comparison. Thus Wilson shows how the preferences of American managers reflect the limitations of a fragmented business community.[41] Sociological network analyses show that firms' positions within networks matter to their political preferences and illustrate the importance of groups to corporate deliberations. Diverging from an older generation of sociologists' emphasis on the social connections between elites, these scholars look to other "mediating mechanisms" by which class unity can be socially constructed: kinship, firm's sector links such as overlapping directorates, and political organiza-

tional Strategy, Structure, and Process (New York: McGraw-Hill, 1978), 5–29; Robert Miles, Coffin Nails and Corporate Strategies (Englewood Cliffs, N.J.: Prentice-Hall, 1982).

[39] Martin Sklar, The Corporate Reconstruction of American Capitalism (New York: Cambridge University Press, 1988); Tony Freyer, Regulating Big Business (New York: Cambridge University Press, 1992); Jacoby, Modern Manors; Robert Wiebe, The Search for Order (New York: Hill and Wang, 1967); Elliot Brownlee, Federal Taxation in America (Washington, D.C.: Woodrow Wilson Center, 1966); and Liepietz, Mirages and Miracles.

[40] Raymond Bauer, Ithiel de Sola Pool, and Lewis Anthony Dexter, American Business and Public Policy (New York: Aldine, 1963); Richard Harris, "Politicized Management," in Remaking American Politics, ed. Richard Harris and Sidney Milkis (Boulder, Colo.: Westview Press, 1989), 2161–285; James Post, Edwin Murray Jr., Robert Dickie, and John Mahon, "Managing Public Affairs," California Management Review 26, no. 1 (1983): 135–50.

[41] See the important works of comparative scholars including Graham Wilson, Interest Groups in the United States (New York: Oxford University Press, 1981); Philippe Schmitter, "Interest Intermediation and Regime Governability in Contemporary Western Europe and North America," in Organizing Interests in Western Europe, ed. Suzanne Berger (Cambridge: Cambridge University Press, 1981). Peter Swenson, "Bringing Capital Back In," 513–44; Bo Rothstein, "State and Capital in Sweden," Scandinavian Political Studies 11, no. 3 (1988): 235–60.

tions.[42] But these insufficiently differentiate between types of networks that matter, and have generally not attempted to produce a model applicable to multiple levels of analysis. In the following section I develop a model of microlevel decision making based on institutional analysis that can be applied to various levels of analysis and explicitly addresses corporate deliberations about policies for human capital investment.

A Theory of Corporate Preference: Setting the Economic Stage

In thinking about why managers at times support human capital investment policy, economic factors are a critical initial consideration but do not tell the entire story. Characteristics such as size, unionization, and labor-intensity seem to affect a company's support for human capital investment policies, because large, unionized, capital-intensive firms are more likely to provide benefits. Providers of social benefits certainly have different concerns from nonproviders. Small firms generally offer fewer benefits and have a lower percentage of high-skilled workers; therefore, they are likely to oppose policies that place any additional labor costs on firms.[43] Since small firms are often the source of cost shifting, they resist efforts "to level the playing field." With the exception of high-tech companies, small firms tend to be less involved in international markets and have less incentive to ensure that the skill levels of workers meet European standards.[44] Large and small companies often have very different cultures, just as big cities seem far removed from Main Street America.

Empirical data confirm that large and small companies in general have very different patterns of investment in human capital. Company training benefits differ enormously between large and small firms. Nearly all medium and large companies offered some training in 1993, while only 69 percent of small companies did so. Types of training also varied between

[42] DiMaggio and Powell, *New Institutionalism;* Laumann and Knoke, *The Organizational State;* Mark Mizruchi, *The Structure of Corporate Political Action* (Cambridge: Harvard University Press, 1992), 13–22; Douglas Schuler, "Corporate Political Strategy and Foreign Competition," *Academy of Management Journal* 39, no. 3 (1996): 720–37.

[43] Charles Brown, Jamer Hamilton, and James Medoff, *Employers Large and Small* (Cambridge: Harvard University Press, 1990). A similar economic divide also separates the manufacturing from the service sector. Carolyn Pemberton and Deborah Holmes, eds., *EBRI Databook on Employee Benefits* (Washington, D.C.: Employee Benefit Research Institution, 1995), "Compensation Costs by Establishment Size," 33; "Benefits Provided over Time: Insurance and Leave," 42, "Compensation Costs by Industry Group," 29–30.

[44] "Benefits Are a Substantial Component of Total Compensation," *EBRI Notes,* January 1994, 7–10.

the two groups: 19 percent of the large firms but only 2 percent of the small ones trained workers in basic skills.[45]

Large and small companies provide quite dissimilar health benefits. In 1986 all sampled firms with over five hundred employees offered health benefits, while only 55 percent of small companies had programs.[46] In a 1994 study small firms with under one hundred workers spent eighty-four cents per hour worked (5.7 percent) on health benefits, while large companies with over five hundred workers spent $1.84 (7.9 percent) on health benefits. Small companies may be reluctant to provide benefits due to their higher costs of coverage, but they are also aware that many workers can obtain coverage through spousal plans at larger firms and explicitly pursue a cost-shifting strategy.[47]

Large firms are also leaders in work-family benefits. While only 8 percent of small companies offered paternity leave in 1992, 53 percent of large and medium companies provided it in 1993. The American Management Association found that companies with fewer than fifty employees were much more likely to fear a negative impact on operational stability from the Family and Medical Leave Act (55 percent) than larger companies (28 percent).[48]

Distinctions also separate manufacturing and service sectors. Manufacturing generates 19 percent of private-sector jobs but accounts for 23 percent of wages and salaries. In 1994 the retail trade spent $2.03 an hour on all benefits for its employees, or 22 percent of total compensation. Manufacturers spent $7.03 an hour on all benefits or 34 percent of total compensation.[49]

Yet there are problems with assuming interests from the economic characteristics of the firm. Sorting companies by economic characteristics suggests a simplistic division that fails to account for significant differences. Although size seems to be important, large firms and small have huge variation. Small high-tech firms have different human capital investment needs from grocers; large insurers' interests in health restructuring are unlike those of large auto producers. The lagging profitability that drove

[45] Harley Frazis, Diane Herz, and Michael Horrigan, "Employer-Provided Training," *Elan Monthly Labor Review* 118, no. 5 (1995): 5.

[46] Brown, Hamilton, and Medoff, *Employers Large and Small,* 41–43.

[47] Pemberton and Holmes, *EBRI Databook,* "Compensation Costs by Establishment Size," 33; "Benefits Provided over Time: Insurance and Leave," 42; "On Small Business Benefits, Conventional Thinking Is Wrong," *Business and Health* 12, no. 7 (1994): 10.

[48] Pemberton and Holmes, *EBRI Databook,* "Compensation Costs by Establishment Size," 33, "Benefits Provided over Time: Insurance and Leave," 42; "AMA Survey Reveals Perceptions of FMLA," *HR Focus* 70, no. 10 (1993): 11.

[49] "Manufacturing Matters," *Modernization Matters,* May 1966, 3; Pemberton and Holmes, *EBRI Databook,* "Compensation Costs by Industry Group," 29–30.

some companies such as Chrysler to ardently lobby for national health reform made others reduce government affairs expenditures and withdraw from politics. Even within industries firms differ enormously. These limits to economic explanations suggest additional attention to the cognitive and institutional dimensions of corporate preference formation.

A Theory of Preference: Corporate Policy Capacity

The central thesis of this book is that business managers' support of human capital investment policy depends on their corporate policy capacity, or their perception of a connection between this policy and economic growth, and their ability to take action in support of this policy. Corporate policy capacity highlights the cognitive dimension in preference formation, yet it rests on the important institutional insight that preferences transcend the individual and are collectively constructed. Thus mine is an institutional model of corporate preference formation that analyzes how managers receive their information about public policy. Corporate policy capacity has three institutional components: private-sector expertise in policy, business group organization, and social policy legacies within business.[50]

Corporate Deliberation and Private Policy Expertise

First, building on the institutionalist argument that the cognitive and organizational resources of the core activists matter, a study of the development of business preferences should investigate the resources available to the primary supporters of human capital investment policy, the private experts on policy in the business world. An expansion of private policy expertise should increase receptivity to human capital initiatives, because these experts share both language and perspective with policy analysts in government and academic sectors. Laissez-faire thinking usually enjoys a "policy monopoly" in the business world, but this prevailing theory is challenged when private experts bring ideas from the external community of policymakers back to others within the firms.[51] These experts may also

---

[50] These correspond to the institutional characteristics that affect state decision-making. See Skocpol, "Bringing State Back In."

[51] Frank Baumgartner and Bryan Jones, *Agendas and Instability in American Politics* (Chicago: University of Chicago Press, 1993); Richard Harris, "Boundary Spanners, Legitimacy, and Corporate Communications," unpublished, chap. 14, 309–28.

wish to accentuate the importance of the issues over which they have jurisdiction in order to enhance their own position within the firm.[52]

Additional information about public policy may change corporate thinking, in part, because knowledge makes managers confront the complexities in social problems and solutions. Ideology, by definition, lacks nuances and simplifies experiences; knowledge introduces complexity and shades of gray where black and white have ruled before. Assuming that most business managers begin on the ideological right with regard to government interventions, a broader range of ideas about public policy should move them closer to the political center.

The stratum of private experts on policy has expanded greatly with the growth in company benefit plans, because human-resource managers must study policy to cope with the social needs of their workers. Expertise in health, for example, dates from the forties, when firms began to provide their own medical benefits. Health benefits began as a strategy by unionized companies to avoid wage increases; over time health benefits also became a way for firms to attract talented employees. The duties of benefits managers have grown with recent concerns about the cost of fringe benefits. Consulting firms offering technical assistance in human-resource issues have also grown enormously; for example, the sales of private training firms increased from $1.5 billion in 1984 to $3 billion in 1989.[53] Although there has been a reduction in the number of benefits personnel at some companies during the downsizing trend in the 1990s, in most firms benefits employment has remained at least stable.[54]

Government affairs departments are another location for private expertise in policy. The past few decades have seen enormous growth in these departments (although they have been targets for recent downsizing). The Labor Department tabulated 106,000 personnel and labor relations managers in 1983; this figure jumped to 130,00 by 1988.[55] Only 10 percent of companies had public-affairs departments in the 1960s, but nearly one-third had them by 1980.[56]

Evidence suggests that companies with a strong role for experts in public policy have different goals from those without this functional role. For

[52] Lauren Edelman, Steven Abraham, and Howard Erlanger, "Professional Construction of the Law: The Inflated Threat of Wrongful Discharge," *Law and Society Review* 26 (1992): 47–84.

[53] Office of Technology Assessment, *Worker Training,* 139, 136.

[54] The Conference Board found 37 percent of its surveyed firms reducing benefit staff, 53 percent maintaining current levels, and 10 percent increasing. Brian Hackett, *Transforming the Benefit Function,* Report Number 1135-RR (New York: Conference Board, 1995), 9.

[55] U.S. Department of Labor, *Handbook of Labor Statistics, 1988* (Washington, D.C.: U.S. Government Printing Office, August 1989), table 18, 79, 90.

[56] Post et al., "Managing Public Affairs," 136.

example, when Washington government affairs representatives determine PAC spending, decisions are more pragmatic than those in firms in which top managements provide the guiding voice.[57] Human-resource professionals have been important in bringing companies to comply with equal opportunity regulations.[58] A Conference Board speaker views as "paradoxical" "the tendency of those of us who monitor Federal regulation to get caught up in what are essentially Washington activities."[59] Putting it positively, one umbrella association staff member remarks about firm dynamics, "You need the foot soldiers—need a strong commitment throughout the firm. People usually think that if you [get commitment] at the CEO level, it's in the bag. But you need buy-in from others in the company." Edwin Feulner Jr. of the Heritage Foundation views with alarm the growing power of policy experts, which has moved some firms away from more conservative corporate views:

> [W]e apparently suffer a credibility problem with the top corporate leadership, in terms of the validity of our ideas at corporate headquarters. Sometimes this is because of the filtering process where corporate support goes through a corporate contributions office, which tends to be controlled by individuals who aren't very sympathetic to the corporate philosophy. . . . We have to remind ourselves that business is not always in favor of free enterprise.[60]

One might protest that it is not surprising that an organizational commitment to policy experts means greater willingness to buy the arguments of policy expertise. Whether companies have government affairs offices might simply reflect the deeper and more mysterious phenomenon of the firm culture: companies likely to establish government affairs offices are by definition more interested in public policy. Indeed, to some extent isomorphism, idiosyncrasy, and the simple twists of fate are as important to corporate decision making as they are to the choices of other rational actors. Firms have very distinctive cultures that influence a range of strategic choices.

Yet linking government affairs offices to a corporate pro-policy culture ignores the origins of these units within the firm. Government affairs

[57] Edward Handler and John Mulkern, *Business in Politics* (Lexington, Mass.: Lexington Books, 1982), 8, 27.

[58] John Sutton, Frank Dobbin, John Meyer, and Richard Scott, "The Legalization of the Workplace," *American Journal of Sociology* 99, no. 4 (1994): 944–71.

[59] Robert H. Moore, "Monitoring Federal Regulation," *Public Relations Society of America Journal*, April 1984, 16.

[60] Interview with umbrella organization participant, summer 1996; Edwin Feulner Jr., "Building the New Establishment," interview by Adam Meyerson, *Heritage Foundation Policy Review* 58 (fall 1991): 6.

departments were developed (largely in the 1970s) to protect firms' interests against what corporate leaders perceived as the overzealous spirit of new regulation activists in government.[61] Experts within government affairs departments were expected to protect the firm; but in the process they offered information about the regulatory setting and technical issues, and dramatically elevated collaboration between business and government. The public-affairs function, initially developed to protect the firm from excessive regulation, became the venue for co-optation by government.[62] The evolution of this new political stratum within the firm continued a trend begun with the managerial revolution of an increasing bureaucratic mentality and a decreasing separate political consciousness. Culture became less salient as issues moved beyond old left-right distinctions and were treated as practical problems. While activism may characterize a firm's culture, finite resources dictate that companies must make choices about which political issues to pursue; institutional factors may matter to these choices.

Now one must add that there is something of a paradox about all this new learning within firms: even as companies are gaining new expertise in human capital investment issues, they may be losing some capacity for action. Although the rise of policy experts within the firm expands the capacity for contemplation, it fragments business political representation at two levels, the association and the firm. Specialization within the modern corporation has provided the opportunity for more information, but at the same time professionalization of social provision within the firm has decentralized decision making, decreased the direct involvement of CEOs in many issues, and created the potential for greater intrafirm conflict between expert units. The executive as Renaissance man is increasingly hard to find. As policy experts become responsible for company positions, CEOs pay less attention to and develop less "ownership" of the issues. When issues are delegated to policy experts within their own fiefdoms, outcomes depend on the intracompany battles between units. Human-resource professionals have very different perspectives from tax experts; both sides struggle to win CEOs' support. At times there appears to be too much information rather than too little; so many technical issues must be taken into account that the easiest course of action may be to do nothing. The firm today is contested terrain. As a human-resource manager put it, "The tax staff are the ones who always bring up the objections

[61] Barry D. Baysinger and Richard W. Woodman, "Dimensions of the Public Affairs/Government Relations Function in Major American Corporation," *Strategic Management Journal* 3 (1982): 27–41.

[62] Harris, "Politicized Management," 270–75.

[to HR proposals]." In addition, human-resource managers are among those being downsized and outsourced. Anthony Carnevale reflects on the disappearing "business responsibility–type" chief executive officer:

Business is less concerned about . . . noblesse oblige—this is gone. It is increasingly the case that capital is global and people are local; so they are less interested in people. Social giving has declined. The current generation of CEOs are the ones that have been tough enough to go through all of the reorganization.[63]

In addition, the experts on policy within the firm have nourished the growing business interest in the linkage between growth and social protection; but these managers also set boundaries on the possibilities for social change. Corporate policy experts wear two hats: they are *both* bearers of the economic interest of the firm and health care policy professionals with knowledge and expertise. As expert participants in the policy debate, firm policy professionals search for broader collective solutions to problems, but as defenders of firm interests they must object to excessive deviation from the status quo. This Janus-faced perspective helps government policymakers when business professionals take technocratic views back to the firm; yet, managers' concerns also constrict options. The contrary nature of these two motivating factors confuses the role of business in public policy.

Corporate Deliberation and Policy Legacies

Second, business support for social initiatives is shaped by prior corporate experiences with private benefits and government policies, or policy legacies.[64] Thus far I have suggested that increasing corporate policy capacity makes business political positions more supportive of government intervention, but policy legacies may move managers in either positive or negative directions, depending on the success of prior experiments.

Prior *positive* experiences with government regulations or programs make it easier for managers to accept new social regulations. Once government intervention in a given area has been deemed legitimate, future deliberations can be more narrowly delimited to questions of means and strategy.[65] In the same way, the private sector's dominance of social provi-

[63] Interview with Anthony Carnevale, February 22, 1996.

[64] Miles, *Coffin Nails;* John Childs, "Organization Structure, Environment, and Performance," *Sociology* 6 (1972): 1–22; Sandra Suarez, "Lessons Learned," *Polity,* forthcoming.

[65] Ann Shola Orloff and Eric Parker, "Business and Social Policy in Canada and the United States, 1920–1940," *Comparative Social Research* 12 (1990): 295–339.

sion makes it difficult to suddenly shift to a public program. The cross-national comparisons discussed in chapter 2 illustrate how important initial corporate responses can be to future social legislation. Past policy legacies contribute to current patterns of vested interests, making us reluctant to give up what we have for the promise of what might be. The proverbial bird in the hand works against radical action.

Conversely, *negative* experiences with public or private welfare plans influence future deliberations.[66] When managers believe that prior intervention by the state has not accomplished its goal, they may advocate private solutions. Likewise, when private welfare plans fail, firms may move toward government solutions. In the case of health reform, managers became increasingly frustrated with company interventions to control health costs and finally moved in desperation toward a government reform. Historically contingent policy legacies have limited predictive powers, but they shed light on many idiosyncratic characteristics of policy realms.

New directions in social provision often have a faddish quality, as managers become collectively impressed by a policy proposal or private-sector innovation. As one manager put it, "There is a tendency to follow the leader out of necessity, since no one wants to let the other guy get the competitive advantage." Another reminisced about health reform, "It's amazing that you can have such fervor and then it goes away and everybody focuses on the O. J. Simpson trial."[67] Like other people, business managers go through cycles of enthusiasm about reform.[68]

Legacies of private provision have been *both* a source of corporate support for public policies to increase human capital investment and a limit on the scope and level of government initiatives. Private provision of a benefit sensitizes business managers to a problem but makes it harder to move to public programs or to overhaul of the system. In the process of offering benefits, corporate managers develop greater technical understanding of the social problem; therefore, they urge government to take action in this area, and state initiatives often happen where employers have paved the way.[69] But at the same time the legacy of private-sector provision of a social benefit often prevents managers from endorsing comprehensive public-sector reforms; company experts have a vested interest in the status quo. Thus employers often advocate a dual system of provi-

[66] Theda Skocpol, *Protecting Soldiers and Mothers* (Cambridge: Harvard University Press, 1992),

[67] Interviews with managers in October 1992 and May 1995.

[68] James Morone, *The Democratic Wish* (New York: Basic Books, 1990); Massimo Paci, "Long Waves in the Development of Welfare Systems," in *Changing Boundaries of the Political,* ed. Charles Maier (New York: Cambridge University Press, 1987), 179–99.

[69] Berkowitz and McQuaid, *Creating the Welfare State.*

sion, with state social policies relegated to residual populations, means-tested standards, or limited social insurance that allows private providers to continue to play a role.

Group Organization and Corporate Policy Capacity

Finally, corporate policy capacity expands with a high degree of organization in the business community. Groups encourage employer support for social policy in two ways: in getting human capital investment on the business agenda and in influencing how managers engage with the legislative process.

Groups are critical to the cognitive processes that shape preferences, in channeling the new ideas that change people's perceptions of their interests and in fostering broader political identities. Thus groups not only represent their members' interests, but also shape their preferences.[70] For example, firms underwent a collective rethinking in the 1980s with regards to health costs, as images of hypochondriac workers and unimaginative benefits managers were replaced with those of perverse incentives in the broader health system. Groups also constitute resources in movements to put an issue on the public agenda; a tightly run organization and an outpouring of people power compensate for other deficits in the movement's ledger.[71] Participation in groups has been shown to increase dramatically participation in other campaign activity.[72]

Specific patterns of business association affect how employers enter into national legislative debates. Corporatist scholars suggest that characteristics of business organizations such as scope, exclusivity, and degree of centralization influence how national business communities engage in political processes and unify to achieve collective goals. According to this view, West European corporatist associations are more centralized, more encompassing, less voluntary, and less competitive than their U.S. counterparts and are thereby better able to promote collective action for shared

[70] John Turner, "Towards a Cognitive Redefinition of the Social Group," in *Social Identity and Intergroup Relations,* ed. Henri Tajfel (New York: Cambridge University Press, 1982), 21, 27; Curtis Grimm and John Holcomb, "Choices among Encompassing Organizations: Business and the Budget Deficit," in *Business Strategy and Public Policy,* ed. Alfred Marcus, Allen Kaufman, and David Beam (New York: Quorum Books, 1987), 105–18.

[71] Linda Bergthold, *Purchasing Power in Health* (New Brunswick, N.J.: Rutgers University Press, 1990); McAdam, *Political Process.* Relations among firms within groups are certainly not the only way companies are connected. Firms also exchange information at the board level; indeed, corporate interlocks are another unifying force within the business community (Useem, *The Inner Circle*).

[72] Phillip Pollock, "Organizations as Agents of Mobilization, *American Journal of Political Science* 26 (August 1982): 485–503.

goals.[73] Social benefits are (in part) collective goods, and groups encourage members to donate resources to these larger political efforts. On a cognitive dimension, these corporatist associations help their members to support collective goods by focusing participants' attention on their broader, shared concerns. On a behavioral dimension, peak associations adjudicate among conflicting demands: often large, technologically advanced, export sectors can force traditionalists in the small-business sectors to go along with a program of social reform. Members do not have the luxury of leaving and joining another group, should the association not satisfy narrow policy demands, thus giving the association the power to unify corporate preferences. At an emotional level, corporatist groups overcome the limits to collective action by binding firms to negotiated decisions and bringing members to trust that they will not be punished for being committed to longer-term investments in human capital. Thus, the limits to collective action are overcome by trust developed in social networks.[74]

Conventional wisdom has it that a weak business community means more social provision because strong employers defeat social initiatives, but if corporatist scholars are correct, well-organized managers are more likely to favor broad welfare states.[75] As chapter 2 points out, managers in countries with early business political centralization often participated in the creation of government social programs. Centralized associations permitted a broader vision of the needs of society, and modernizing sectors could discipline traditional sectors; consequently, these business communities were more likely to accept government programs that had an equal impact across the economy. In countries with less business centralization many sectors (especially small business) opposed social reforms and prevented the legislation of comprehensive programs. In nations with greater intrabusiness conflict the motivation for some sectors to join forces with government or labor leaders to support social reforms is less likely to be a broad vision of the policy's contribution to growth, than a self-interested desire to impose equal costs on competitors or to gain selective benefits. The policies likely to attract such corporate favor usually take the form of targeted programs with selective benefits.

[73] Graham Wilson, "American Business and Politics," in Cigler and Loomis, *Interest Group Politics,* 227–31; Timothy McKeown, "The Epidemiology of Corporate PAC Formation, 1975–1984," *Journal of Economic Behavior and Organization* 24 (1994): 153–68; William Coleman, *Business and Politics* (Toronto: University of Toronto Press, 1988).

[74] Wolfgang Streeck, "Between Pluralism and Corporatism: German Business Associations and the State," *Journal of Public Policy* 3, no. 3 (1983): 265–84; Rothstein, "State and Capital," 235–60.

[75] For the former view see Castles, *Social Democratic Image;* for the latter see Streeck, *Social Institutions,* 77; Harold Wilensky, *The "New Corporatism," Centralization, and the Welfare State* (Beverly Hills, Calif.: Sage, 1976), 23–25.

One must make some caveats about corporate policy capacity. Not all economic periods are equally advantageous to the expression of social concerns. When business managers fear economic downturns, they are less likely to tolerate social goals that interfere with short-term profitability.[76] Worries about immediate hard times may take priority over concerns about human capital investment and drown out the voices of experts on policy within firms. Especially in the United States, where most companies get their investment capital from the stock exchange, short-term concerns about the financial profiles can shift CEOs' attention from long-term interests in human capital investment.[77] This does not negate the logic of corporate policy capacity, but only means that economic conditions can suppress its significance.

Thus far we have neglected the state's role in shaping corporate interests, but business organization does not happen in a vacuum. Government is essential to the story of employer political activism because state actors and structures influence how managers organize. Four aspects of government influence the expression of employers' political concerns, two shaping business representation generally and two being relevant to policy distinctions.

First, the broad institutional structures of government have an impact on how managers enter into the political process and go far in explaining cross-national differences in the behavior of employers. State fragmentation (separation of powers, federalism, and coalition party rule) generally translates into greater business fragmentation because managers can try to influence successive veto points until they find a sympathetic hearing.[78] When access to government deliberations is limited, managers must discipline themselves to achieve success in their few opportunities for input.

Second, historical business regulations have shaped group organization and engagement in politics. Many governments formally recognize peak employers associations as the legitimate representatives of their members, thus binding employers to policy outcomes and enabling these groups to transcend the limits of pluralism.[79] These peak associations can help employers to generate industry-wide positions on public policy that are more enduring than the epiphenomenal business inputs one finds in countries without formal structures for corporate involvement.

[76] Vogel, *Fluctuating Fortunes.*

[77] Dertuzos et al., *Made in America.*

[78] Dietrich Rueschemeyer, Evelyn Huber, and John Stephens, *Capitalist Development and Democracy* (Chicago: University of Chicago Press, 1992); Coleman, *Business and Politics.*

[79] Gerhard Lembruch, "Concertation and the Structure of Corporatist Networks," in Goldthorp, *Order and Conflict,* 60–80. Labor may also bring managers to unify. John Bowman, "When Workers Organize Capitalists," *Politics & Society* 14, no. 3 (1985): 289–327.

Third, specific pieces of policy matter to the activism of employers. In the short term the details of specific proposals must be both politically feasible and sufficiently different from the status quo to solve the problem. Policies are more politically feasible to employers when packaged as technical adjustments to (rather than as ideological attacks on) core market principles, compatible with private initiatives, and voluntaristic.[80] In the long term, patterns of public policy divide interest groups in subsequent political battles. Thus the U.S. mixed system of social provision with participation from both the private and public sectors means that citizens' interests will be more diverse than they are in countries with universal programs and influences how citizens pursue their collective goals.[81]

Finally, politicians' political strategies vis-a-vis employers influence corporate mobilization, in some cases giving rise to comprehensive policy-level groups. Weak labor and party organization in the United States means that policy entrepreneurs have not been able to rely solely on working-class support for social initiatives but have been forced to bring in other allies.[82] By bringing managers into broad-based coalitions, political leaders may help to overcome some of the fragmentation in the business community. When politicians organize business from the top down, they can sometimes leverage corporate participants into restraining their narrow concerns for a larger goal and can shift the debate to a higher level.[83]

Politicians' strategies may shape the manner in which managers articulate their preferences for policy. Top-down coalitions that focus on broad themes and negotiate between difficult trade-offs change how business participants view their options. Divided government can influence both the *degree* of business leverage and the *kind* of corporate preferences expressed. Institutional rivalry between parties and branches can motivate political leaders to seek out the help of business by using corporate leaders to bolster their positions with skeptical legislators. When weak congressional parties frustrate executive leadership in policymaking, presidents may solicit outside assistance to help push their initiatives through Congress.[84] But partisan conflict may make it more difficult for a leader to build corporate consensus. During bidding wars, highly competitive parties seek to attract corporate sponsors with concessions, and managers

[80] Martin Rein, *Enterprise and Social Benefits after Communism* (New York: Cambridge University Press, 1997).

[81] Weir, *Politics and Jobs.*

[82] Rueschemeyer, Huber, and Stephens, *Capitalist Development and Democracy.*

[83] Martin, *Shifting the Burden;* McConnell, *Private Power;* Peter Katzenstein, *Between Power and Plenty* (Madison: University of Wisconsin Press, 1978), 17; Peterson, "Interest Mobilization."

[84] Benjamin Ginsburg and Martin Shefter, *Politics by Other Means* (New York: Basic Books, 1990).

can search until they find a politician or bureaucrat amenable to their concerns. In these frenzies of legislative deal-making, the two parties offer ever more generous concessions to special interests in exchange for endorsement of the bill.[85]

The politics of bipartisanship has a very different role for corporate players. During periods of partisan cooperation, when there is agreement about policy goals and willingness to share credit for legislative accomplishments, the multiple veto points are not very useful and managers are unable to divide and conquer. Party leaders may "circle the wagons" to keep all private interests at bay; or they may bring business participants into bipartisan coalitions supporting their legislative initiatives.[86]

Case Comparisons: Investigating Corporate Policy Capacity

Employer associations in the United States generally fare badly in corporatist measures of associational power, and one might assume that American business has little to offer to political initiatives that promote investment in human capital.[87] These widely noted, national-level incapacities in business organization, however, do not account for all variation in employers' political lives. One finds important deviations from the national pattern in the policy-specific groups that organize a broad spectrum of businesses concerned with the issues the group addresses. Consequently, at the policy level one occasionally finds broad-based groups that dominate the issue, resemble national peak associations within their narrow field, and enjoy formal or informal recognition as the legitimate representatives for their concerns. These policy-level groups must justify their existence, and their claim to fame is a greater capacity for political action. Thus, they may be more willing to take positions that alienate some members and, like corporatist organizations in other countries, may attempt to discipline their business members to present a unified voice. Thus, centrally positioned business groups may suspend the general tendencies in the United States toward fragmentation and a least-common-denominator business politics.

[85] Parties engage in bidding wars when each side wants to win but will not share victory with the other party due to disagreement on policy goals or competition for glory. Bidding wars typically happen in tax, trade, and other areas of policy with many selective benefits; but they have an impact on social policies in that they often entail serious revenue loss.

[86] Kent Weaver, *Automatic Government* (Washington, D.C.: Brookings Institution, 1988).

[87] Robert Salisbury, John Heinz, Edward O. Laumann, and Robert Nelson, "Who Works with Whom? Interest Group Alliances and Opposition," *American Political Science Review* 81 (1987): 1217–34.

The focus of these groups on a single issue makes it easier for them to avoid a pattern of least-common-denominator politics than groups covering all issues. Most (if not all) companies have some special interests that diverge from the collective concerns of their peers. For example, managers are generally interested in low rates of inflation but welcome increases in the price of their own products. When a business group purports to cover all issues and competes with other groups for members, it is reluctant to take positions that harm some members' special interests even if these stands are acceptable to the majority. If the group took the majority position in each issue and if members with special interests in each of these issues departed as a result, the group could be left with no members. By comparison, single-issue groups can afford to lose a few members whose special interests diverge from the general concerns of the group.

The following section offers subnational comparisons of corporate policy capacity, recognizing deviations from the broad patterns of U.S. business organization. Subnational comparisons are important for three reasons. First, they offer a more complete picture of U.S. business than broad, cross-national comparisons portray.

Second, subnational comparisons offer insight into the microprocesses by which managers determine their interests. Because corporate policy capacity varies across countries, areas of policy, and firms, its institutional components should have a similar effect on the formation of businesses' preferences and political participation in macrolevel welfare state development, on corporate engagement at the policy level, and on the microprocesses by which managers in firms form their preferences for public policy. Therefore, I chose the research design in order to demonstrate the similar effects of corporate policy capacity at different levels of analysis. I also hoped to address a criticism of new institutional analysis, that unlike a rational-choice approach it fails to provide a microlevel model of deliberation, and to move toward addressing the problem of the macro-micro link.[88]

Third, subnational comparisons make a methodological contribution by allowing us to pinpoint the specific contributions of institutions. If variations in institutional patterns at the policy and firm levels influence outcomes while keeping constant ideology, culture, and countervailing powers, cross-national generalizations about the importance of business organization gain more validity. Thus institutional "exceptions that prove the rule" reinforce observations about the limits of American business organization.

---

[88] Jonas Pontusson, "From Comparative Public Policy to Political Economy," *Comparative Political Studies* 28, no. 1 (1995): 117–47.

The empirical basis of the book consists of two sets of case comparisons to evaluate corporate policy capacity: a firm-level study of companies' preferences for national health reform and a policy-level comparison of business involvement in training, health, and work-family acts.

The first study, a comparison of company's positions on national health reform, surveyed randomly selected firms during the seven-month period after Clinton's election in 1992 (as the Clinton health plan was first being introduced) with follow-up contacts until the spring of 1995. The dependent variable or object of explanation in this quantitative study was company support for the Clinton health plan. Using advanced statistical methods, I tested measures of corporate policy capacity as well as economic characteristics often argued to influence firm decision making.

The study found the institutional measures to be statistically significant in determining company positions on national health reform. How companies viewed their interests (and whether they bought into the high-performance workplace perspective) depended in large part on how they got their information. Firms with government affairs offices in Washington, D.C., and those that participated in groups that exposed them to detailed analyses of health-financing problems were more likely to believe that the health system needed systemic reform and to back employer mandates. Respondents were often confused about health reform before their groups studied the issue. But the process of sharing their experiences in collective settings and learning about expert opinion brought them to a greater understanding.

A Policy-Level Case Study

The second study was a comparison of the corporate policy capacity of business networks at the policy level, specifically looking at health, training, and work-family initiatives. My objective was to explain the differential involvement of business in these three areas. I questioned why—when business opinion polls revealed that a majority among managers supported these initiatives—did managers acting collectively in groups make tangible, public expressions of support for these initiatives only in the training area? Using qualitative, case study methods I compared measures of corporate policy capacity, showing how differences in policy-level business organization, private policy expertise and policy legacies mattered to business participation in the legislative process.

I chose these three cases because a vast literature connects each to worker productivity and to economic growth. Similar linkages are not made to other areas of social policy, for example to welfare, and all three are areas of growing interest to employers. I selected the actual bills to be discussed within each area by picking the most significant initiatives of the Clinton administration: the Health Security Act, the Family and Medical Leave Act, and the Goals 2000 and School-to-Work Opportunities Partnership Acts in the area of training. These constitute the major initiatives in human capital investment in recent years.

There is, of course, a danger in making assessments about an interest group's support (or lack thereof) for specific acts as opposed to concepts, because the barriers to support may lie in how broad goals are translated into legislative bills. The acts themselves may be seen as suspect, even though the societal actors desire the ends the initiatives aim to achieve.

For example, Clinton chose a very contentious policy tool to fund his goals, the employer mandate. In advance, mandates seemed to many to be a fine strategy for solving problems without creating new government programs (important to budgetary constraints), and mandated benefits often lagged behind the provision of services already offered by many big firms. Mandates were also careful not to redistribute income in any dramatic way.[89] Yet the right convincingly framed employer mandates as new entitlements and hidden taxes. Novack and Banks portrayed mandates as the latest example of Democratic "tax and spend" politics.[90]

To deal with the problem of understanding whether managers are responding to the goals or to the legislative format of the goals, I begin my case investigations with business input during the agenda-building and proposal development stages. I ask why managers were able to get a satisfactory (to them) training proposal but not satisfactory health reform. I assume that business influence is important not only to the ultimate success of the legislation, but to the development of proposals. A high degree of business unity in support of a proposal greatly increases the likelihood that government entrepreneurs will choose the form of the policy supported by managers. The cases examined here reveal that large employers entered into these legislative debates in very different ways from the very beginning, and the institutional features of the business networks organized around these issues were important to the variation.

One might also protest that managers responded differently to the initiatives because of different economic concerns about these issues. Support voiced in poll data is not enough to assume equal economic interests in the various policies or comparable economic barriers to managers' participation in the legislative campaigns to enact them.

---

[89] "For Three Banks, Family Leave Is No Big Deal," *ABA Banking Journal* 85, no. 4 (1993): 7; Ruth Shalit, "Family Mongers," *New Republic,* August 16, 1993, 12.

[90] Janel Novack and Howard Banks, "Put Up the Price of Beans," *Forbes,* April 6, 1987, 32.

Let me highlight the problems with such an unadulterated economic argument by focusing on the training and health cases. In both cases opinion polls revealed a majority of managers supporting government involvement, and in both cases the Clinton administration designed its proposal to build on ideas that had been gaining attention in the business community. But in one case managers voiced support for the proposal through their collective associations, while in the other they did not.

An argument restricted to economic considerations fails to explain the divergence in these cases in many ways. At the most simplistic level, one could argue that if it were a simply a matter of economics, one wold expect to see expressed positions in both cases since a majority of managers claim to have interests in both policy initiatives. If we take them at their word, then it is legitimate to wonder why some business organizations failed to support the health plan even when a majority of their members supported it.

But one must consider the possibility that there was a difference in intensity of feelings between supporters in the two cases, that managers cared more about training policy than they did about health reform and were more determined to do something about it. The issues are not entirely fungible and may involve different incentives for employers, even though they both fall into the category of policies said to enhance the productivity of workers. Training policy aimed to develop workers' skills. Health reform appealed to business both as a mechanism to improve the competitiveness of U.S. firms by restraining health costs and to enhance worker productivity. The key question is whether these differences in incentives constituted a reason for one policy to gain express corporate support where another failed, yet it is hard to imagine that companies were more concerned about workers' skills than about international competition.

One might argue that it was harder for managers to reach a consensus position in the health area than it was in training due to stronger sectoral differences in the former. Policies nearly always affect industrial sectors differently, and those having the most diverse effect on sectors may have a more difficult time gaining collective corporate support.

Sectoral differences among firms could be an obstacle to corporate political action in both cases, but the effect of industrial structure on company interests in itself did not make managers more divided in the case of health care than in the case of training. Companies have vastly different training needs because workers' skills vary enormously across sectors. One could easily imagine a zero-sum politics developing in the area of training, in which manufacturing sectors lobbied for school-to-work programs while low-skill, low-wage sectors demanded rudimentary skills training in the three Rs for their poorly educated workforce. Thus sectoral analysis would acknowledge that support for training has grown with the rapid technological change in industrial production and the corresponding need for a more highly skilled workforce. But it would expect to find advocates of training only in the high-tech sectors that place a priority on workers' skills.

The facts suggest otherwise. While it is true that many corporate sponsors (e.g., Motorola) came from these sectors, others came from companies, such as Aetna, that used a lower-wage workforce in desperate need of basic skills training. Although the politics of training could easily have been constructed as a zero-sum contest between high- and low-wage sectors, it has not unfolded in this manner. What is impressive about the training issue is that although sectors have vastly different needs from training, managers have constructed their interests in a manner that minimizes the economic divides.

In comparison, mandated health benefits (especially with subsidies to low-wage firms) might appear on the surface to be an easier sell, as all enterprises need healthy workers. Of course complicating the health story is the private policy legacy of the employer-based system, which has brought firms with similar industrial structure characteristics to have very different material concerns because they offer divergent benefit packages. But in this case an institutional arrangement, rather than industrial structure, creates the economic divisions among firms.

The two cases might also vary in the strength of the opposition. Economic arguments recognize a collective-action problem for managers who are acting in broad, collective areas far removed from their core economic activities, or cases where managers act as consumers rather than producers. Thus the collective-action problems for business may have been greater in health because of the many health providers and insurers in the political arena; business consumer interests may have been swamped by the producer interests of the providers.[91]

Health opponents were certainly highly mobilized by the end of the legislative cycle while the training case experienced no such fierce opposition, yet the seemingly united front of opponents in health developed long after the early departure of the business community. As Graham Wilson has pointed out, the medical industry was originally quite divided over health reform, with many physicians supporting the Clinton plan.[92] Collective-action theory suggests that dominant sectors may overcome collective-action problems and facilitate action. Yet an irony in the health case

[91] Olson, *Logic of Collective Action*.

[92] Graham Wilson, "Interest Groups in the Health Care Debate," in *The Problem That Won't Go Away,* ed. Henry Aaron (Washington, D.C.: Brookings Institution, 1996), 110–30.

was that major small-business associations, with less economic power, wielded much more organizational, political power than the economically dominant large firms.

It is also possible that one policy initiative was more redistributive than the other, thus diminishing corporate enthusiasm. The irony is that although health reform was quite redistributive, its major impact was to redistribute some of the health burden from nonproviders to providers. This was not a reason for the big-business community to reject the bill, as large employers were already paying for the uninsured and saw reform as a way both to shift the burden back onto nonproviders and to end cost shifting by the federal government. In comparison the training legislation's target group was working America; therefore, by definition this legislation was redistributive between business and labor.

One might protest that it is inappropriate to compare the initiatives, since they were quite different in scope. The training package could be more easily passed because it was smaller, voluntary, cheaper, and more modest in its goals.

While it is true that the health and training bills had different parameters, the original initiatives to promote training (as conceptualized by the Clinton transition team) were to have broader ambitions; indeed, the 1.5 percent training mandate was even more controversial than the health mandate. The proposal was quickly dropped in response to corporate objections; thus, business action simultaneously enhanced the political fortunes of the act and limited its reach. Because managers were so well organized, government entrepreneurs were forced to adopt the broad corporate view. But although the core supporters rejected the mandate, they did want a policy vehicle to increase training by all firms and lobbied for a tax credit, which they viewed as a replacement for the mandate. This was rejected by legislators as too expensive in our tight budgetary climate. Next, training business activists began planning a drive to increase private training within firms, but this campaign was abandoned after the 1994 election.

In addition while dropping the mandate made the training package an easier sell than the more dramatic health package, the other training initiatives were not simply window dressing. The school-to-work proposal was originally viewed with suspicion by many managers. As a pillar of active labor market policy in West Europe, it was seen as involving too much government. But visits to European programs, considerable study, and a process of social learning led to a slow transformation of the issue in the collective corporate consciousness. The proposal really was a stretch for the U.S. business community that has been characterized as fearful of state power and committed to laissez-faire thinking. Although school-to-work began as a small, pilot program, so did many of our important welfare state initiatives. Most participants believed that the program would have been expanded quite a bit in years to come.

In addition, the legislation was heavily contested after 1994 and managers were deeply committed to protecting it. If business had merely signed on as a passive player, it would have ducked when the Republican right began shooting real bullets. But this did not happen. Administration officials report that business allies helped enormously in nullifying right-wing attacks on the bills both before and after 1994.

As Weir has pointed out, training has historically occupied a small space in the American political landscape; indeed, there has been practically no active labor market policy of the type found in West European countries. She links this phenomenon to the narrow interpretation of Keynesian ideas and to the early linkage between training and welfare.[93] Thus one must explain how training, and especially active labor market policies, gained in standing as a business issue.

Business involvement in health care played out quite differently. When managers objected to aspects of the bill, the administration promised to remedy these problems during the legislative process. Yet even after these assurances, large employers ultimately failed to participate as coalitional partners for reasons that can only be explained by an institutional analysis. In addition, although health care had a much broader impact on the economy, large employers claimed to have very strong financial stakes in solving the health crisis. Presumably this was not an area of policy that companies would turn away from lightly. Therefore, it is necessary to understand the disappearance of corporate support for health reform.

When the institutional measures of corporate policy capacity are introduced to the causal mix, the divergence in business behavior in these two areas becomes more comprehensible. In the following sections I explain how institutional differences in business networks shaped managers' involvement with health, training, and work-family initiatives.

Corporate Policy Capacity and Health Reform

In the area of health reform, private expertise in policy grew considerably in the years leading up to Clinton's proposed Health Security Act, and managers did much to put the issue on the public agenda. Yet the legacies of private-sector provision interfered with employer support at the point of legislation. Managers wanted collective cost containment but were unwilling to sacrifice some of the benefits they enjoyed from their private health care system. They worried that the Clinton proposal for re-

---

[93] Weir, *Politics and Jobs*. See also Donald Baamer and Carl Van Horn, *The Politics of Unemployment* (Washington, DC: CQ Press, 1985).

gionwide health alliances would erode firms' market leverage to secure low health rates from providers.

Big-business failure to support health reform also reflected the absence of a policy-level mediating organization to aggregate the interests of likely big-business supporters and to represent broad corporate concerns about health financing. Although the National Association of Manufacturers (informally) and the Chamber of Commerce (formally) both initially favored reform, minority factions forced the two groups to switch directions (despite Clinton's assurances that corporate concerns about the plan could be addressed). Small-business opposition also contributed substantially both to the failure of the Clinton health plan in Congress and to large companies' relative inaction.

President Clinton made matters worse in health reform, offering a complicated plan and pursuing a questionable strategy. The multitude of interests made it very difficult to make zero-sum trade-offs. Caught between conflicting demands of mass and elite opinion, Clinton opted for an anticorporate attack that undermined the spin control of corporate policy experts who were trying to present health reform as a growth-oriented investment in human capital rather than as redistribution.

Corporate Policy Capacity and the Family and Medical Leave Act

Business inaction also contributed to the lengthy delay in enacting the Family and Medical Leave Act, which built on existing private-sector policy legacies and simply ratified the status quo for many big firms. Yet big-business experts in work-family issues had practically no involvement with the national legislative debate due to very limited corporate policy capacity in this area.

Experts in work-family policy have a much more tenuous position within the firm than, for example, training experts who are located in human-resources departments with close connections to government affairs. Work-family experts are likely to be situated in special departments created to deal with the rather new issues connected to two-career families. Work-family managers are predominantly women, and the issue's feminist overtones have done little to increase its viability as a corporate concern.

This relatively new issue also has no policy-level encompassing business political organization, which further limits the big-business presence in debates over policy. Without a group sponsor to organize business followers, to spread the word in the larger business community, and to push the issue in the public arena, managers have largely ignored the political arena. Rather than pursuing national public policy, work-family activists concentrate on community-level activities to enhance child care resources and to create family-friendly policies within the firm. Big-business inaction on the work-family issue was matched by small-business hyperactivity, as a coalition called the Concerned Alliance of Responsible Employers (CARE) made fighting family leave its cause celebre in the 1980s.

Corporate Policy Capacity and Training Initiatives

From a cross-national perspective, American training programs are quite fragmented and, until recently, have included nothing resembling the active labor market policies that one finds in many industrialized countries. This fragmentation undoubtedly reflects the way that business and labor negotiate labor policy. Lacking a centralized collective-bargaining structure, U.S. social partners do not engage in the sort of cooperation that has given rise to collaborative initiatives to promote training that one finds in other countries.[94]

But in recent years American employers have struggled to overcome their comparative fragmentation, making employment and training policy the partial exception that proves the rule in the tale of big-business deadlock. Corporate politics is characterized by accumulated expertise in policy, beneficial policy legacies, and the commanding presence of a corporatist-style business organization, the National Alliance of Business (NAB). Considerable corporate policy capacity in training helped recent (though limited) training acts to pass in a noncontentious fashion.

Training legislation received much big-business support due to the growth of the training profession within the firm. Driven by a blend of professional concern about the issue and career building within the firm, these trainers have led the quest for a high-skilled workforce. The employment and training intiatives proposed by Clinton were also accepted fairly easily by large employers because they built on the legacies of business interest in education policy and on findings of previous administration's bipartisan commissions.

Finally a very strong organizational base enhanced training's fortunes as a political issue among big-business managers. A multisector, broad-based association, the NAB, has set out to overcome the narrow focus found in many other business groups, to organize coalitions of other business groups, and to develop broad support for training initiatives. The recent acts were small in scope and resources, but broad employer support for training did demonstrate that managers at times support high-performance workplace arguments made to them by highly organized corporate activists.

---

[94] Thomas Kochan, Harry Katz, and Robert McKersie, eds., *The Transformation of American Industrial Relations* (New York: Basic Books, 1986).

A National Predisposition for a
Least-Common-Denominator Politics

The subnational exceptions to the rule illuminate the micro foundations for the widely noted organizational weakness of American business.[95] Despite subnational exceptions, American employers have limited corporate policy capacity from a cross-national perspective. Many voices claim to speak for business, and these voices have only proliferated in recent years. John Tierney and Kay Schlozman found a tenfold increase from the organizations listed as representing business in the *Congressional Quarterly* in 1960 (about three hundred) to those having a Washington office in 1980 (about 3,060).[96] Companies increasingly hire law firms to represent their interests, rather than rely on trade associations to put forth their concerns. Government affairs offices also create the means for identifying a firm interest separate from the interests of the sector or business community as a whole. As Howard Vine of the NAM put it, "Associations used to be clubs on long leashes—you shared their theology, so you gave." This has changed to an attitude of "What's in it for my company?"[97]

A least-common-denominator politics within the big umbrella associations (the most likely sources of centralized thinking and planning among business leaders) further limits collective thinking. As noted above, U.S. managers have no single peak association to aggregate their interests at a class level. Rather, the Chamber of Commerce and the National Association of Manufacturers compete to represent the entire business community, and the Business Roundtable claims to represent big business. Competition for members makes groups risk-adverse and unwilling to alienate their constituents with controversial stands. Because umbrella associations lack jurisdictional monopoly, they act more like sales organizations than like decision-making bodies and tend to cater to minority preferences. Unable to make difficult choices, employer organizations tend to defer to vocal minorities and to neglect the sentiments of the more silent majority. Since change always offends somebody, groups find it easier to voice objections than to endorse positive action. The art of offending no one leaves big-business groups in a kind of political limbo. Like feisty two-year-olds, they are good at saying no to regulations that offend their

---

[95] Ian Maitland, "House Divided: Business Lobbying and the 1981 Budget," *Corporate Social Performance and Policy*, vol. 5 (Greenwich, Conn.: JAI Press, 1983), 1–25; Wilson, "American Business and Politics"; McKeown, "Epidemiology of PAC Formation"; Theodore Lowi, *The End of Liberalism* (New York: Norton, 1969).

[96] Kay Lehman Schlozman and John Tierney, *Organized Interests and American Democracy* (New York: Harper and Row, 1986), 75–77.

[97] Victor, "Step Under My Umbrella,"1063.

narrow self-interests, but bad at saying yes to policies that further their long-term, collective concerns.

Weakness in the political organizations that represent employers makes it more difficult for American managers to generate collective positions and to take collective action toward common goals than it is for their counterparts abroad. These constraints typically do not affect action toward the narrowly targeted self-interests of companies. In areas where a few large firms or even sectors have direct economic interests, producers tend to dominate the policy process. But where a wide spectrum of companies shares a broad collective goal, employers are hard-pressed to find common ground. Companies are very good at securing their firm- or industry-specific concerns but less good at expressing collective interests.[98]

Perhaps we should not be startled by this failure of coalescence. Common perceptions of a problem do not translate into consensus over its solution. One might protest that it is impossible to unify all corporate interests in a single perspective—the economy is simply too large and diverse. Indeed, references to "the business community" as some anthropomorphic creature evoke equally implausible images of conspiracy for one end of the political spectrum and salvation for the other.

But large employers are concerned about how their views are represented. In a 1983 Harris poll, two-thirds of the executives sampled believed that business views were poorly or only fairly represented. NAM was rated highly effective by only 30 percent, the Business Roundtable by only 33 percent, and the Chamber of Commerce by just 17 percent.[99] Firms that belong to several organizations complain that they have a hard time knowing which organization's perspective to accept. As one manager put it, "We get conflicting reports from NAB, NAM, and AEA."[100]

Much has been made of American companies' short-term perspective in economic investment; a similar dynamic may constrain managers' perceptions of their political and social interests.[101] Business observers routinely decry the reactive nature of large corporations. Thus Joseph Nolan wrote that "the business community has been anything but a major player in the agenda-setting arena, despite the flamboyant claims of political action committee critics that business PACs have 'seized control' of the national

---

[98] Wilson, *Business and Politics;* James Q. Wilson, *The Politics of Regulation* (New York: Basic Books, 1980).

[99] "Executives Take a Dim View of Their Image-Makers," *Business Week,* March 7, 1983, 14.

[100] Interview with John Tobin, May 23, 1996.

[101] Robert Hayes, Steven Wheelwright, and Kim Clark, *Dynamic Manufacturing* (New York: Free Press, 1988).

agenda."[102] Joseph O'Neill of the American Retail Federation complained, "Unless there is a consensus, a lot of associations become eunuchs in terms of lobbying."[103] Vernon Loucks Jr., CEO of Baxter, lamented,

> While business may enjoy a measure of economic power, most businessmen don't have true political power and don't purport to understand it or use it. No change will come to our schools that isn't approved in some form by our political process. Yet put us in the political arena on a public policy question like education, and we in business are often totally in the dark.[104]

Groups occasionally try to shift gears, but usually get pushed back into neutral. In the early years of the Clinton administration the Chamber of Commerce tried to offer leadership in public policy. Its revenues had dropped from $71.7 million in 1989 to $65.8 million in 1991, and some considered the group's political incapacities to be responsible for the drop-off in membership. Allan Cors of Corning reported, "We had become upset with its [the Chamber's] ideological mind-set and obstructionist positions. The chamber was so predictable and so far out that it was not a player, in my view. When we cut our dues, we made it clear that we were sending a message."[105]

But the organization's friendly interest in President Clinton's policies made it a lightning rod for conservative criticism. Daniel Wattenberg in the *American Spectator* charged William Archey, vice president of the Chamber of Commerce, with fashioning "a career as a liberal Trojan horse within the walled cities of conservatism."[106] Ultimately the organization moved back into the least-common-denominator mode.

Also part of the unique profile of American business representation is the political power of the small-business trade associations, which have managed to move beyond a least-common-denominator politics. The political power of small business is somewhat surprising. Interest group theory predicts that widely dispersed interests (such as the multitude of small companies) will have a more difficult time than larger firms in overcoming collective-action problems.[107] Small firms have historically given much less money to political candidates, generally enjoy less prestige, and are too numerous to produce the star-quality CEOs offered by large corporations. Large firms in industries are thought to control their smaller breth-

---

[102] Joseph Nolan, "Political Surfing When Issues Break," *Harvard Business Review* 63, no. 1 (1985): 72.

[103] Victor, "Step Under My Umbrella," 1063.

[104] Vern Loucks Jr., "Business and School Reform," *Vital Speeches,* May 15, 1993, 466.

[105] Kirk Victor, "Deal Us In," *National Journal,* April 3, 1993, 805.

[106] Daniel Wattenberg, "Clinton's Echo Chamber," *American Spectator,* June 1993, 18–23.

[107] Olson, *Logic of Collective Action.*

ren; in interfirm alliances large manufacturers are considered to coerce their small-business suppliers and customers.[108]

Although this may be an accurate perception of the economic distribution of power, small business is a political powerhouse in Washington today. The fragmentation of business organization in the United States has meant that large employers have never been able to force small business to acquiesce to modernizing economic and social changes.[109] Thus, small employers in America have always enjoyed a strong political voice, and with the rise of groups such as the National Federation of Independent Business (NFIB) this voice has grown louder in recent years.

Before surveying reasons for the political power of small business, let me make absolutely clear that I am referring to the primary small-business trade associations, the groups described in the popular press as the small-business lobby. Although small firms are a varied lot, the primary trade associations representing them, such as NFIB, generally reflect the interests of low-wage, low-skilled enterprises. Small technology companies lack the manpower to participate in the forums that aggregate the interests of large companies with whom they often share interests, such as investment in human capital. Consequently, small entrepreneurial firms do not have an effective system of political representation and have little voice in national politics beyond participating in a few issues in specific industries such as biotechnology and semiconductors.

To some extent small employers have an easier task of wielding political power in Washington. On most social issues they have opposed government intervention, and it is easier to oppose than to promote. Small employers perceive family leave and health mandates as payroll deductions directly linked to their bottom line rather than as social supports with productivity implications; consequently, they are more strongly committed to political action in these areas than their big-business counterparts. Large employers are more likely to save their political capital for more relevant battles. These multinational firms may be so preoccupied with trade issues that they have been willing to leave domestic social issues to small firms.[110] Political action committees on behalf of small firms have been limited but are growing in number, and small-business groups tend to target their funds to legislators who share their policy predilections.[111] Small firms exercise considerable leverage on large companies as customers; large companies have no such reciprocal power.

---

[108] Fligstein, *Transformation of Corporate Control*.

[109] While created to prevent cartels, antitrust laws actually increased corporate concentration and widened the gap between large and small firms. Freyer, *Regulating Big Business*.

[110] Interview with Anthony Carnevale, February 22, 1996.

[111] Brown, Hamilton, and Medoff, *Employers Large and Small*, 70.

But small-business groups also have an unambiguous organizational advantage over large firms. Several qualities give them comparative advantage in the political arena. First, small-business groups are better able to play to the media, an important quality today when the ability to exercise spin control has become so important to political outcomes. Small businesses evoke the same nostalgic reminiscences as farmers, increasing their approval ratings among outside publics; for example, small-firm proprietors were found credible by 71 percent of journals in 1982, but only 50 percent believed CEOs of big corporations.[112]

In this "going-public" world the ability to demonstrate a public show of organizational force carries more weight than it did when Washington was a closed community.[113] The very weakness of small employers in the old days—their numbers, diversity, and lack of prestige—is a source of strength today. The well-heeled corporate lobbyist that wielded such power behind closed doors lacks the television charisma of hundreds of restaurateurs storming Congress. Innovations in computer technologies have augmented the advantage of small-business groups: grassroots computer mailings first made popular by public-interest groups are perfectly suited to their large and varied membership.

Second, these organizations have developed rules for making decisions that augment the natural advantages of a broad-based, numerous membership. NFIB avoids the least-common-denominator politics of larger umbrella groups by grounding its positions on policy in regular polls of members. The association polls its five hundred thousand members every two months and immediately makes the data available to legislators. This practice gives the organization's positions a legitimacy that they might otherwise lack and makes decisions that adversely affect a minority of members easier. In 1995 *Roll Call* called NFIB the most powerful group in Washington.[114]

One might protest that small-business groups have an easier time developing positions on policy because they are more homogeneous than umbrella organizations that include both large and small employers. Indeed, the Chamber of Commerce has suffered from a sort of schizophrenia over the years, flip-flopping between its large- and small-business constituents. After a period of relative inaction, the Chamber grew dramatically in the late 1970s and early 1980s, moved to the ideological right, and developed a grassroots operation called Citizen's Choice, which organized mass tele-

---

[112] Brown, Hamilton, and Medoff, *Employers Large and Small*, 73.

[113] Samuel Kernell, *Going Public* (Washington, D.C.: Congressional Quarterly Press, 1986).

[114] "NFIB Named 'Most Powerful,' " *Capitol Coverage* (Washington, National Federation of Independent Business), December 1995, 1.

phone calls to legislators before key congressional votes. The Chamber's budget for research and political action increased threefold between 1974 and 1980.[115] This period marked a close relationship with its small-employer members (about 59 percent have fewer than ten workers), whom the organization viewed as an enormous source of power in lobbying Congress.[116] The move rightward alienated the Chamber's big-business members, however, and in the late 1980s the organization shifted dramatically toward its international, high-technology, big-business wing. But in 1993 the Chamber moved right again.

But small business enjoys less ideological homogeneity than one might think; in fact, opinion polls show much polarization among small employers. Some want no government intervention in areas such as health and work-family policies; others want even more government involvement than do large employers, believing that small firms on their own cannot hope to provide sufficient investment in human capital. Thus NFIB found a quarter of its members favoring a government single-payer plan in health reform.[117] In a *New York Times*/CBS business poll, 52 percent of the firms with sales less than $99 million supported an employer mandate for health care.[118]

Third, small-business groups have overcome the least-common-denominator syndrome with single-issue coalitions. Large employers sometimes join these coalitions; for instance, Pepsico was an important actor in the Health Equity Action League, which helped defeat the Clinton health plan. But groups such as the National Federation of Independent Business, the National Association of Wholesaler-Distributors, the National Restaurant Association, and the National Retail Association are typically the leaders in organizational efforts. Indeed, the small-business lobby has tried to establish itself as an independent voting bloc. In the words of NFIB's grassroots organizer R. Marc Nuttle, "Christians did not realize how big they were. Pat Robertson put a face on them and I intend to do that for small business."[119] NFIB recently passed on to its members David Broder's rhetorical question, "Is there a small business voting bloc?" The association's response was predictable: "Your personal involvement can help make the answer 'Yes.' "[120]

[115] Richard Kirkland Jr., "Fat Days for the Chamber of Commerce," *Fortune*, September 21, 1981, 144–58.

[116] Carol Matlack, "Mobilizing a Multitude," *National Journal*, October 17, 1987, 2592.

[117] Interview with NFIB staffer, June 1992.

[118] *New York Times*/CBS News Business Poll, "Business Executives Survey," December 1–9, 1992, in Roper Library, "CBS News and CBS News/The New York Times Poll Releases—1992 (2)" file.

[119] Cindy Skrzychi, "Dome Alone II," *Washington Post*, January 6, 1995, B1.

[120] "Building Bloc?" *Capitol Coverage* (Washington: National Federation of Independent Business), December 1995, 1.

Coalitions typically evolve because employers are dissatisfied with the limitations of the umbrella associations' least-common-denominator politics and believe that a forum dedicated to a single issue can make tougher decisions. Coalitions are usually organized to address a single issue and to influence a specific bill, although some outlast their precipitating legislation. They may be organized by business groups or by public-sector policy entrepreneurs. Groups organized by political figures tend to have greater direction:

> There is a big distinction between a coalition that has an elected official and one that doesn't. The Reagan administration was very adept at providing leadership from the top down. They had a goal and mobilized folks that shared that goal and provided leadership. That type of leadership gave a sense of direction and position that you don't have without that type of leadership.[121]

Not all coalitions achieve the desired discipline, but the most successful have developed rules for making decisions that keep participants committed to general objectives. Participants can hope for action on their special issues, but must promise to support the coalition's entire package, to avoid side deals, and to restrain pushing individual issues in favor of the broad legislative agenda. These single-issue coalitions have an explicit mandate to take political stands and have no other reason for existing; therefore, they cannot afford to slip into inaction. Like policy-level groups discussed in what follows, these coalitions find it easier to alienate potential members because only one issue is at stake. (When groups try to take tough stands on many issues and when these groups are not compulsory, they run the risk of driving away many subsets of their membership.) Thus the major small-business associations have been able partially to overcome the least-common-denominator politics that handicaps big-business managers.

Finally, small-business groups have gained power in their close connections to the Republican Party. Recent years have witnessed a growing split between the Republicans and big business. As the party has moved to the right under the sway of evangelical Christians, large employers increasingly are uneasy, a clash described by *Fortune* as a culture war.[122] Katherine M. Hudson, CEO of W. H. Brady Company, explained, "It's easier to

---

[121] Interview with Dirk Van Dongen, National Association of Wholesaler Distributors, summer 1994.

[122] Sixty percent of the new House Republicans were elected with the blessing of the Christian Right; whereas only 4 percent of a Fortune survey of CEOs advocated school prayer, and 59 percent were strongly pro-choice. Another study found big business contributing $3.42 to progressive issues for every $1 given for conservative causes. Richard I. Kirkland Jr., with Patty de Llosa, "Today's GOP: The Party's Over for Big Business," *Fortune*, February 6, 1995, 50.

teach economics to Democrats than abortion [rights] to Republicans."[123]
Many Republicans also grew frustrated that large employers demonstrated so little commitment to the party. There has always been a split
between Wall Street and Main Street Republicans, but after the 1994 election it seemed more pronounced than ever, causing Haley Barbour, chairman of the party, to declare, "Ours is the party of small business, not big
business." Dick Armey was even more forceful: "We call them prags. . . .
These big-business guys love peace more than freedom. . . . If anybody's
been carrying their water in Washington, it's been the Democrats."[124]
Edwin Feulner Jr. of the Heritage Foundation reflected this view that large
employers were not sufficiently ideological: "We can talk about the in-
credible influence of the business community, but half the time the business community is split in three different directions. Even when the business community is marching in lockstep, there's very little conservative
grass-roots mobilization."[125]

Since Reagan's first term, the Republican Party has been quite aware
of the superior strength of small-business groups and has mobilized small
employers to accomplish ends as varied as changes in family leave and
corporate taxation. For example, the Republican-organized Tax Reform
Action Coalition (TRAC) pushing tax reform in 1986 was to become a
model for other ad hoc groups. Composed of firms and associations from
high technology, wholesale, retail, food processing, and other small-business sectors, TRAC focused its members' attention on legislation that cut
corporate tax rates, urging them not to make narrow demands that could
push rates up again. TRAC had an elaborate vote-counting operation and
moved the bill along at critical points.[126] More recently, the Republicans
turned to small business for help in battles over family leave, health reform, and components of the Contract with America.

Implications for Business Theory and the Welfare State

This chapter has developed an institutionalist model of business interests
in policies affecting human capital investment. I have argued that the corporate capacity to grasp ideas about policy matters greatly to how managers view social proposals. Under certain institutional conditions managers
may view social initiatives as growth-supporting measures and join forces
with supporters in government and labor.

---

[123] "How the Election Looks from the Corner Office," *Business Week,* November 21,
1994, 36.
[124] "Big Business vs. the GOP?" *Wall Street Journal,* March 13, 1995, A14.
[125] Feulner, "Building the New Establishment," 6.
[126] Interviews with industry participants, November 1989; Martin, *Shifting the Burden.*

This model has implications for current debates about the influence of business and the future of the welfare state. First, too much time has been spent debating the tools of business power without attending to factors that shape corporate preferences. Discussions of corporate power primarily have focused on employers' ability to keep certain policies off the public agenda, but this is an overly constricted way of defining business's ability to get what it wants from government. One must also investigate employers' capacity to put collective concerns *on* the agenda. The *institutions* facilitating business mobilization are critical to the exercise of corporate power, something that the old corporate-power debate all too frequently ignores. Thus, corporate organization matters to both the *content* of business demands and employers' *ability to mobilize* around those demands.

Ideas and interests are often portrayed as distinct and mutually exclusive explanations for the origins of policy, yet this study suggests that ideas shape managers' perceptions of interests. Firms' preferences and political actions depend on the organization of professional expertise and the networks that expose managers to new ideas about social issues. We must put these insights into perspective: other policy spheres may have different politics.[127] Interests are undoubtedly more fixed in areas closest to the production process; social-welfare initiatives may give business participants somewhat more freedom.[128] But managers are intrigued by ideas just like the rest of us and reevaluate their interests accordingly.

Second, the institutional model of corporate preference has implications for welfare state development. Corporate liberal theory (with its rather static view of preference) has been the only approach to take seriously a role for business, but cannot account for managers' preferences. My perspective adds to corporate liberal theory by fleshing out the institutional conditions under which managers may support policies to increase human capital investment. In addition it recognizes the reciprocal relationship between managers and other actors. Unions and government bureaucrats often take the lead in seeking social legislation and may need cross-class coalitions to pass their initiatives when labor is too weak or the state insufficiently autonomous.

Third, this argument has implications for the future of economic growth and social renewal in the global age and the role of business mobilization in this process. Scholars have recently suggested that corporate support is necessary to future social initiatives, as the fragmentation of

[127] Theodore Lowi, "American Business, Public Policy Case Studies, and Political Theory," *World Politics* 16 (1964): 667–715.

[128] Walter Salant, "The Spread of Keynesian Doctrines and Practices in the United States," in Hall, *Political Power,* 37; Peter Hall, "Keynes in Political Science," *History of Political Economy* 26, no. 1 (1994): 137–54.

labor undermines the social democratic underpinnings of the welfare state. Due to structural changes in the organization of work and the polarization of skilled and unskilled workers, organized labor, the historic champion of social causes, is losing ground.[129] If labor unity becomes harder to achieve because of such structural changes, support from business for the welfare state may become more urgent. Yet the literature on the welfare state has not posited the bases for shifts in employers' thinking. My institutional model explores the conditions under which such a paradigm shift may occur.

But as the following pages make clear, there are limits to what corporate support can do to further social policy initiatives. First, postindustrial growth may be producing a decline of labor power and an increased need for cross-class coalitions. But the declining number of jobs associated with new manufacturing forms makes it increasingly difficult to base social-welfare initiatives on employment. When social policies are disconnected from economic growth, it is much harder to attract corporate sponsors. Slower growth rates have increased zero-sum battles between the various sectors of American business, working against collective solutions, even while increasing globalization makes these solutions more urgent.

Second, the U.S. business community is increasingly torn between employers in low-wage sectors who largely produce for the domestic economy and those in high-technology sectors who produce for international markets. This is both a source of cross-class support for specific policies and a possible political deterrent to their passage.

Third, policymakers may believe that cultivating corporate allies is necessary to future initiatives promoting human capital investment, yet they may be ultimately disappointed in this political strategy. Business partners in political coalitions tend to favor state interventions that do not disrupt existing private innovations. The legacy of the employer-based system provides the groundwork for business awareness of human capital investment issues but also interferes with support for the more far-reaching changes many policy entrepreneurs desire. In addition, there is a tension for many companies between trying to maintain their existing levels of social provision and opting out. Political coalitions with business are inherently unstable as long as firms can relocate their manufacturing operations at any time. Faced with a shortage of skilled workers in an era of capital mobility, companies may choose exit as an alternative to voice.

---

[129] Swenson, "Bringing Capital Back In, " 513–44; Scott Lasch, "The End of Neo-Corporatism," *British Journal of Industrial Relations* 23, no. 2 (1985): 215–39. Frank Longstreth, "From Corporatism to Dualism?" *Political Studies* 36 (1988): 413–32.

TWO

A CENTURY OF BUSINESS INVOLVEMENT

IN SOCIAL PROVISION

I N STORIES of welfare state development, business usually plays the role of villain: the force in society that derails the good fight of labor movements or disrupts the cautious plans of government bureaucrats. These stories, as it turns out, are more fiction than fact. Business managers throughout the century and throughout the world have backed a wide range of social programs.

History is constantly redrawing the boundaries between the social and economic realms. Every age has its own vision of peace and prosperity and its own version of the social conditions necessary for economic growth. Peasants obviously had very different educational needs from those of computer-aided-design technicians. When families routinely numbered in the double digits, infant mortality did not pose the economic threat that it does today. A society that depends on women working has had to address work-family issues that would seem bizarre when mothers were expected to tend the home fires.

Within each economic era, social policies have also varied enormously across countries. In some countries health and retirement benefits are universally offered to just about everybody; in others benefits are means-tested, or available only to those whose incomes fall below a certain level. Government budgets for social spending span a wide range, and policy instruments take many forms. Some governments administer programs directly, while others finance programs through social insurance but do not actually offer services.[1]

This chapter takes a historical look at the successive logics connecting social policies to economic growth and considers the contribution of business politics to national divergence in social development. The chapter scans the changing historical connections between growth and social policy, concluding with the current debate over policies for human capital investment, and describes business's involvement in prominent debates. Managers across the industrial world have taken a surprisingly wide range of positions on social provision. While employers elsewhere have often favored the policy pillars of their nation's welfare state, U.S. manag-

---

[1] Richard Titmuss, *Essays on the Welfare State* (London: Unwin Books, 1958).

ers have largely stayed out of the social policymaking process, beyond relaying information to lawmakers about private plans.[2] The chapter investigates employers' involvement with social policy in the early decades of the twentieth century, in response to the Great Depression, in the 1960s, and since the 1970s.

The chapter also considers the relationship between the political organization of business at the cross-national level and the positions managers take on social initiatives, focusing in particular on the institutional organization of employer groups and on legacies of past policies. This wide-sweeping summary does not apply the same research methodology to historical employer preferences that is relied upon in later empirical chapters and does not make the same claims about causality. In addition, it is beyond the scope of this book to explore all the factors contributing to cross-national differences in development of the welfare state, and the ruminations presented here are not intended to contradict arguments about the impact of labor strategies and state structures on social innovation. Rather, this exercise offers a comparative and historical backdrop for the subsequent probes into contemporary business activities, because managers' responses to perceived social needs today are conditioned by policy choices in the past.

Historical comparisons suggest that the organization of associations of employers and the legacies of private and public provision matter to how managers view new social initiatives. First, broadly organized, corporatist business groups have been more likely to support public social initiatives than fragmented political groups. Western European employer associations have often backed government programs and regulations to meet social needs, while their U.S. counterparts have largely rejected such programs, preferring instead to address social concerns through private, voluntary channels.[3] The history of social innovation in the United States reveals episodes of infighting between segments of capital over alternative views of social initiatives. Some large employers have been drawn to social reforms but have been generally unable to win over small businesses to their perspective; consequently, business associations have usually taken negative or neutral positions on the social debates of the day.

Second, the corporate responses at each critical juncture have shaped subsequent initiatives, by contributing to legacies that influence future political battles. In the United States the path toward private social provision by the company was begun quite early. These private-sector plans worked against future interventions by the government because companies were unwilling to consider initiatives that threatened their own turf.

---

[2] Berkowitz and McQuaid, *Creating the Welfare State*, 1.
[3] Rein, *Enterprise and Social Benefits*.

Thus the system of business representation contributed to the emergence of the distinctly American patchwork system of public-private provision. Let us now turn to stories of these business struggles over social provision and economic growth.

Social Policy in the Age of Innocence and the Roaring Twenties

Every age has its panic buttons, those images of decay that cause throats to constrict and stomachs to knot. If today *productivity* or *competitiveness* conjures up images of the Japanese burying us under a pile of consumer electronics, late-nineteenth-century Cassandras worried about losing a war to socialism at home and to imperialism abroad. Revolutionary workers and healthy German soldiers were objects of terror to that generation in much the same way that talented Japanese engineers are to our own.

Turn-of-the-century debates about social protection focused on two perceived needs: to maintain national colonial advantages and to resist urban unrest. First, some nations were concerned about losing their empires. Britain received its wake-up call with the Boer War, when thirty-five thousand untrained South African Boers initially threatened (but subsequently bowed to) the full powers of the English war machine. Muckraker Arnold White revealed in 1899 that 70 percent of the would-be enlistees at a Manchester depot were rejected by the army as physically unfit.[4] A hue and cry immediately sounded about the failings of this lumpen proletariat and its contribution to national degradation and military weakness. Nations worried about the powerful German war machine. Still smarting from the loss of Alsace and Lorraine, the French in 1906 could call up only 386,000 men to Germany's 1.2 million recruits to military service.[5]

In England concerns about national security and supremacy inspired a generation of imperialists to advocate social policies to improve the physical condition of the citizenry. Suddenly the entire future of the imperialist project seemed to hang on the physical well-being of the street urchin. The concern for the destitute that Dickens tried to inspire finally became implanted in the British consciousness; but nationalist panic rather than pity was the route to social reform. As Bentley Gilbert remarked, "The

[4] Arnold White, *Efficiency and Empire* (Brighton: Harvester Press, 1973), 103, 106.
[5] J. M. Winter, *The Great War and the British People* (Cambridge: Harvard University Press, 1986), 12–16, 7.

white man's burden had to be carried on strong backs."[6] Thus the fate of empire helped to launch the modern welfare state.

The business-oriented, Unionist Balfour administration considered a voluntary, contributory old-age pension, when party-member Joseph Chamberlain pointed out that half of the working class ended up as elderly paupers. Prime Minister Balfour expressed enough interest in Chamberlain's plan to appoint a committee on physical degradation. Chamberlain's pension plan had moral overtones and sought to preserve the class structure rather than to reduce social inequities; yet it differed from the earlier poor laws in containing seeds of the social-rights language that was to underlie later British social reform: "The industrious poor have really some claim on the Society that they have served and on the State as its representative."[7]

But the Unionists were opposed by the Friendly Societies, an odd marriage of Elks Club and insurance company, who feared that a government-sponsored pension program would put them out of business. When the Unionists lost to the Liberals, the debate became moot and the new government legislated a nonvoluntary, tax-based pension program.[8] Gilbert observed that the Unionists missed an opportunity "to establish themselves as the true friends of the working man in the tradition of Tory democracy."[9] But before and after the change in government, many employers were quite interested in legislating social insurance, for example, contributing much to the enactment of the National Insurance Bill of 1911.[10]

A second draw for social policy during this period was concern about unrest among workers and the rising appeal of socialism. Industrialization in the nineteenth century had turned autonomous, highly skilled craft producers into interdependent, less-skilled cogs in the factory wheel. The new factory system greatly expanded industrial output and corporate profits, but at the same time it made workers much more vulnerable to social and economic risk. Worldwide depression in the 1870s and 1880s caused many to leave their agricultural havens in search of subsistence,

---

[6] Bentley B. Gilbert, *The Evolution of National Insurance in Great Britain* (London: Michael Joseph, 1966), 61.

[7] Joseph Chamberlain, "Old-Age Pensions," *National Review,* February 1892, 726–27, 724.

[8] James Treble, "The Attitudes of Friendly Societies toward the Movement in Great Britain for State Pensions, 1878–1908," *International Review of Social History* 15 (1970): 272; E. P. Hennock, *British Social Reform and German Precedents* (Oxford: Clarendon Press, 1987), chap. 9.

[9] Gilbert, *Evolution of National Insurance,* 158.

[10] J. Roy Hay, "Employers' Attitudes to Social Policy and the Concept of 'Social Control,' " in *The Origins of British Social Policy,* ed. Pat Thane (London: Croom Helm, 1978), 119–20.

but the dark, closed factories of Dickens's days were living hells for farm boys turned industrial proletariat.

Industrialization and urbanization demanded dramatically revised schemes of social protection, and the modern welfare state can be dated from this era. Before the ascendancy of the factory system, social protection had incarcerated the destitute in prisonlike facilities. The old system limited the mobility of labor, but factories needed mobile workers. Poor laws assumed that the natural order linking landowners and peasants would cover all but the most deviant; but liberalism, emphasizing individual pursuit of self-interest, offered no such communal protections.[11] The new social-insurance system of protection permitted labor mobility, recognized the expanded risks associated with industrial capitalism, and compensated for reduced communal care for the sick and aged.

The German welfare state reflected these concerns when Bismarck, advisor to Kaiser Wilhelm II, invented a "welfare monarchy" system of government-administered social insurance that would prevent more radical solutions to the ills of the day and tie the industrial worker firmly to the state. Bismarck's compulsory social insurance drew considerable backing from German employers, led by iron and steel industrialists Ludwig Baare and Carl Stumn. Germany's rapid transition from an agricultural to an industrial economy relied on trade protections to shelter indigenous industry from foreign competition; therefore, employers were used to a high degree of intervention by the state. Yet German employers diverged from Bismarck's original plan, successfully demanding that firms rather than government administer old-age pensions and industrial-accident insurance so that business would appear to be the source of social largesse. In an impressive policy shift Bismarck caved in to business demands and created corporative associations to administer workmen's compensation and other benefits. Meanwhile trade unionists and leftists denounced Bismarck's plan as blatant political machination, not unlike the crumbs delivered to the starving masses at the end of the Roman Empire.[12]

Other countries were influenced by German deliberations about social problems. Danish employers backed government provision of social benefits at a very early stage (thereby permitting easier legislation of future government programs). The Danish Conservative Party, representing urban employers, had resisted compulsory government programs before 1890, preferring instead the liberal program of voluntary social benefits. But during the same period that Danish employers became organized into

---

[11] Quadagno, *Transformation*; Gaston Rimlinger, *Welfare Policy and Industrialization in Europe, America, and Russia* (New York: John Wiley and Sons, 1971), 36–37, 58.

[12] Rimlinger, *Welfare Policy and Industrialization*, 108–13, 117–22: Ralph Bowen, *German Theories of the Corporate State* (New York: McGraw-Hill, 1947), 154–56.

a centralized peak business association, managers began to accept comprehensive and compulsory social provision. The Conservative change was inspired by findings of a Workers Commission set up by the Conservatives to explore social reform and influenced by Bismarck's social-insurance experiments. The commission persuaded the Conservatives to join with the rich farmers' party to support the first mandatory, tax-financed old-age pension (albeit means-tested) available to all occupational groups and administered largely through government.[13] Thus even before achieving a parliamentary democracy in 1901, Denmark had laid the groundwork for a modern welfare state.

The extensive public system of social provision was aided by the strong organization of Danish business (and ironically the Social Democrats opposed many of these early social reforms). Danish employers organized centrally in 1896–98 before both their Swedish counterparts and Danish workers and viewed their interests in broad collective terms. The early centralization of Danish business was due to a relatively uniform economic base of small manufacturers, to a history of collectivism dating from the medieval guilds, and to employers' early frustrations with labor negotiations. Even though resisting labor was an early motivation for the unity that employers displayed, Danish business quickly determined that its interests would be best served by a stable, peaceful workforce and encouraged workers to form a centralized labor federation. Employers actually asked unions to refuse to work for companies that did not join the centralized employers' federation, thus using labor to discipline members of the business community.[14]

American social reformers were also highly influenced by European social innovations but made little headway. Even limited state-level pensions did not emerge until the 1920s, and unemployment insurance was absent from the policy landscape until the thirties. Vogel has argued that the unusual centralization of authority among American business during the Progressive Era made it possible for reform-oriented capitalists to speak for their entire industries in some regulatory areas.[15] But this prerogative did not extend to the more collective arena of social legislation.

The absence of early social regulation partially reflects labor's mistrust of government, dating from the courts' energetic promotion of corporate interests in the nineteenth century; consequently, workers were reluctant to approach the state as a protector of their rights.[16] Skocpol argues quite

---

[13] Iver Hornemann Moller, *Den danske velfaerdsstats tilblivelse* (Frederiksberg: Samfundslitterature, 1992), 55–125.

[14] Galenson, *Danish System*, 2–8, 58, 69–72, 91. See also Peter Baldwin, *The Politics of Social Solidarity* (New York: Cambridge University Press, 1990).

[15] Vogel, "Why Businessmen Distrust State," 70–71.

[16] Christopher Tomlins, *The State and the Unions* (New York: Cambridge University Press, 1985); Stevens, "Labor Unions, Employee Benefits."

convincingly that the American failure to enact early social-insurance programs reflected bureaucrats' inability to mobilize much support from the weak labor movement, while better-organized women's groups succeeded in obtaining programs for mothers.[17]

Political structures also contributed to the early absence of labor rights and social regulation. Nineteenth-century employers initially responded to instability in the market, brought about by industrial capitalism, with cartels and other forms of collusion. But the Sherman Antitrust Act made cartels illegal, while permitting mergers; therefore, firms solved stability problems by becoming more concentrated. Antitrust law's prohibition of collusion by employers in economic matters increased their antagonism to public policy and to cooperation in the social realm as well. Although some nineteenth-century employers had tried to use organized labor to stabilize industry, as industries came to be dominated by a few large firms there was less need for labor's assistance. In addition, federalism made interstate business-labor cooperation nearly impossible. Diverging from the German model, the federal government did not directly assist corporations in economic development, making them turn elsewhere for solutions to social concerns.[18]

The laggard status of the United States also reflected the absence of a unifying business organization to reconcile the perspectives of large and small employers. Other countries, such as Britain, had similar divisions between large and small firms, but they were overcome by means of self-regulation.[19] In turn-of-the-century America two groups represented business interests in the area of social policy. The National Association of Manufacturers, organized in 1895 to lobby on trade issues, began a vigorous antilabor campaign when taken over by small and medium-sized firms in 1902. Although some within NAM believed that certain social policies were advantageous to economic growth, they failed to convince their skeptical compatriots. Thus, Frank Schwedtman, chair of NAM's Committee on Industrial Betterment, tried to persuade his colleagues to work with government on social-insurance legislation, but opponents feared that such insurance would increase their costs, and they rejected compulsory systems.[20]

The National Civic Federation (NCF), dominated by large employers but also including representatives of labor, saw organized labor and social

[17] Skocpol, *Protecting Soldiers and Mothers,* 161, 158.

[18] Sklar, *Corporate Reconstruction,* 164–65; Freyer, *Regulating Big Business,* 7–9; David Robertson, "Voluntarism against the Open Shop," *Studies in American Political Development* 13, no. 1 (1999).

[19] Britain also had no urban-rural split (Freyer, *Regulating Big Business,* 7–9).

[20] Irwin Yellowitz, "The Origins of Unemployment Reform in the United States," *Labor History* 9 (fall 1968): 353–56; Robert Wesser, "Conflict and Compromise: The Workmen's Compensation Movement in New York, 1892–1913," *Labor History* 12 (1971): 345–72.

benefits as important deterrents to socialism. The NCF's investigations into social benefits and labor protections reflected the West European innovations of the era. Although the NCF steered away from national policy solutions, it encouraged both uniform state-level social regulations and the provision of benefits by companies. But the NCF could not persuade the "business anarchists" at NAM to endorse its conciliatory stance toward labor, other than to sign onto workmen's compensation.[21] Small-business backing for workmen's compensation was not surprising, as workers, in exchange for fixed monetary compensation, gave up the right to sue.[22]

In those nations that had not created public social programs in the early years of the century, big corporations often started providing their own social benefits to employees when in the 1920s mass production began to create new problems for employers and for workers. Thus "welfare capitalism," as opposed to "welfare monarchy," launched social provision in several countries, including the United States.

Mass production created several kinds of problems to which social policies responded. First, mass production eliminated jobs. Henry Ford's assembly lines were a miracle of modern management—automobiles multiplied like the biblical loaves and fishes—but streamlined production processes created surplus labor. Older workers especially had problems keeping abreast of increasingly sophisticated technology. Retirement pensions were an obvious solution, allowing employers to move less productive folks out of the workforce and to retain the more productive ones. Many large manufacturers developed old-age pensions during this period; by 1935 these plans purported to cover as much as 80 percent of the workforce, although only a small percentage of workers actually met the service requirements.[23] Health benefits were another part of the social-insurance package; many firms retained on-site company doctors. By 1926 over four hundred large firms offered on-site medical care to their workers.[24]

A second problem posed by mass production was to find buyers for all the goods that factories could now produce. The enormous gains in productivity greatly enhanced supply, making adequate demand a poten-

[21] Weinstein, *Corporate Ideal,* 6, 31.

[22] Joseph Castrovinci, "Prelude to Welfare Capitalism: The Role of Business in the Enactment of Workmen's Compensation Legislation in Illinois, 1905–12," in *Compassion and Responsibility: Readings in the History of Social Welfare Policy in the United States* (Chicago: University of Chicago Press, 1980), 267–75.

[23] Myles, *Old Age,* 29, 12–13; Graebner, *A History of Retirement;* Gordon, "New Deal, Old Deck," 171.

[24] Stuart Brandes, *American Welfare Capitalism* (Chicago: University of Chicago Press, 1976), 99.

tially serious problem. Thus, Henry Ford was attracted to welfare capitalism's Doctrine of High Wages in order to increase the purchasing power of the emerging American consumer. Retail and banking firms also promoted welfare policies to ensure aggregate demand.[25]

Third, the growing factory system brought workers together under one roof, making it much easier for unions to organize. Some employers responded to labor militancy with a strategy of social provision to curb unrest. For example, the National Civil Federation offered technical expertise to firms desiring to set up welfare programs in such areas as child care, housing, health, and training.[26] Other employers suppressed labor organization with violence and coercion. Immediately after the Great War companies (led by the steel industry) sought to prevent an increase in working-class power with a "red scare" attack on labor militancy: tactics included industrial espionage, blacklisting labor activists, strikebreaking, and yellow-dog contracts (in which employees agreed never to join unions). One labor leader estimated that two hundred thousand industrial spies were operating in 1928. The governor of Pennsylvania estimated that the private coal and iron police exceeded public cops by a ratio of twenty to one.[27]

Welfare capitalism's popularity swelled in the 1920, as employers sought to replace the crude instruments of power with more subtle efforts to maintain the imbalance in class relations. For instance, reformers saw vocational education as a mechanism to wrest control over the training of skills away from the workers themselves and to develop a stratum of foremen who would be immune to the enticements of union activity. In this vein NAM's Committee on Industrial Betterment wrote, "It is plain to see that trade schools properly protected from the domination and withering blight of organized labor are the one and only remedy for the present intolerable conditions." Company unions also became popular, allowing workers some voice within the firm without tying employers to a larger labor movement.[28] Welfare capitalists also endorsed better working conditions (higher wages, shorter hours) to improve efficiency.

Some historians argue that these private programs were minimalist interventions to prevent greater unrest among workers, and there is much to justify this view. Four hundred and ninety companies set up unions during the conflict-ridden years of 1919–24, while only seventy-three developed them from 1924 to 1928. Firms used pensions to enhance loyalty

[25] Irving Bernstein, *The Lean Years* (Boston: Houghton Mifflin, 1960) 179; Gordon, "New Deal, Old Deck," 165.

[26] Weinstein, *Corporate Ideal*, 17–19.

[27] Bernstein, *The Lean Years*, 148–49; Brandes, *American Welfare Capitalism*, 2.

[28] Bowles and Gintis, *Schooling in Capitalist America*, 193; David Brody, *Workers in Industrial America* (New York: Oxford University Press, 1980), 55.

to the company, as when the Endicott-Johnson Shoe Company explained to its employees that "your own selfish interest, now, demands that you protect this business."[29] In the iron, steel, and metal sectors—a breeding ground for welfare capitalism—there were more than five times as many strikes in 1916 as in 1924; but where welfare capitalism was practically nonexistent, the building trades, the strike rate dropped by only 33 percent between those years. Finally, welfare capitalism occasionally moved into ridiculous forms of social control; thus, a Phelps Dodge social hall prohibited dancing cheek to cheek.[30]

Others believe that welfare capitalists had at least some genuine concern about the well-being of their workers.[31] Regardless of employers' motivations, however, the absence of national social legislation and the creation of private company plans during the first two decades of the twentieth century laid a foundation for future debates over policy in the United States. This trajectory was significantly different from the early emergence of state welfare programs elsewhere.

The Great Depression and the New Social Contract

When the Great Depression undermined the world economy, corporate voluntary solutions proved inadequate to the enormous demands for social protection. Countries throughout the industrial world that did not already have government safety nets in place began to develop more comprehensive public systems of social security.

The subset of employers drawn to the new social initiatives believed that these policies would help to secure labor peace and to revive the legitimacy of the economic system. In some countries business and labor signed onto a historic compromise destined to reduce class conflict for half a century. Workers would give up the socialist dream of doing away with private property and accept capitalist control over productive resources and an unequal distribution of wealth. In exchange business managers would agree to share the fruits of their enterprise with labor in the form of tax transfers and protection from risk.[32]

Managers' interest in social-welfare expansion in the 1930s reflected changing views about economic growth. Some believed that the depression stemmed from a crisis of underconsumption, or insufficient demand

[29] Bernstein, *The Lean Years,* 157; Gordon, "New Deal, Old Deck," 171.

[30] Brandes, *American Welfare Capitalism,* 136; Bernstein, *The Lean Years,* 182.

[31] Jacoby, *Modern Manors;* David Fairris, "From Exit to Voice in Shopfloor Governance," *Business History Review* 69 (winter 1995): 493–529.

[32] Adam Prezeworski and Michael Wallerstein, "Democratic Capitalism at the Crossroads," *Democracy,* July 1982, 54–55.

for the enormous outpouring of goods produced by the new techniques of mass production. Because geographical expansion had reached an end, industrial countries could no longer colonize third-world countries to buy cheap raw materials and to sell goods produced in the mother country. Internal sources of demand were constrained by the limited buying capacity of the American worker: the frenzied growth in the 1920s never trickled down to the average American family. Despite Henry Ford's "Doctrine of High Wages," employers barely raised wages between 1925 and 1928; thus the growth of a mass-consumption society was cut short by the very limited gains in the real wages of workers.[33]

Social democratic political parties and organized labor were the unambiguous leaders in the social reforms of the 1930s and 1940s, but employers played varying roles in this process. Swedish managers were active partners in the new social contract. After being badly defeated in 1928, Swedish Social Democrats moved to the center to attract support for their program of social reform and to build a broader electoral base. The alliance between workers and farmers is well documented, but Social Democrats also wooed employers with the fundamental economic tenet that equality and growth were mutually supportive. Social democracy was dependent on a growing economy; consequently, capital formation, promotion of exports, technology development, and social interventions were all part of a package deal. Thus Social Democrat Ernst Wigforss argued to private industry that neither the Right nor the Left could eliminate the other; the two sides had best work together. In 1938 workers and employers signed a broad agreement at Saltsjorbaden that institutionalized disciplinary power at the level of the peak association, and other social and industrial reforms.[34]

The expansion of Danish social policy in the early 1930s also drew considerable business support, as parties at both ends of the political spectrum struggled to cope with the Great Depression. Because domestic-oriented Danish manufacturers were used to receiving economic protections from the government in the form of tariffs, asking for social protection was an easy transition.[35] Conservatives were quite involved in the reforms in unemployment insurance passed in June 1932. Party member Hans Thyge

---

[33] Bernstein, *The Lean Years,* 179–80.

[34] Timothy Tilton, "A Swedish Road to Socialism," *American Political Science Review* 73 (1979): 515–16, 509. Swedes across the political spectrum were also worried about population loss. Lisbet Rausing, "The Population Question," *European Journal of Political Economy* 2, no. 4 (1986): 545–46.

[35] Cameron says that openness makes for welfare-oriented countries, but in Denmark it was the opposite. Svend Aage Hansen and Ingrid Henriksen, *Dansk Social Historie 1914–39* (Copenhagen: Gyldendalske Boghandel, 1984), 292–94; Iver Hornemann Moller, *Velfaerdsstatens udbygning* (Frederiksberg: Samfundslitteratur, 1994), 111–60.

Jacobsen claimed that "without a doubt, Conservative initiative and leadership in negotiation drove the passage of the unemployment law."[36]

Although Conservatives ultimately opposed the Social Democratic pension reform, it was because the proposed program was too limited. The Social Democrats fashioned a means-tested pension system to be funded from general revenues; the Conservatives wanted a comprehensive social-insurance system financed by payroll taxes. Social Democrats feared that the lowest-paid workers could not pay more taxes, but the net effect of the Social Democratic victory was to accelerate the development of a private pension system for all but the most impoverished.[37]

Ironically, when pensions were expanded to all income levels in the 1960s (a project initiated by Conservatives), the Conservatives and Social Democrats had switched sides. Social Democrats now wanted a supplemental pension scheme funded by payroll taxes; managers preferred a tax-financed program because they feared that payroll taxes would add to the wage rate and because they wanted to protect the now extensive private pension system. The employers won, and the Right was to brag that "no decisive step in this expansion [of the welfare state] has been undertaken without support from all these parties."[38]

In some other countries employers were absent from the political coalitions supporting governmental solutions to the crisis. Although some U.S. employers were quite interested in passing Social Security legislation, they lost the internal power struggle within their political organizations, and business stayed away from the final legislation.[39] In the early days of the Roosevelt administration many leaders of big business realized that the existing welfare framework could not handle the depression. Companies found pensions to be increasingly costly and wanted the government to

[36] Hans Thyge Jacobsen, "Sociallovgivningen," in *Konservatismens Historie I Danmark,* ed. Alfred Bindslev (Odense: Kulterhistorisk Forlag, 1937), 149–58.

[37] The issue was resolved by a secret pact between the Social Democrats/Radical Venstre government and Venstre in which the Conservatives were shut out. The furious Conservatives charged that the Social Democrats were motivated by a desire to win electoral gains and had wanted to paint the Conservatives as an enemy of reform (Jacobsen, "Sociallovgivningen," 149).

[38] Henning Friis, "Issues in Social Security Policies in Denmark," in *Social Security in International Perspective,* ed. Shirley Jenkins (New York: Columbia University Press, 1969); Baldwin, *Politics of Social Solidarity.*

[39] Ferguson, "Normalcy to New Deal," suggests that social legislation enjoyed support from high-tech, export-oriented big companies who constituted the cutting edge of American industry. Skocpol, *Protecting Soldiers and Mothers,* disagrees, arguing that business support failed to materialize for the state-initiated social programs. Both theorists have points in their favor; yet Ferguson exaggerates the ability of big business effectively to express its political concerns, and Skocpol misses that the limits to business backing were institutional rather than merely ideological.

help bear the burden; for example, DuPont's welfare benefits jumped from 2 percent of payroll in 1930 to 5 percent in 1934. Those who provided benefits were anxious to force their competitors to assume similar costs; thus, the Ohio Manufacturers Association supported state unemployment insurance because its largest members provided benefits. The business-loaded Advisory Council on Economic Security offered recommendations to the president's Committee on Economic Security; corporate liberals favored an approach allowing for experimentation and variation.[40]

Ultimately big business contributed little to the passage of the Social Security Act due to internal conflict within employer organizations. Proponents of the social-insurance concept were largely drawn from the pool of big companies in competitive industries, with small firms generally opposed. The Chamber of Commerce actually endorsed social insurance until May 1935, when the Chamber's task force participants and staff were overruled by (in their words) a "minority group with selfish political and business interests."[41] Roosevelt grew frustrated with the lack of unity in business; working-class militancy proved to be a stronger attraction than corporate disunity, and the increasing radicalism of the New Deal agenda pushed big business further away from the administration. Although business ultimately did very little to pass Social Security, the legislation did reflect corporate concerns that it not interfere with private programs, especially in its 1939 amendments. Rather than replace the system of private pensions, FDR created a minimum provision that protected the growing private system. In fact, much of the Social Security Administration was patterned after the private sector's experiments.[42]

The U.S. social policy framework developed in the 1930s was expanded in the decades thereafter. The public/private combination of social provision was to become an enduring theme of the system: in addition to the Social Security system, U.S. employers continued to expand private company benefits. In part the expansive private pension system reflected dynamics of labor-management relations. Although unions were initially hostile to company plans, viewing benefits as weapons to halt the advance of collective bargaining and to trap workers in onerous jobs, the creation of the National War Labor Board (NWLB) precipitated a dramatic expansion of the employee benefit system. Anxious to prevent inflation, the NWLB specified acceptable wage increases but allowed benefits to be calculated separately; therefore, labor (and sometimes management) negoti-

---

[40] Gordon, "New Deal, Old Deck." Many employees from the Rockefeller-created Industrial Relations Counselors (IRC) were hired by the committee. Edwin Witte, *The Development of the Social Security Act* (Madison: University of Wisconsin Press, 1962).

[41] Peter Swenson, "Arranged Alliance," *Politics and Society* 25, no. 1 (1997): 66–116.

[42] Berkowitz and McQuaid, *Creating the Welfare State*.

ated increases in benefits as a way of expanding the total compensation package. The excise profits tax also pushed the growth of benefits, because companies could pay for benefits with pretax dollars.[43]

The national innovations of the 1930s, created under conditions of extreme economic crisis and working-class mobilization, were only reproduced (and then in much paler form) in the 1960s, when Lyndon Johnson managed another surge of social policy with considerable involvement by business. But diverging from the New Deal experience, Johnson seemed to recognize the constraints on U.S. social-welfare expansion—the organizational weakness of business and the strength of private policy legacies—and packaged the Great Society as a centrist measure to protect private plans and to promote economic growth. Confronted by the skepticism of Republicans and southern Democrats, LBJ viewed Fortune 500 leaders as more amiable allies in his social experiment. Henry (Joe) Fowler, the Treasury secretary, praised this business-government partnership, writing "of the remarkable feats that American government and American business can accomplish when they work as allies rather than as antagonists" and seek "common cause in the national interest."[44] As Johnson himself put it,

[The American economy] is an economy where the health of business benefits all the people. It is an economy where the prosperity of the people benefits the health of business. It is an economy where, in large measure, the fortunes of each are tied to the fortunes of all.[45]

These themes dominated the 1964 presidential campaign as Johnson articulated a vision of the good life, tying social rejuvenation to economic growth and minimizing the conflict in interests between haves and have-nots. This approach made the Democrats more palatable to those of a conservative hue, especially because the president deliberately left vague many details of the Great Society. The Democrats also portrayed Goldwater as a right-wing radical who could hardly be taken seriously except in his ability to lead the country to the brink of nuclear war.[46]

[43] Stevens, *Complementing the Welfare State,* 13–19.

[44] "Remarks by the Honorable Henry H. Fowler, Secretary of the Treasury, to the Business Council at the Homestead, Hot Springs, Virginia," Fowler Archives, Roanoake College Library, Salem, Virginia, Treasury Series, Speeches/Statements, "Business Council at Hot Springs Virginia—May 8, 1965," 1–4.

[45] As cited by Henry Fowler, "Remarks by the Honorable Henry H. Fowler Secretary of the Treasury before the Economic Club of New York, Waldorf-Astoria Hotel," Fowler Archives, Treasury Series, Speeches/Statements, "Economic Club of New York, November 8, 1965."

[46] Memorandum from Jack Valenti to LBJ, September 7, 1964, Johnson Presidential Library, WHCF PL, "Ex PL2 9/6/64—9/14/64"; John Kessel, *The Goldwater Coalition* (Indianapolis: Bobbs-Merrill, 1968), 245.

Business was essential to the centrist electoral strategy. Johnson wanted to attract managers across the corporate spectrum, beyond the coterie of corporate liberals who had favored Democrats since the New Deal. Cliff Carter suggested developing a business committee "in order that we may try to pre-empt this field while the Republicans are scrambling around for a nominee." The resulting National Independent Committee grew to "read like a Who's Who of Eastern big business."[47]

After the 1964 election, President Johnson expanded efforts to mobilize business on behalf of the social concerns of the Great Society. Much of the Great Society program was developed by expert task forces; by 1966 thirty business advisory groups had been developed.[48] According to one observer, the statement of support written by twenty-two CEOs for John-son's housing initiatives sounded like it came from the AFL-CIO:

> Our cities are being submerged by a rising tide of confluent forces—disease and despair, joblessness and hopelessness, excessive dependence on welfare payments, and the grim threats of crime, disorder and delinquency. America needs the demonstration cities act."[49]

In the 1960s and early 1970s opinion polls evidenced a surprising ideo-logical openness among businesspeople to social programs and regula-tions. The Opinion Research Corporation found that 73 percent of the executives polled in consumer manufacturing and 59 percent in industrial manufacturing favored or already had programs to hire inner-city hard-core unemployed. In 1971 a majority of business leaders in a sample of Fortune 500 firms backed Nixon's Family Assistance Plan, and 81 percent disagreed with the proposition, "Too much is done for the poor in this country."[50] Another study identified broad-based support for pension re-form to protect employees; thus, 58 percent supported conflict-of-interest regulations for pensions. Managers also seemed generally open to social

---

[47] Memorandum from Cliff Carter to LBJ, January 7, 1964, Johnson Presidential Li-brary, WHCF PL, "EX PL2 1/4/64—1/31/64"; "Toward an 'Independent Citizens for John-son,' " memorandum from Henry H. Fowler to James Rowe and Clifford Carter, July 24, 1964, attached to letter from LBJ to Fowler, September 5, 1964, Johnson Presidential Li-brary, WHCF PL, "PL2 8/26/64—9/5/64"; Rowland Evans and Robert Novak, *Lyndon B. Johnson: The Exercise of Power* (New York: New American Library, 1966), 470.

[48] John T. Connor, address to inaugurate the American University Lectures in Business-Government Relations, December 1, 1966, in Fowler Archives, attached to letter from Fowler to John Connor, Treasury Series, Subject Files, "General Business/Government," 8.

[49] Theodore Levitt, "The Johnson Treatment," in the House of Representatives, *Con-gressional Record* 113, no. 20, February 9, 1967, H1210.

[50] Opinion Research Corporation, "Corporate Social Responsibility: Executives Appraise Inner-City Programs to Hire the Hard-Core Unemployed," *ORC Public Opinion Index* 29, no. 16, end of August 1971, 2; Allen Barton, "Determinants of Economic Attitudes in the American Business Elite," *American Journal of Sociology* 91, no. 1 (1985): 63, 64.

responsibility: thus 56 percent of another sample saw "no contradiction between earning a profit and being socially responsible," and a majority thought that stockholders' activism aimed at increasing corporate responsibility was a good thing.[51] Theodore Levitt was to remark at the time:

> Whether they know it or not, the leaders of the economically most significant sector of the American business community—the top executives of the larger corporations—are just completing what may turn out to be the most remarkable ideological transformation of the century. . . . there is abundant evidence that the American business has finally and with unexpected suddenness actively embraced the idea of the interventionist state.[52]

The Current Debate on Growth and Social Policy

By the 1960s, government's role in promoting growth was confined to quibbles over fine tuning.[53] Even Richard Nixon proclaimed, "We are all Keynesians now." But in the 1970s problems with Keynesian demand management, increased pressures from global competition, and profound changes in manufacturing processes led to renewed disagreement over the role of government in sustaining economic growth and in pursuing social initiatives.

In the past few decades, employers' interest in private and public social programs has largely been concentrated in the areas of human capital investment, that is, training, health care, and work-family programs that are said to improve workers' skills, productivity, and attendance. For example, *training* is alleged to have an impact on productivity, turnover, and earnings. Some companies operating below their expected levels of labor productivity see significant increases in productivity after introducing training programs.[54] Such programs influence employees' earn-

---

[51] Opinion Research Corporation, "Executives' Attitudes toward Pension Reform," *ORC Public Opinion Index* 31, no. 22, end of November 1973, 1, 6; Opinion Research Corporation, "Business Trends: Executives' Views on the Goals and Tactics of Corporate Reformers," *ORC Public Opinion Index* 30, no. 11, mid-June 1972, 7, 2.

[52] Levitt, "The Johnson Treatment," H1211.

[53] Robert Collins, *The Business Response to Keynes* (New York: Columbia University Press, 1981).

[54] Ann Bartel, "Productivity Gains from the Implementation of Employee Training Programs," *Industrial Relations* 33, no. 4 (1994): 411–25; Harry Holzer, Richard Block, Marcus Cheatham, and Jack Knott, "Are Training Subsidies for Firms Effective? The Michigan Experience," *Industrial and Labor Relations Review* 46, no. 4 (1993): 625–36; John Bishop, "Job Performance, Turnover, and Wage Growth," *Journal of Labor Economics* 8 (1990): 363–86.

ings, attendance, turnover, and job performance.[55] Some believe that American private-sector training is less effective than that in other countries because of its applied, job-specific approach, in which the skills of workers are only marginally improved. On-the-job training may produce initial higher productivity growth rates, but these fall considerably after six months, and job-specific training benefits are not helpful when workers change jobs.[56]

Interventions in health care have also been connected to productivity, absenteeism, and job performance. Wellness programs and other benefits that improve the physical and mental functioning of workers affect job performance and absenteeism.[57] Cost-benefit analyses of workplace programs to promote health demonstrate positive returns on investment and benefits in areas such as productivity and absenteeism.[58] Because health benefits are important to workers, they affect job satisfaction, which in turn influences organizational commitment and turnover.[59] Health benefits have implications for economic growth in a more systematic way: the high cost of health provision (due in large part to the irrationality of the financing system) adds to the price of U.S. goods, thus hurting companies' market positions.[60] Chrysler estimated that it paid $5,300 for health care per worker in 1983, while its Japanese competitor Mitsubishi paid $815.

[55] Alan Krueger and Cecilia Rouse, "The Effect of Workplace Education on Earnings, Turnover, and Job Performance," *Journal of Labor Economics* 16 (1988): 61–94; Charles Brown, "Empirical Evidence on Private Training," in *Research in Labor Economics,* ed. R. Ehrenberg (Greenwich, Conn.: JAI Press, 1990), 97–113; Lee Lillard and Hong Tan, "Private Sector Training: Who Gets It and What Are Its Effects?" in Ehrenberg, *Research in Labor Economics,* 1–62.

[56] Lynch, "Payoffs to Alternative Strategies," 68, 72–77, 81–85.

[57] Bertera, "Effects of Health Promotion"; Roy Shephard, *The Economic Benefits of Enhanced Fitness* (Champaign, Ill.: Human Kinetics Publishers, 1986); Blank, "Larger Social Safety Net," 161–62.

[58] T. Golaszewski, "A Benefit-to-Cost Analysis of a Work-Site Health Promotion Program," *Journal of Occupational Medicine* 34, no. 2 (1992): 1164–72; K. Warner, "Health and Economic Implications of a Work-Site Smoking-Cessation Program," *Journal of Occupational Environmental Medicine* 38, no. 10 (1996): 981–92.

[59] E. Davis and E. Ward, "Health Benefit Satisfaction in the Public and Private Sectors," *Public Personnel Management* 24 (fall 1995): 255–70; R. Tett and J. Meyer, "Job Satisfaction, Organizational Commitment, Turnover Intention, and Turnover," *Personnel Psychology* 46 (1993): 259–93; A. E. Barber, R. Dunham, and R. Formisano, "The Impact of Flexible Benefits on Employee Satisfaction," *Personnel Psychology* 45 (1992): 55–72.

[60] Schramm, "Living on Short Side"; Walter McNerney, "A Macroeconomic Case for Cost Containment," *Health Affairs* 9, no. 1 (1990): 172–74; Stuart Altman, Susan Goldberger, and Stephen Crane, "The Need for a National Focus on Health Care Productivity, *Health Affairs* 9, no. 1 (1990): 107–16. For the counterargument see Uwe Reinhardt, "Health Care Spending and American Competitiveness," *Health Affairs* 8, no. 4 (1989): 5–21.

The high costs of health benefits also reduce available resources for other needs such as training and investment in research and development.[61]

Studies have also linked *work-family benefits* to factors such as productivity, absenteeism, and turnover.[62] By giving parents greater flexibility, family leave policies reduce turnover and retraining costs. Access to good child care programs reduces absenteeism and enhances productivity.[63]

Interest in human capital investment has grown in the past decades for several reasons. First, rapid technological change connected to advances in information technology have signaled significant economic restructuring and made managers rethink their production needs.[64] Although analysts disagreed somewhat about how new technology would change the organization of work, most believed that computer-age machines would require more highly skilled operators.[65] Many believed that future workers would need high skills, because rapid technological change required flexibility and the education to adapt readily to shifts in production technologies. The baffling slowdown in the growth of productivity expanded the concerns about all kinds of investments, human and capital. (U.S.

[61] Carol Cronin, "Next Congress to Grapple with U.S. Health Policy, Competitiveness Abroad," *Business and Health* 4, no. 2 (1986): 55; David Brailer and Lawrence Van Horn, "Health and the Welfare of U.S. Business," *Harvard Business Review* 71, no. 2 (1993): 128.

[62] Nancy Brown Johnson and Keith Povan, "The Relationship between Work/Family Benefits and Earnings," *Journal of Socio-Economics* 24, no. 4 (1995): 571–84.

[63] Galinsky, Bond, and Friedman, *The Changing Workforce;* Dana Friedman, Ellen Galinsky, and Veronica Plowden, eds., *Parental Leave and Productivity* (New York: Families and Work Institute, 1992); Committee for Economic Development, *Why Child Care Matters;* Friedman, *Linking Work-Family Issues;* John Fernandez, *The Politics and Reality of Family Care in Corporate America* (Lexington, Mass.: Lexington Books, 1990), chap. 2; Sandra Burud, Pamela Aschbacher, and Jacquelyn McDroskey, *Employer-Supported Child Care* (Boston: Auburn House, 1984), 21–64; Kraut, "Organizational Research."

[64] Larry Hirshorn, *Beyond Mechanization: Work and Technology in a Post-industrial Age* (Cambridge: MIT Press, 1984); Manuel Castells and Yuko Aoyama, "Paths toward the Informational Society: Employment Structure in G-7 Countries, 1920–90," *International Labour Review* 133, no. 1 (1994): 6.

[65] Some feared that automation would eliminate jobs and/or deskill the workforce. H. Allan Hunt and Timothy Hunt, *Human Resource Implications of Robotics* (Kalamazoo, Mich.: W. E. Upjohn Institute for Economic Research, 1983), ix–xi; Harry Braverman, *Labor and Monopoly Capital* (New York: Monthly Review Press, 1974). Others thought that automation would eliminate many of the most mundane tasks in direct labor, leaving workers to carry out more complicated, abstract, and challenging aspects of work. Shoshana Zuboff, "New Worlds of Computer-Mediated Work," *Harvard Business Review* 60, no. 5 (1982): 144–48; David Buchanan and David Boody, *Organizations in the Computer Age* (Hampshire, England: Gower, 1983); Koji Okubayashi, "Work Content and Organizational Structure of Japanese Enterprises under Microelectronic Innovation," *Annals of the School of Business Administration,* Kobe University, no. 31 (1987); Richard Cyert and David Mowery, *Technology and Employment Innovation and Growth in the U.S. Economy* (Washington, D.C.: National Academy Press, 1987), 89.

productivity grew annually at a rate of 3.3 percent from 1948 to 1966, 2.1 percent from 1966 to 1973, and 1.2 percent from 1973 to 1978.)[66]

Second, global competition further increased interest in human capital investment, as many analysts came to believe that the United States would only survive as a manufacturing power in high-wage, high-skilled markets. Industrialized countries such as Japan and West Germany were competing with the advantage of newer capital as a result of the devastation caused by World War II, and newly industrialized countries were able to price aggressively due to much lower labor costs. Competition based on low prices was a dead end for companies in high-wage countries that could never hope to undersell their third-world opponents.[67] Thus, Piore and Sabel argued that countries could maintain their high standards of living only if they moved into flexible, specialized production, offering high-quality goods at higher prices to be sold in upper-end, niche markets. Streeck took a slightly different track, disputing that nations could build manufacturing strategies around niche markets and recommending instead "diversified quality production," a manufacturing process that used advanced technology to make high-volume quality goods.[68] (Of course, some companies dealt with the wage differentials by outsourcing, or manufacturing components of domestically produced goods elsewhere; 20 percent of what we think of as American output is actually produced by foreign workers.)[69]

Third, some economists and managers believed that the new rules of competition demanded greater participation by workers in decision making and more consensual labor relations; human capital investment could contribute to these consensual relations. Technology can be implemented in many different ways depending on strategies in labor relations chosen by managers.[70] Product development is most successful when companies

---

[66] Edward Wolff, "The Magnitude and Causes of the Recent Productivity Slowdown in the United States," in *Productivity Growth and U.S. Competitiveness,* ed. William Baumol and Kenneth McLennan (Oxford: Oxford University Press, 1985), 32, 36.

[67] Tim McKeown, "The Global Economy, Post-Fordism, and Trade Policy in Advanced Capitalist States," in *Continuity and Change in Contemporary Capitalism.*

[68] Michael Piore and Charles Sabel, *The Second Industrial Divide* (New York: Basic Books, 1984); Streeck, *Social Institutions,* 5–6, 32–34.

[69] Robert Reich, *The Work of Nations* (New York: Knopf, 1991), 120, 140.

[70] Paul Adler, "Rethinking the Skill Requirements of New Technologies," Harvard Business School Working Paper, HBS 84–27, October 1983; Maryellen Kelly, "Programmable Automation and the Skill Question," *Human Systems Management* 6, no. 33 (1986): 223–41; Steven Miller and Susan Bereiter, "Modernizing to Computer-Integrated Production Technologies in a Vehicle Assembly Plant," paper presented to NBER conference, Cambridge, August 26–28, 1985, 2; Barry Wilkinson, *The Shopfloor Politics of New Technology* (London: Heinemann Educational Books, 1983), 89–90; Steven Davis and John Haltiwanger, "Wage Dispersion between and within U.S. Manufacturing Plants, 1963–1986,"

can capture shopfloor learning; cooperative relations encourage valuable input from workers.[71] Adversarial labor-management relations can dampen growth in productivity because a more cooperative workforce is quicker to accept new technology and the elimination of less-productive jobs. Thus the Work in America Institute argued that employment security makes it easier for workers to embrace technical change, to give up obsolete work rules, and to participate in the industrial restructuring so necessary to productivity growth.[72] Osterman suggests that "high commitment work places" seek to enhance productivity by using workers' expertise and fortifying employees' commitment to quality products.[73]

Others believed that global competition demanded fewer concessions to workers rather than more benefits.[74] The modern firm must be flexible and able to make decisions about production unhindered by government meddling or by labor contracts. This flexibility motivates a movement away from the paternalistic firm with cradle-to-grave benefits. An irony is that the logic of global trade *both* rewards lower labor costs and demands efficient social reproduction of the workforce.[75]

Despite much interest in expanding investment in human capital, economists and managers alike disagreed about the role of public policy in this process. Participants in this debate gravitated toward two camps:

Brookings Papers on Economic Activity (1991): 115–80; Marc Maurice, Francois Sellier, and Jean-Jacques Silverstre, *The Social Foundations of Industrial Power*, trans. Arthur Goldhammer (Cambridge: MIT Press, 1982).

[71] Harry Katz, Thomas Kochan, and Kenneth Gobeille, "Industrial Relations Performance, Economic Performance, and QWL Programs," *Industrial and Labor Relations Review* 37, no. 1 (1983): 14; Hayes, Wheelwright, and Clark, *Dynamic Manufacturing;* David Teece, ed., *The Competitive Challenge* (Cambridge, Mass.: Ballinger, 1987).

[72] Work in America Institute, *Employment Security in a Free Economy* (New York: Pergamon Press, 1984), 323–45; Ronald Dore, *British Factory, Japanese Factory* (Berkeley and Los Angeles: University of California Press, 1973); C. F. Pratten, *Labour Productivity Differentials within International Companies* (Cambridge: Cambridge University Press, 1978), 55–56.

[73] Osterman, "Work/Family Programs." See also Joel Cutcher-Gershenfeld, "The Impact of Economic Performance of a Transformation in Workplace Relations," *Industrial and Labor Relations Review* 44, no. 2 (1991): 241–60. Positive worker attitudes have produced higher total factor productivity and lower unit costs of production in the U.S. automobile industry. J. R. Norsworthy and Craig Zabula, "Worker Attitudes, Worker Behavior, and Productivity in the U.S. Automobile Industry, 1959–1976," *Industrial and Labor Relations Review* 38, no. 4 (1985): 544. Paper mill plants with lower grievance rates have been more productive. Casey Ichniowski, "The Effects of Grievance Activity on Productivity," *Industrial and Labor Relations Review* 40, no. 1 (1986): 75–89.

[74] For discussion see Alfred Pfaller, Ian Gough, and Goran Therborn, *Can the Welfare State Compete?* (London: Macmillan, 1991).

[75] Graham Vickery and Gregory Wurzburg, "Flexible Firms, Skills, and Employment," *OECD Observer*, October 20, 1996, 17–21; John Dunning, *The Globalization of Business* (New York: Routledge, 1993), 326–28.

adherents of laissez-faire and advocates of a high-performance workforce. The former considered government social policy detrimental to economic goals; the latter thought it a necessary inducement to investment in human capital. Business managers took sides in this debate, sharing the goal of protecting profits but disagreeing about the best way to achieve this goal.

Those advocating a laissez-faire stance by government feared that social regulations would interfere with market efficiencies. For example, the Organisation for Economic Co-operation and Development (OECD) warned that excessive labor market regulations had reduced long-term employment in Europe. Many agreed with the Committee for Economic Development that problematic government policies, including excessive regulation and high taxes, contributed to the slow growth of capital spending.[76] Critics attacked social policy in general; for example, AFDC was alleged to erode fathers' sense of responsibility for their children, to encourage teenage pregnancy and illegitimacy, and to contribute to the development of an underclass. Programs designed to compensate for the breakdown in traditional structures of family and community were thought to be weakening other traditional social structures.[77] Thus one solution was to "roll back the intrusions of the therapeutic state" and to restore power to the individual and to more "natural" social groupings.[78]

Although much of the laissez-faire critique focused on means-tested programs for the poor such as Aid to Families with Dependent Children, similar questions were raised about social initiatives designed to enhance human-resource investment. Thus Glazer argued that national training programs have an abysmal record. Heckman suggested that the costs of a national training program would be astronomical and that the German model is deeply flawed; instead, development of skills is best left to the market.[79] Gill maintained that government subsidies for and regulation of child care disadvantaged families with stay-at-home moms, forcing them (through taxes) to contribute to other families' needs for child care. Broude

[76] Organisation for Economic Co-operation and Development, *Flexibility in the Labour Market* (Paris: OECD, 1986), 111, 91; Robert Holland, "The Committee for Economic Development Report on United States Technology Policy," in *Technology, International Economics, and Public Policy,* ed. Hugh Miller and Rolf Piekarz (Boulder, Colo.: Westview, 1982), 87–92; Paul McCracken et al., *Towards Full Employment and Price Stability* (Paris: Organisation for Economic Co-operation and Development, 1977).

[77] Charles Murray, *Losing Ground* (New York: Basic Books, 1984), 146; Lawrence Mead, *New Politics of Poverty* (New York: Basic Books, 1992); Nathan Glazer, *The Limits of Social Policy* (Cambridge: Harvard University Press, 1988), 3–6.

[78] William Schambra, "The Old Values of the New Citizenship," *Policy Review* 69 (summer 1994): 32–38.

[79] Nathan Glazer, "A Human Capital Policy for the Cities," *Public Interest* 112 (summer 1993): 27–49; James Heckman, "Is Job Training Oversold?" *Public Interest* 115 (spring 1994): 91–115.

argued that advocates of national policy have underestimated the negative impact of day care on children, fearing that such evidence could damage their political cause.[80] Herzliner suggested that Clinton's health reform proposal threatened the quiet revolution already set into motion by small health provider entrepreneurs. Because industries with a few big firms tend to avoid price competition, managed competition would discourage small entrepreneurs from getting a foothold in the industry and would actually increase costs.[81] Finally, even if one accept the merits of such policies, questions have been raised about the ability of government to fashion effective policies (without succumbing to the demands of special interests) in the areas of human capital investment and industrial policy.[82]

Those advocating a high-performance workplace thought that government policies were essential to achieve adequate levels of investment in human capital. Human capital falls into the category of broad collective good, and the benefits of the investment cannot be contained to the companies that devote resources either to private provision or to lobbying for public policies. Consequently, individual firms are unlikely to make sufficient investments in these goods. Human capital differs from physical capital in three ways: It cannot be owned; consequently, capitalists are more reluctant to invest in it. Investments in human capital require longer time horizons than are generally allowed by capitalism. They also require a social context, something "completely foreign to the individualistic orientation of capitalism." Because employers today are competing with firms in countries that enjoy many policy supports, government must attempt to level the playing field.[83]

Advocates of the high-performance workplace wanted policies targeted to human capital investment, even while many criticized existing social programs (as no longer appropriate to the growth requisites of the new age and as doing nothing for the problems of the most disadvantaged).[84] For example, frustration with the traditional training programs prompted the initiatives of the Clinton administration. Traditional public-sector

[80] Richard Gill, "Day Care or Parental Care?" *Public Interest* 105 (fall 1991): 3–16; Gwen Broude, "The Realities of Day Care," *Public Interest* 125 (fall 1996): 95–105.

[81] Regina Herzlinger, "The Quiet Health Care Revolution," *Public Interest* 115 (spring 1994): 72–90.

[82] Phillips, *Staying on Top*, 149–51.

[83] Thurow, *The Future of Capitalism*, 281, 16; Grahame, *Losing Time*, 65; Anthony Carnevale, *America and the New Economy* (San Francisco: Jossey-Bass, 1991); George Lodge, *Perestroika for America* (Boston: Harvard Business School Press, 1990).

[84] Claus Offe, "Smooth Consolidation in the West German Welfare State," in *Labor Parties in Postindustrial Societies*, ed. Frances Fox Piven (New York: Oxford University Press, 1992), 124–46; John Myles, "Decline or Impasse? The Current State of the Welfare," *Studies in Political Economy* 26 (1988): 73–107; David Ellwood, *Poor Support* (New York: Basic Books, 1988).

training programs have a mixed record in improving earnings and enhancing productivity, with those to improve the material circumstances of the economically disadvantaged doing least well in cost-benefit analysis. Public training programs for dislocated workers fare better, although programs for this population have been studied less. Not surprisingly, longer-term, costly programs work better, and women seem to benefit from training more than men or and adolescents. LaLonde notes that the "modest investments" in traditional public training programs have produced "modest gains" in terms of income and workforce participation.[85]

The Clinton administration hoped to escape the limits of these traditional public-sector training programs. It believed that traditional training inappropriately separated the classroom and the workplace and sought to reintegrate these settings. The new approach hoped to overcome the problems of past public-sector training programs while realizing the great need for a comprehensive training system. Stressing the interconnections within firms between social benefits and economic growth, Robert Reich wrote,

> Decisions about health care needs, for example, will be related to decisions about needs for retirement benefits or for retraining assistance. . . . A decision to expand into a new technology may require special emphasis on retraining, relocation, and day care assistance. . . In short, rather than two separate systems that interact only incidentally—one geared to production and the other to passive dependency—we will have one system, serving both economic and human development.[86]

Reagan and the Triumph of Laissez-Faire

At the end of the 1970s political coalitions everywhere seemed poised to embrace laissez-faire ideas. Conservative parties with considerable corporate backing worked (with varying success) to cut back the welfare state in countries throughout the world. Margaret Thatcher tried to sell off a considerable share of public housing and initiated a broad drive to expand private pensions. Sweden experimented with a conservative regime after

---

[85] Robert LaLonde, "The Promise of Public Sector-Sponsored Training Programs," *Journal of Economic Perspectives* 9, no. 2 (1995): 149–68; Department of Labor, *Study of the Implementation of the Economic Dislocation and Worker Adjustment Assistance Act—Phase II* (Washington, D.C.: U.S. Government Printing Office, 1993); Department of Labor, *The National JTPA Study* (Washington, D.C.: U.S. Government Printing Office, 1993).

[86] Reich, *The Next American Frontier*, 248–49; W. Norton Grubb, *Learning to Work: The Case for Reintegrating Job Training and Education* (New York: Russell Sage Foundation, 1996).

thirty years of social democracy. Even the French socialists under Francois Mitterand embraced the austerity politics of rightist regimes.[87]

Ronald Reagan attacked the welfare state with a two-pronged proposal for cuts in taxes and spending. Although the spending cuts did little to change the shape of social provision, tax reductions in 1981 and 1986 created a budgetary crisis that put future spending decisions in a zero-sum context, in addition to inflating the dollar and exacerbating the trade deficit. David Stockman's remarkable confession acknowledged that the administration viewed the tax cuts as a tool for reducing the welfare state.[88] Reagan's policies were to redistribute the tax burden greatly between rich and poor. The families in the poorest quintile lost 18 percent of their income between 1968 and 1986; the income of the richest quintile increased 8 percent. Almost 23 million lived in poverty in 1973, but over 32 million were poor in 1986.[89]

As a nominee, Ronald Reagan originally had limited corporate support; most business managers preferred John Connally or George Bush. Most of Connally's PAC financing (88 percent) came from corporate groups, labeling him the candidate of big business. Reagan received most corporate money only after victory was certain and long after he first began leading in the public-opinion polls.[90] The *Economist* attributed Reagan's victory to his ability to capture the center of American politics and predicted that he would "abandon that centre-right ground at his peril."[91]

Yet as Reagan won the nomination and the presidency, a wide array of business managers signed onto his policies on taxes, spending, and deregulation, putting to rest their concern about the budgetary implications of supply-side economics. The Reagan administration was quite successful at mobilizing business support for specific policy initiatives. Wayne Valis at the Office of Public Liaison built a coalition of five hundred business groups to push through the spending cuts in 1981. A similar group supported the huge tax reductions in the same year.[92] As if to build corporate approval for its program of deregulation, the administration asked one hundred large companies and trade associations about the regulations

[87] Ramesh Mishra, *The Welfare State in Crisis* (New York: St. Martin's Press, 1984); Pierson, *Dismantling the Welfare State.*

[88] David Stockman, *The Triumph of Politics* (New York: Harper and Row, 1986); John Palmer and Isabel Sawhill, eds., *The Reagan Experiment* (Washington, D.C.: Urban Institute Press, 1982).

[89] Bennett Harrison and Barry Bluestone, *The Great U-Turn* (New York: Basic Books, 1988) 131, 135.

[90] William J. Lanouette, "PAC Gifts to Presidential Candidates Include Some Political Surprises," *National Journal,* August 9, 1980, 1309–11.

[91] "Warts and All," *Economist,* November 8, 1980, 13.

[92] Dick Kirschten, "Reaganomics Puts Business on the Spot," *National Journal,* December 19, 1981, 2229; Martin, *Shifting the Burden.*

that most oppressed them. Firms were asked to identify specific problems with the regulations and estimate their costs. This deregulation hit list was widely touted in the popular press as evidence of business-government collusion of the most egregious sort. In fact, according to a high-ranking government official, the lists were used to pressure firms to accept less tolerable aspects of the president's agenda.[93]

The shift rightward partly reflected the increasing influence of a southern and western Sunbelt with an ideological orientation different from the old Wall Street Republicans. But the Wall Street Republicans themselves seemed to become more conservative during the Reagan years: witness eastern-establishment John J. McCloy's move to the conservative Olin Foundation.[94]

Managers were also drawn to Reagan because they began to rethink the relationship between economic prosperity and social security, wondering if they could now afford the expansive private and public social benefits that had helped to secure labor peace. Social costs could be less easily absorbed in a highly competitive climate; therefore, social regulations that added to the costs of products, either as taxes or as part of the social wage, came under more intensive cost-benefit scrutiny.[95] Global pressures were compounded by the tendency of nonpaying companies to shift social costs onto the paying ones: many large companies provide health benefits to the spouses of their workers, when these spouses cannot obtain coverage through their own employers. Large firms were frustrated when they invested in training for workers who then moved to smaller firms. The Committee for Economic Development laid out the logic for cutbacks in social provision:

> The changes accompanying the new economy mean that many of our social and economic institutions created to deal with labor market adjustment and economic security need reform. Support systems, such as unemployment insurance or public and private systems of health and retirement benefits, were designed primarily for workers with long-term attachments to a single employer, an arrangement that is becoming less relevant for a significant proportion of the labor force.[96]

[93] William H. Miller, "A Plea for Help from Reagan's Deregulators," *Industry Week,* June 1, 1981, 58; interview with government official, 1984.

[94] Mike Davis, "The New Right's Road to Power," *New Left Review,* July–August 1981, 28–49; Kirkpatrick Sale, *Power Shift: The Rise of the Southern Rim and Its Challenge to the Eastern Establishment* (New York: Random House, 1979); Thomas Ferguson and Joel Rogers, *Right Turn* (New York: Hill and Wang, 1986), 103.

[95] Alfred Pfaller with Ian Gough and Goran Therborn, "The Issue," in *Can Welfare State Compete?* 1–6.

[96] Frank Doyle and Anthony Carnevale, "American Workers and Economic Change," Committee for Economic Development, 20–21.

The internationalization of American production eroded the old mer-
cantilist arguments that citizens share a common interest in the economic
prosperity of their nation and, therefore, in their country's major corporations. Because business's support for policies expanding human capital
investment depended on its perception of a connection between the nation's and firm's economic well-being, the severing of that link lowered
business backing for social policy.[97]

Managers also began scaling back services within the firm and shifting
social risk to their workers. In 1982, 84 percent of employees were guar-
anteed monthly pensions upon retirement through defined-benefit plans.
By 1994 only 56 percent were in such plans; the remainder were given a
monthly allowance (defined contribution) that they could invest as they
saw fit. *Business Week* remarked that

> the relationship [between company and worker] isn't what it was. The new
> compact between company and worker dismisses paternalism and embraces
> self-reliance. Big farewell to unconditional lifetime employment, even at the
> bluest of blue-chip companies that once implicitly turned on such an ethic.[98]

The Post-Reagan, Postindustrial World

Yet, despite much hoopla about the death of the welfare state, ultimately
the laissez-faire view failed to establish itself as the indisputable new or-
thodoxy either in government policy or in business thinking.[99] Although
managers were drawn to Reagan's supply-side magic that promised tax
cuts, deficit reduction, social-spending cuts, and military increases in one
marvelous package, over time many employers became less sanguine
about the Reagan plan. Vague unease about the economic future in the
late 1980s fostered some business interest in policies to expand human
capital investment. Some managers shared the Democratic view that markets alone are insufficient to spur international competitiveness and that
government must assist industry through incentives strategically calculated to maximize America's competitive advantage. In 1984 *Business
Week* observed that "American business executives are on the brink of a
profound change in their view of the future of U.S. industry."[100]

---

[97] Reich, *The Work of Nations,* 280.

[98] "Business Rolls the Dice," *Business Week,* October 17, 1994, 89; "The New World
of Work," *Business Week,* October 17, 1994, 76.

[99] Ramesh Mishra, *The Welfare State in Capitalist Society* (Toronto: University of Toronto Press, 1990), 1–4; Houghe and Marks, "The Making of a Polity."

[100] "A Cautious Nod to 'Industrial Policy,' " *Business Week,* March 19, 1984, 15.

Although managers often favored the general Republican goal of reducing aggregate public social spending, many promoted specific initiatives in human capital investment. Thus eight out of ten of the *Business Week* 1000 companies wanted new education and training programs, and 65 percent were even willing to pay higher corporate taxes for educational improvement; 68 percent believed that the inadequate education of poor and minority children had a major impact on economic competitiveness. Another poll found 70 percent of its sample of employers desiring increased federal spending on training in 1992.[101] The managers who strongly agreed that we were "facing a health care crisis" went up from 30 percent in 1985 to 54 percent in 1990.[102]

Managers today are much more sanguine about the climate for business than they were at the beginning of the 1990s. Productivity growth rates in the manufacturing sector have rebounded, the trade deficit has been scaled back, and inflation has remained quite low. Although good economic news usually instills fear of inflation in the hearts of traders, the stock market has enjoyed one of its longest booms in history. Information technology and globalization may finally be enabling higher rates of productivity. The *New York Times* recently pointed to themes of "triumph" and "self-satisfaction" in the American psyche.[103]

Yet as this book is being written, business managers continue to show conflicting views about the proper role of government social policy in spurring investment in human capital. Shortly after President Clinton took power many big-business managers seemed interested in the new administration's ambitious social programs. Interest in human capital investment did not translate into a sudden upsurge of support for the Democratic Party: *Chief Executive* found that only 3 percent of its sample CEOs favored Clinton in 1992. But Robert Rubin of the White House National Economic Council claimed that "a lot of the administration's accomplishments have been in coordination with business."[104] When business soured

[101] Louis Harris and Associates, "A Survey of the Reaction of the American People and Top Business Executives to the Report on Public Education by the Task Force on Teaching as a Profession of the Carnegie Forum on Education and the Economy," Study no. 864011, Roper Library, "Harris for Carnegie Forum 08/1986" File; Prepared for the Nightly Business Report by Yankelovich Clancy, Shulman, "Health Care and Health Insurance," (June 10–19, 1992) obtained from the Roper Center, "Yankelovich for the Nightly Business Report Surveys of Executives 01/93" file.

[102] William M. Mercer, Inc., *Employer Attitudes toward the Cost of Health Care* (New York, 1990).

[103] Louis Uchietelle, "Puffed Up by Prosperity, U.S. Struts Its Stuff," *New York Times*, April 27, 1997, E1.

[104] "And Then There Were Two," *Chief Executive*, September 1992, 14–15; David Broder and Michael Weisskopf, "Business Prospered in Democrat-Led 103rd Congress," *Washington Post*, September 25, 1994, A1.

on Clinton in 1994, *Business Week* gave the administration something of a backhanded compliment: "leadership and character issues outweigh gains on trade and jobs."[105]

Then the sweeping election of a Republican Congress in November 1994 was initially heralded in the press as a triumph of business interests and conservative thought. Many big-business managers liked the Republican Contract with America's promise to curb product liability suits; even the big auto manufacturers, supposedly the champions of Clinton's attempt to reform health care, embraced the Republican's proposed changes in personal-injury law. The National Association of Manufacturers organized a one-thousand-company group to promote risk assessment and to cut back environmental regulations.[106]

Yet after a few months fissures between big business and the Republicans became the story of the hour. Big-business managers share class, educational background, and social values with many Democratic elites, but they share only economic conservatism with Main Street Republicans. Considerable disagreement about policy also divided large employers from conservative Republicans. Big-business managers had serious concerns about the Republican's plan to devolve decision making to the state level, since multistate employers would find themselves having to answer to a multitude of social and environmental regulations.[107] Business managers were much more interested in the reduction of budget deficits than in tax cuts; for example, a Chamber of Commerce survey found its members ranking tax issues numbers 12, 14, and 15 out of twenty on a list of priorities. A 1992 CBS/*New York Times* poll found that only 12 percent of its corporate sample actually favored cuts in spending; the majority (53 percent) wanted immediate attention to deficit reduction, and 33 percent wanted an increase in budgets for social programs.[108] Business managers worried about the right-wing populist rejection of the North American Free Trade Agreement (NAFTA) and the General Agreement on Tariffs and Trade (GATT). Said one business association representative: "I'm a conservative Republican, but on trade I'm a flaming liberal compared to some of these new House Republicans. They can do enormous damage."[109] Many large manufacturers want to retain Commerce Department

---

[105] "Why Business Hates Clinton," *Business Week,* October 10, 1994, 38–40.

[106] Bob Davis, "Big Business, Striking It Rich in GOP 'Contract,' Stands by as Clinton's High-Tech Plans Get Cut," *Wall Street Journal,* March 7, 1995, A20; Howard Banks, "They're Killing the Environmental Law Monster," *Forbes,* March 13, 1995, 37.

[107] "Gingrich's Plan Sounds Fishy to Business," *Fortune,* March 20, 1995, 24.

[108] Howard Gleckman, with Richard Dunham and Richard Melcher, "The GOP's Tax Cuts Are Falling Off the Table," *Business Week,* February 27, 1995, 42; CBS/*New York Times* Poll, "Business Leaders Feb. 18–March 6, 1992," Press Release, March 12, 1992, Roper Library, "CBS News and CBS News/The NYT Times Poll Releases—1992" file.

[109] Lee Walczak, "The New Populism," *Business Week,* March 13, 1995, 72.

programs to encourage exports and subsidies for research and development; small business would exchange "corporate welfare" programs for
the tax reductions in the Republican Contract.[110]

Conclusion

Contrary to widely accepted stereotypes, business managers have backed
many social initiatives in the past century, both at home and especially
abroad. Although labor leaders and government bureaucrats typically
lead these struggles for social reform, managers have none the less entered
into the fray. That we find this surprising reflects a narrow appraisal of
the goals of social policy: in addition to redistribution (which fails to
appeal to managers for the obvious reasons) social policies may promise
to enhance workers' skills, to expand demand, to secure labor peace, or
to force all companies to provide commensurate benefits.

Judging from the past, one concludes that American managers find it
difficult to translate their interest in policies that promote human capital
investment into legislative support. Indeed, at critical junctures, the major
business groups gave voice to the skeptics within their ranks and rejected
social initiatives. Large employers then moved onto develop their own in-
house social benefits, establishing a legacy of private provision to shape
future deliberations over policy.

Business managers continue to debate the relative costs and benefits
of human capital investment policies. Proponents of a high-performance
workplace find them indispensable, while those preferring a laissez-faire
approach by government are unlikely to see merit in these policies. The
goals of profit and productivity are ubiquitous, but the preferred means
for achieving these ends are subject to very different interpretations. Thus
ideology is not the unilateral stumbling block to government intervention
that we often hold it to be; indeed, internal corporate deliberations are
marked by conflict between opposing ideological perspectives.

What is lacking in many accounts of employers' responses to policy
initiatives from both parties is a systematic account of how managers
develop their political preferences. The following chapters delve into the
process by which managers choose between competing worldviews and
formulate their positions on policy.

---

[110] Richard Dunham and Mary Beth Regan, "Let the Wild Rumpus Start!" *Business
Week,* January 16, 1995, 28; David Sanger, "Backing Deficit Reduction, Executives Are
Wary of Deep Cuts," *New York Times,* May 14, 1995, 22.

THREE

NATURE OR NURTURE?

COMPANY PREFERENCES FOR

NATIONAL HEALTH REFORM

CORPORATE ANXIETY about economic growth is like a recurring nightmare, yet business managers cope with this primal fear in varied fashion. One person's palliative is another's quackery. Chapter 2 surveyed business's historical debates over social policy and growth. Some leaders of industry joined government and labor in supporting social legislation, while others rejected it as damaging to economic prosperity. Although managers' regard for growth may be enduring and archetypal, their view of the relationship between growth and social policy is more indeterminate.

Historical and cross-national examples indicate a willingness among corporations to consider social solutions to economic problems but tell us little about how, when, and why it arises. When do social policies gain significant backing from business? How do new ideas win corporate confidence? What is the process by which managers become involved in the political realm?

Skeptics want evidence. And social scientists—like stockbrokers, parole officers, and weather forecasters—must isolate the factors essential to prediction. This chapter moves us from exploring the possible to questioning the probable, and to isolating the factors that bring some companies to connect social policy with economic growth. Specifically, this chapter surveys the economic and institutional characteristics that lead Fortune 200 companies to endorse employer mandates for health benefits.

In this chapter I show that certain institutional characteristics make companies more likely to encounter high-performance workplace arguments and, hence, to favor government policies to expand human capital investment. First, companies with a functional role within the firm for policy experts (that is, those companies maintaining government affairs offices in Washington, D.C.) are significantly more likely to favor employer mandates. Second, firms' participation in politically focused groups significantly enhances support for employer mandates. Finally, legacies of frustrating private interventions, while not statistically significant, seem to enhance a company's willingness to embrace government policy.

Thus, the positions a firm takes are shaped by the cognitive assessments and organizational memberships of the people within its ranks. Support for national health reform developed when the stratum of private policy professionals within the firm worked to put this issue on the business agenda. Sharing their experiences collectively in professional groups and forums, these private experts came to believe that health financing was a problem of enormous scope, exceeding the capacities of an individual firm, and worked to bring top management to share this perspective. Growing weary of failed market interventions, they embraced governmental reform.

Two Views of Firms' Preferences

The division between economic and institutional explanations of political action, described in chapter 1, emerges in discussions of firms' preferences. Many investigations of company positions on public policy find causality in the economic characteristics of the firm, or in the structure of the industry to which it belongs. Others suggest that an exclusive focus on material characteristics such as industrial structure masks the real dynamics of political deliberation within companies.

Preference is rather easily assumed from the company's material conditions in the economic model; therefore, it is correspondingly simple to predict which firms should support health reform. To identify those likely to accept an expanded social regulation such as employer mandates, one looks at how policy change would affect the balance of power among winners and losers in the current system.

Size should matter because larger firms are more likely to provide benefits to their workers.[1] Company *health costs* should have an influence because companies that provide rich health benefits want to stop cost shifting from other companies and because those with lower health costs do not want to lose their competitive edge.[2] *Profitability* should matter, because less profitable companies have a harder time coping with rising health prices and are more likely to seek government help. (Profitability could also work in the opposite direction: richer companies might be better able to afford to develop policy stands, and poorer companies with limited benefits might have reason to fear mandates that demand more expansive provisions.) A firm's *capital-labor ratio* is important because

[1] Alexander Hicks and Duane Swank, "On the Political Economy of Welfare Expansion," *Comparative Political Studies* 17, no. 1 (1984): 81–119.

[2] One might protest, as many economists do, that firms simply shift benefit costs to workers; therefore, the price of health does not matter. But firms often oppose corporate taxes and mandated benefits as a matter of public policy, even if they ultimately do not bear the burden.

when labor costs are a small proportion of total production costs, companies can afford to pay more for benefits in order to achieve industrial peace.[3] *Unionized* companies might favor reform to force their competitors to bear health costs, to reduce their commitments to their unions, and to induce government to take over the provision of benefits.

Two types of *industrial sectors* are more likely to accept government intervention: regulated sectors and troubled sectors. Troubled sectors accustomed to asking for government subsidies should be more willing to accept regulation; however, troubled sectors that do not provide high levels of health benefits may be more fearful of mandates. Regulated sectors by definition are resigned to government intervention and should be less cautious about new controls.[4] (Even though regulated sectors have become more deregulated in the past two decades, they have a history of interacting with government.) Many companies have entered the business of providing health care services, especially with the expansion of for-profit facilities in the past decade; obviously these companies have much less interest in controlling costs.[5] Finally, *export-oriented* companies that compete in foreign markets with firms having lower health costs might prefer systemic restructuring.

For institutionalists the economist's skeletal view of firms' motivations is akin to deriving the full range of human emotion from bone structure. To say that profits drive all corporate action is like saying that sustenance underlies all human behavior. Of course these primal instincts are at the base of our behaviors. But eating in the poststructuralist world can signify an art form, an act of friendship, self-destruction, a sacred taboo, or a sexual overture. Similarly, many possible actions might satisfy the ultimate profit motive; political preference depends on the interpretation of economic circumstance. Disagreements about ends and means, comfort of habit, or force of reason shape the processes by which firms satisfy their ultimate goals.[6]

How companies view their interests should depend on where they get and how they process information. Support for policies to promote human capital investment requires a leap of faith, but also a leap of thought. Firms must be exposed and receptive to an alternative worldview, in which high-performance workplace concepts challenge views antithetical to government intervention. The nut of the prob-

---

[3]   Ferguson, "Normalcy to New Deal."

[4]   Handler and Mulkern, *Business in Politics,* 24–29; Val Burris, "The Political Partisanship of American Business," *American Sociological Review* 52 (1987): 732–44.

[5]   J. Warren Salmon, "Introduction, Special Section on the Corporatization of Medicine," *International Journal of Health Services* 17, no. 1 (1987): 1–6.

[6]   Thompson, "Firm as Dispersed," 233; Michael Best, *The New Competition* (Cambridge: Harvard University Press, 1990).

lem, then, is to figure out what enables companies to make this leap of thought.

This chapter argues that deliberation over interests within the firm reflects three institutional factors. First, in-house expertise affects how managers think about their interests. Government affairs and human-resource departments are usually staffed by individuals with professional training in their substantive fields who share a language with their peers in the public and nonprofit sectors. If these private experts on policy gain the confidence of their CEOs, they can influence the way that top management considers the company's interests.

Second, participation in deliberative groups improves the odds that companies will endorse policies of human capital investment. Participation in groups and networks channels new ideas from both the corporate and noncorporate realms and increases companies' exposure to current ideas about policy. Part professional, part social, these groups help participants to define problems and to identify with the goals of the group. Thus, groups not only represent their member firms' interests, but shape their members' preferences.[7]

Third, policies legacies from past efforts guide corporate deliberations. Business managers struggle to correct, and to learn from, past failures.[8] As a company exhausts the range of interventions in a social area that are available to the individual firm, it may become disillusioned with market solutions and move on to collective, governmental solutions. At the same time vested interests in past experiments can prevent a firm from accepting changes that stray too far from the status quo.

The Economics of Health Reform

Before moving to identifying the companies supporting employer mandates, we should ponder why employers might be drawn to health reform. After all, decades of bills to contain costs have faltered under the attack of the medical industry, and managers rejected earlier comprehensive reforms as costly, invasive of physicians' power, and ideologically incorrect. Marmor et al. noted in 1980 that "national health insurance generates an ideological intensity matched by few other issues in American politics. The antagonists in the debate are well defined and well known, and they have remained relatively stable over time."[9]

---

[7] C. Oliver, "Strategic Responses to Institutional Processes," *Academy of Management Review* 16 (1991): 145–79; J. D. Auerbach, *In the Business of Child Care* (New York: Praeger, 1988); Grimm and Holcomb, "Choices among Encompassing Organizations."

[8] Miles, *Coffin Nails,* 169–76, 186.

[9] Theodore Marmor, Judith Feder, and John Holahan, *National Health Insurance: Conflicting Goals and Policy Choices* (Washington, D.C.: Urban Institute, 1980), 7.

Beginning in the late 1980s, however, the escalating costs of health care triggered a collective anxiety attack, and for the first time in fifteen years a fundamental national overhaul of the health-financing system appeared on the public agenda. Leaps in health care spending did not deliver vastly improved outcomes: for example, the United States ranked number 11 in the world in infant mortality. Combined with rising costs was the continuing problem of some 35 million uninsured persons, many of whom were working poor.[10] The baroque eligibility rules of many health plans kept workers from improving their employment circumstances. Rates varied wildly, with small firms and the self-employed paying much more than those in government or large-firm insurance pools; indeed, insurance plans for individuals could easily cost more than housing. Even those lucky enough to get top-rate care were receiving less service for more money every year. The buildup of the medical industrial complex, like the arms race, was frustrating in its lack of tangible benefits.

Managers shared other Americans' distress about spiraling health costs. Almost two-thirds of our nonelderly population are covered through employers, and this private health care system has increasingly been threatened.[11] Health care costs have risen dramatically in the past forty years, increasing from 5.3 percent of the GNP in 1960 to 11.6 percent in 1989, with a large share falling on corporate employers. In 1965 households funded 60.5 percent of the nation's health care; business, 17 percent; and government, 20.7 percent. By 1989 each sector paid about one-third. Rising corporate costs can be traced to cost shifting in which governments negotiate ever lower rates, leaving business and commercial insurers to pay more. Hospitals make up Medicare and Medicaid payment shortfalls with whopping bills to private payers. Lewin-ICF estimated that such "cost shifting" totaled $20.1 billion in 1989 (11 percent of total hospital costs) and was likely to expand to $34.6 billion by 1992.[12]

Health benefits have become a much larger source of labor strife over time, causing only 18 percent of strikes involving over one thousand workers in 1986 but 78 percent in 1989. Health benefits really were a fringe benefit when they cost employers 2.2 percent of salaries and wages in 1965, but they became a major drain on companies' bottom line when they jumped to 8.3 percent by 1989.[13] In 1991 U.S. employers spent on

[10] Victor Fuchs, "The 'Competition Revolution' in Health Care," *Health Affairs* 9, no. 2 (1988): 9.

[11] Marilyn Field and Harold Shapiro, "Summary," in *Employment and Health Benefits,* ed. Marilyn Field and Harold Shapiro (Washington, D.C. National Academy Press, 1993).

[12] Lewin-ICF, Allen Dobson and James Roney, "Cost-Shifting: A Self Limiting Process," prepared for the Healthcare Financial Management Association (April 1992).

[13] Kirk Victor, "Gut Issue," *National Journal,* March 24, 1990), 704, 706; Levit et al., "National Health Care Spending, 1989," 117, 127–29.

average $3,573 per worker on health insurance, a gain of 13 percent from 1990.[14]

Fierce international competition over both export opportunities in foreign countries and our own domestic market share has driven U.S. firms to search for new ways to cut costs. Health care supposedly adds $700 to the price of an American-made car, but only $200 to an auto made in Japan. Health costs for each hourly Canadian steelworker are $3,200 a year; the American counterpart costs $7,600 a year.[15]

In a remarkable reversal of fortune, national health reform became associated with keeping costs down rather than driving them up, making many managers (at least initially) quite open to a comprehensive overhaul of the health-financing system. For this reason there was a broad perception before Clinton proposed his bill that large employers would join the reform coalition.[16] Cantor et al. found that 80 percent of the 384 Fortune 500 executives in their study believed that "fundamental changes are needed to make it [the health care system] better" and that 53 percent favored employer mandates. *Business and Health* found 30 percent of its corporate respondents in favor of, and 25 percent neutral toward, national health insurance.[17] A survey of Conference Board CEOs found half believing that government action was necessary to control health costs. One corporate lobbyist put it, "Business from the far right has moved to the center in saying that the federal government needs to be involved."[18]

Four major reform proposals for restructuring the health-financing system organized the national debate before the Clinton administration came to office: the single-payer, play-or-pay, Heritage tax credit, and managed-competition proposals.

The single-payer approach created a single pool into which all would pay, usually through taxes rather than through premiums; this pool would negotiate with hospitals and doctors. Advocates claimed that a Canadian-style single-payer system would save $69 to $83.2 billion in administrative costs.[19] Critics retorted that the Canadian federal government is shift-

---

[14] Health Policy Briefs 1, no. 6, Bethlehem Steel Corp, Human Resources Dept., 2.

[15] William Schneider, "Is There a Cure for America's Medical Inflation?" *National Journal,* April 21, 1990, 983; Walter Williams, "United States Senate Committee on Finance Hearing on Health Care Costs, April 16, 1991," *Healthwise* 2, no. 2 (1991): 2.

[16] Mark Peterson, "The Politics of Health Care Policy," in Weir, *Social Divide.*

[17] Joel Cantor, Nancy Barrand, Randolph Desonia, Alan Cohen, and Jeffrey Merril, "Business Leaders' Views on American Health Care," *Health Affairs* 11, no. 1 (1991): 99–101; Robert Wisnewski, "The 1990 National Executive Poll on Health Care Costs and Benefits," *Business and Health* 8, no. 4 (1990): 36.

[18] "CEOs Worried about Still-Spiraling Health Care Costs," *Business Wire,* July 2, 1992; interview with industry lobbyist, May 1991.

[19] Steffie Woolhandler and David Himmelstein, "To Save a Penny Two Are Spent," Division of Social and Community Medicine, Harvard School of Public Health, unpublished

ing costs to the provinces.[20] Others worried that the national government was not competent to administer the plan and that quality would decrease without competitive market pressures.

A second approach, incremental market reform, provided the basis for most Republican proposals and consisted of an assortment of small-market, malpractice insurance, and other changes. Parts of the plan offered by President George Bush drew from more comprehensive market-oriented reform concepts, such as the Heritage tax credit or voucher system, that sought to reintroduce competition into the health care market and to change all employment-related benefits into direct wages. Under this system workers would pay for premiums directly.[21]

A third approach, the "play or pay" plan, was a mixed public-private system that would impose global budgets to limit costs, regulate rates to reduce inequities, and create employer mandates to expand coverage. The "play or pay" feature meant that employers would either *play* and offer health insurance, or *pay* a new payroll tax of 5 to 8 percent to expand the public program.[22]

A final approach, the managed-competition proposal based on the work of Alain Enthoven, sought to change the market incentives for both providers and consumers. On the demand side, consumers would be aggregated into large purchasing cooperatives, or health alliances, that would evaluate plans, negotiate rates, and offer their members a choice of the best plans.[23] On the supply side, a national board would determine a standardized benefit package, and only plans that provided the package would be certified as "accountable health plans." According to its advo-

---

paper, 8. Some plans would abolish private insurance but others allowed private insurers to administer the public plan.

[20] Barry Brown, "How Canada's Health System Works," *Business and Health* 7, no. 7 (1989): 29.

[21] In this system individuals and families get tax credits from the government, adjusted for income, and all heads of households are required to buy at least catastrophic insurance. The plan limits malpractice suits and "experience rating" by insurers and encourages the use of a single, universal insurance claim form. Edmund Haislmaier, "The Principal Culprit in Health Insurance Is the Current Tax Treatment of Benefits," *Roll Call,* May 4, 1992, n.p. In its pure form, the Heritage plan entailed considerable government monitoring of private markets, but the Bush variant was not comprehensive and included no realistic funding strategies.

[22] Play or pay imposed a payroll tax of 7 percent. Funds from this tax would be used to create a new public insurance plan called AmeriCare, which would also absorb Medicaid. Edward Kennedy, "An Affordable Health-Care Plan for All," *Boston Globe,* June 6, 1991, 21.

[23] States would be responsible for regulating the purchasing cooperatives, but the entities could take various forms. Jeremy Rosner, "A Progressive Plan for Affordable, Universal Health Care," in *Mandate for Change,* ed. Will Marshall and Martin Schram (New York: Berkeley Books, 1993), 111–15.

cates, managed competition would move all consumers to the managed-care market and would accomplish dramatic changes in the health care landscape without excessive government intervention. But since the plan stipulated both mandates and regulatory boards, the government would remain very involved.[24]

Clinton's managed-competition proposal was something of a hybrid between Enthoven's market strategy and play or pay. In keeping with the spirit of play or pay Clinton proposed that all employers be mandated to pay 80 percent of insurance premiums for all employees.[25] To contain costs Clinton proposed state-level spending targets for the amount to be spent on health care. The administration combined these regulatory efforts to contain costs with the Enthoven-inspired managed-care proposal for nongovernment purchasing cooperatives.

A Study of Firms' Preferences for Employer Mandates

In a research project *cum* road trip, I visited corporate headquarters to find out what business managers thought about national health reform and how they contributed to the policy debate. From Seattle to Jacksonville, New York City to Newton, Iowa, a common theme echoed through big-city skyscrapers and suburban industrial parks: health care was killing American business. Just as fast-food and motel chains create a seamless web of interstate culture, pervasive concerns about health costs defied regional distinctions; yet companies varied widely in their views of the appropriate role for government in containing the cost of health care.

The primary empirical goal of my study was to identify economic and institutional factors that persuaded companies to favor employer mandates.[26] Critical to financing the plan and focal in legislative debate, the employer mandate merited the attention of anyone interested in corporate support for social regulation.

Some of the data were provided from a series of structured interviews, lasting on average two hours, with high-level managers from a sample of companies. I visited corporate headquarters in the fall of 1992 and the

---

[24] Edmund Faltermayer, "Let's Really Cure the Health System," *Fortune,* March 23, 1992, 58; Michael Abramowitz, "Pushing Bush to a Market-Led Health Solution, Enthoven Sees Competition as Best Antidote for Rising Costs," *Washington Post,* January 26, 1992, H1.

[25] U.S. Department of Commerce, National Technical Information Service, *President's Health Security Plan* (Springfield, Va.: Random House, 1993).

[26] It is important to note that firms did not develop positions on this issue unless they wanted to become involved; therefore, those companies in the top category were truly politically active on health reform.

spring of 1993 and made follow-up telephone calls to fill in missing data in June 1993. In all cases the benefits managers of the firm were interviewed, and in many I also met with the senior vice presidents for human resources and/or with personnel in the Washington, D.C., government affairs office. The sample was a random selection of Fortune 200 manufacturing companies and the American firms on the list of Fortune 500 international service companies.[27] Sixty-six percent of a sample of eighty-nine companies participated.[28]

The dependent variable of firm preference was operationalized as the firm's formal endorsement of employer mandates. It consisted of a scale, moving from a formal political position opposing employer mandates to a formal political position supporting employer mandates; thus, firms that were politically inactive on the issue occupied the middle ground.[29] The scale reflected both whether the firm had taken a formal position on employer mandates as well as the content of that position.

The earlier discussion suggested seven economic hypotheses about the causal determinants of support for health reform. The *cost* of health care was obtained by asking the firms to calculate their annual contributions to health benefits per worker. (This figure also included company-provided benefits for dependents).[30] The *profitability* measure, taken from 1992 Fortune 500 lists, represented net income as a percentage of sales.[31] *Size* was measured as the total sales of the company, taken from Securities and

---

[27] The sample was chosen from a list sorted by size and sector; every third firm was selected. "It Was the Worst of Years," *Fortune,* April 20, 1992, 212–315. Data for the service sector firms were taken from the comparable *Fortune* figures for the international five hundred largest service corporations. "It was a Very Bad Year," *Fortune,* August 24, 1992, 208–44.

[28] I anticipated that there would be some selection bias in that active companies would be more willing to participate than inactive ones. While this was true to some extent, this tendency was overcome by an opposing tendency for the inactive firms to welcome me as a source of additional information about the health care debate. In addition, some known activists in health care refused to see me because they were experiencing severe fiscal constraints and did not wish to share information about their health costs or could not afford the resources to participate.

[29] If there was no formal position, the position of the highest-ranking respondent at the firm was used as a proxy for content. The benefit manager's view in general seemed to be an accurate reflection of the general views of top management (except in eight cases where the company was quite divided). Cases without a formal position but with supportive managers were presented in the answer "no formal position but respondent favored mandates." The fact that the two measures (taking a formal position and favoring mandates) were correlated at nearly .5 supports the use of a scale.

[30] Based on self-reported and seemingly quite reliable data.

[31] Taken from "It Was the Worst of Years," 212–315 and "It Was a Very Bad Year," 208–44.

SCALE 3.1
Firm Positions on Employer Mandates

Answer	Value	Frequency	Percentage
Formal opposition	1	1	1.7
Considering opposition	2	4	6.8
No formal position, but management opposed	3	10	16.9
No formal position, and ambivalent	4	8	13.6
Considering future position but mixed	5	3	5.1
No formal position, but a faction of management in favor	6	8	13.6
Considering support	7	8	13.6
Formal Support	8	16	27.1
Missing data		1	1.7
Total		59	100.0

Exchange Commission reports of firm sales for 1991.[32] *Unionization* was operationalized as the percentage of total employees who belonged to a union.[33] Data about the relative *capital-intensity* of the production process consisted of a ratio of net sales divided by employees.[34] Another economic argument suggested that regulated and troubled manufacturing *sectors* were more likely to support national health reform. The troubled manufacturing sectors included metals, autos, mining, and paper.[35] The regulated sectors included railroads, airlines, utilities, and telecommunications.[36] The final economic variable, a firm's involvement in *international trade,* was measured using annual reports and respondents' calculations of the percentage of total sales devoted to exports and direct foreign investment.[37]

---

[32] Claude Schoch, *Compact Disclosure Version 4.25,* CD-ROM, Digital Library Systems, July 1993.

[33] Based on company-supplied data.

[34] Schoch, *Compact Disclosure Version 4.25.*

[35] These were drawn from a list of the "sick six," which also includes two regulated sectors.

[36] I created a dummy variable to evaluate this effect: firms in regulated and troubled sectors were coded 1 and all others were coded 0. The allocation of a company to a sector was based on the Fortune 500 categorization of firms. See also Handler and Mulkern, *Business in Politics,* 24–29.

[37] U.S. Department of Commerce, International Trade Administration, *U.S. Industrial Outlook '92,* (Washington, D.C.: U.S. Government Printing Office, 1992). In fourteen cases firm data on exports were simply not available; therefore, I substituted a calculation of the industry's exports as a percentage of total sales. This blending of data is unsatisfactory, but the reputed importance of trade concerns motivated the fullest investigation possible.

In addition to the economic variables, I evaluated the institutional determinants of political action linked to corporate policy capacity: in-house policy expertise, experience with private social provision, and participation in policy groups. First, I operationalized internal expertise in policy as whether or not the company had a government affairs office in Washington, D.C.[38]

Second, to evaluate company participation in groups (trade associations that worked on health reform, regional health care coalitions, and national policy groups), I counted the number of such groups in which a company was a member.[39] One might argue that joining a group is a dependent variable: interest in a solution causes one to join the group. But the participating firms entered into these groups before health reform became a national issue; moreover, the sector and regional groups were established for other purposes.

Third, to evaluate the impact of private policy legacies I measured firms' market interventions, looking at the percentage of employees who belonged to managed-care networks and health maintenance organizations. The movement into managed-care networks began in the mid-1980s, and they have been the primary tool for controlling costs at the level of the firm. Please see the appendix for a summary of the statistical methods used to examine the hypotheses.

Findings: Company Preferences for National Health Reform

In the aftermath of the Clinton victory, I found a high level of support for health reform. Over half of the business respondents (54 percent) personally supported mandates whether or not their companies had taken a formal position, and another 19 percent were undecided. Twenty-eight percent of the companies officially backed employer mandates, and another group was seriously considering an endorsement. Almost half of the respondents personally believed that some sort of global cap was necessary to limit aggregate health spending. The increasing disaffection between big business and Bill Clinton is the topic of chapter 5, but let me say here that almost every company that initially backed an employer mandate

---

[38] This dummy variable was coded 1 if the company had a Washington office and 0 if it did not.

[39] I did not include the three major umbrella groups, the National Association of Manufacturers, the Chamber of Commerce, and the Business Roundtable, in these discussions since almost all the companies belonged to these umbrella associations. National groups include Washington Business Group on Health, APPWP, ERIC, EBRI, and the National Leadership Coalition. Firms received one point for sitting on the task force of a group (but could receive only one point).

continued to do so throughout the political process (as of my final telephone follow-up interviews in 1995).

The human-resource professionals interviewed were not naturally drawn to big government solutions. Many had struggled to control health care costs since the early eighties: their conversion to national reform was a product of much deliberation and considerable experimentation with market alternatives. Many business managers embraced government intervention as a necessary corrective to the failings of the market, and this support was often uneasy. One vice president for human resources remarked, "Public policy is like a black hole, but you can't ignore it." Caught in a bind between protecting their firms' profitability from the assault of health costs and maintaining commitments to their workforce, these managers considered radical alternatives to the status quo.

Although my companies were all quite large, they varied greatly in their experiences with national policymaking forums. Although regional location did not seem to affect participation, some companies seemed only peripherally involved with national politics. Thus one midwestern business manager explained, "National politics has an East Coast bias." Other firms' activities had attracted media coverage, guided state-level commissions, and contributed greatly to making national health reform a major issue for the American public.

Economic Characteristics and Company Preferences

As with every catastrophe, companies were not equally victimized by hemorrhaging health costs; the firms in my study were touched by this financial disaster in varying fashion. Company *health care costs per worker* could to some extent be determined by industrial structure: large, unionized firms in regulated and troubled sectors were significantly more likely to spend more on employee health care. (See table 3.3 and the appendix for a discussion of the statistical findings.)

Although broad economic concerns precipitated business interest in health reform, economic characteristics of firms were not decisive for their positions on employer mandates. None of the economic factors contributed in a significant way to whether a company decided to support employer mandates. (See table 3.4, equation 1.)

In part the failure of size to predict a company's position had to do with the fact that I surveyed only Fortune 200 firms, and small companies on average were generally much more hostile to the Clinton plan than large ones. I chose this sample because the largest firms are more likely to take individual political stands; thus, it allowed me to understand the dynamics by which political choices within the firm are made. Size would probably have been significant in a more varied selection of companies, and the sample could have affected the firms' health costs per worker measure (as all the companies provided some health benefits) and the unionization variable (as larger firms tend to be more unionized).

Despite the similarity in size, the firms were enormously varied in many ways. Although all made health care available, some paid the entire cost, while others funded less than a quarter of their workers' health benefits. Some were totally unionized; others had no unionized workers. Profitability varied tremendously, as did the capital-labor ratios of the firms.

The inability of the economic factors to predict a company's position also seemed to reflect that many economic characteristics worked both for and against a firm's backing mandates. Even though companies with certain industrial characteristics seemed to suffer more, they were not of one mind about how to end their suffering. For instance, many of the companies with high health *costs* reported that they favored mandates in order to impose costs on their competitors and to end cost shifting from government recipients and small firms; they also seemed to believe that they had little to lose from mandates. Yet some companies with high health costs believed that firm-level interventions were a more appropriate course of action.

Profitability also seemed to work both ways. More profitable industries, for example in the oil and computer sectors, had the organizational slack to develop political positions. But other profitable companies were not especially concerned about rising health costs. Some managers concluded that low profits prevented their firms from becoming politically involved. Yet respondents at other financially weak companies reported that they had tried everything, were pressed to take dramatic measures, and therefore had turned to government as a last resort.[40]

We tend to think that business is pushed by labor into accepting social reform, but the cases studied demonstrated that unionization could work for or against a company's support for employer mandates. Some firms reported that labor negotiations within the industry produced a commitment from both parties to participate in the national policy debate; in these cases a high rate of unionization correlated with support for employer mandates. For example, companies in the paper and steel industries set into place a "self-education process," with labor-management groups committed to understanding systemic problems in health financing; eventually these companies came to back an employer mandate. But respondents in other heavily unionized companies feared that mandates would only swell concessions to workers. Some companies with fewer

[40] Interviews with company representatives, April 5, 1992, December 9, 1992, May 1993, September 2, 1993.

unions, such as a midwestern appliances company, none the less supported the mandate and viewed their unions as deeply resistant to change
from traditional fee-for-service plans. In these cases management's education took place largely outside of labor negotiations. Some nonunionized
companies, such as one East Coast utility, had extremely high health costs
per worker because they wanted to thwart a big union drive. As my respondent explained, "I don't want people to say, 'Except for you guys
screwing up, we would still be nonunion.'"[41]

The importance of sector seemed to be confirmed by the qualitative
evidence. For example, deregulation of the energy industry and the opening up of distribution channels to new firms made the old utilities turn to
the government for help in controlling health costs. Utilities reported having a hard time passing their costs on to consumers, and as a result were
more interested in government controls. But other regulated industries,
such as telecommunications, were less supportive of mandates.[42]

A fundamental change in the trading context of American business un-
derlay much of the discussion, because export companies who compete
with firms from countries with national health insurance were hurt by
rising costs. But again the pressure of international competition seemed
to move companies in different directions. Some firms in the study argued
for employer mandates and comprehensive restructuring of the health system to improve U.S. competition in world markets, while others shifted
costs to their workers to survive internationally.

Private Policy Experts and National Health Reform

In contrast, corporate policy capacity was critical to explaining why some
firms were willing to back national health reform while others resisted an
expanded role for government. Companies with institutionalized expertise in policy, in the form of a Washington, D.C., government affairs office, were significantly more likely to take a position in favor of employer
mandates. (See table 3.4, equation 1.)

Benefits managers also seemed to play a big role in shaping corporate
perceptions of health issues. When the Financial Accounting Standards
(FAS) 106 regulations were passed in 1989, making companies account
for benefits promised to retirees on their bottom lines, senior management
also began to focus on the issue of health costs. In many cases attention

---

[41] Interviews with company representatives, February 4, 1993, March 26, 1993, April
23, 1993. See also Edward Lawler, Susan Mohrman, and Gerald Ledford, *Employee
Involvement and Total Quality Management* (San Francisco: Jossey-Bass, 1992), 69–76.

[42] Interviews with company representatives, winter and spring 1993.

to the FAS 106 regulations gave benefits managers greater leverage to experiment with their own plans and to push the company to take a public stand on national reform.

One might argue that Washington government affairs representatives and benefits managers exercise such influence only until they are reined in by the CEOs when an issue gains a critical prominence. Indeed, firms are contested terrain: heavy media coverage makes it difficult for companies to take less orthodox positions. But while isomorphic forces influence the outcomes of internal struggles, expertise in an issue also matters, giving specialized managers a great deal of influence, if not absolute power. In-depth interviews with companies reveal the following findings about these struggles.

Companies with little formal connection between the human-resources and government affairs departments tended not to take a supportive position on employer mandates. For example, the HR manager for a large midwestern agricultural-products company complained that the Washington government affairs personnel sent "all kinds of information, most of which we do not have time to read." In comparison, a close working relationship between the benefits and human-resources departments, on the one hand, and the government affairs department made supportive positions on health reform more likely. This cooperative process was made easier when human-resources and government affairs managers reported to the same vice president, as was the case in many of the companies that endorsed mandates. There tended to be a division of labor between the technical and political functions: an eastern oil firm manager reported that "government affairs largely looks to HR for direction." A western oil company manager explained that because the D.C. office had no specialist in health care, the benefits department took the lead in explaining issues.[43] An eastern candy producer recalled the considerable cooperation between the two divisions:

> An inside team was set up to consider the issue consisting of people in human resources and government relations. The two departments report through the same VP, so coordination was made easier. . . . HR provided the technical insights, and government relations provided the political savvy. They enjoyed each other's expertise.[44]

Companies supporting mandates also overwhelmingly described arriving at their positions as a bottom-up process in which, in the words of an airline company vice president, "the push comes from lower down," or as a western oil producer put it, the "lower-level guys run the show." The

[43] Interviews with company representatives, January 7, 1993, March 25, 1993.
[44] Interview with company representative, April 7, 1993.

vice president for a large western utility reported that "the CEO's relative lack of interest in health care made it easier for the upper-level managers below him to take the lead in this area." An office supply manager suggested that firm's impressive profitability gave the board no "excuse to yell at the management"; consequently, the "managers have a lot of leeway" and "can basically do anything they have the guts to do." A vice president for human resources in the chemical industry explained the basis for managerial discretion: "If the CEO were spending more time on it [health care], he wouldn't be doing his job adequately. It is the responsibility of the human-resources department, and I want the CEO to think that our guys have it by the throat."[45]

In some companies the activist benefits managers simply spoke for the company in public settings, asserting a position even though none had been formalized. When asked about this practice, one person explained, "I'm paid to be the expert on this." Another manager for a southern utility acknowledged the downside of such action:

> Someday my boss may read something and say, "We're saying that?" But he hired me to get the job done. If I had to go back and ratify everything, we'd be nowhere. I can strongly defend everything that I am supporting.[46]

Companies supporting employer mandates also seemed more likely to have a centralized benefits function in the firm and better data about health costs. Many of these huge conglomerates had historically handled health costs at the division level; yet in recent years companies were dissatisfied with the lack of information about health costs and moved to centralize benefits. An eastern oil company manager explained, "There is the feeling that there is not the capacity at the local level to deal with the magnitude of the problem."[47] Concentrating responsibility for health costs in the corporate benefits office made managers more willing to embrace a political solution, because passing costs down to the divisions concealed the magnitude of the problem.

Companies in which political positions on health care were largely made by human resources and government affairs were more likely to support employer mandates. Tax and finance personnel were generally seen as resistant to mandates. A manager with a chemical company remembered circulating a draft that summarized the national debate over policy in order to move the firm toward a position:

[45] Interviews with company representatives, December 9, 1992, January 6, 1993, January 13, 1993, February 17, 1993, May 1993.

[46] Interview with company representative, March 17, 1993.

[47] Interview with company representatives, March 1993, February 13, 1993, April 5, 1993.

Some had a social position; some said it was not the government's business. There was some role influence: the benefits people preferred play or pay. The medical directors wanted universal coverage but no cost controls and did not want a tax-based system. The finance people favored the Bush plan with some cost controls but limited government intervention. So even before we tried to take it to the board of directors we could not get any consensus. As a result, we never tried to push it at a higher level.[48]

Many respondents also reported a tendency for issues to be considered in more ideological and less practical terms at higher levels of the organization. In addition, managers—such as one from an eastern aerospace company—encountered "a reluctance at the senior level to waste clout on health care. . . . There is a natural tendency at the senior management level to save their energy for issues critical to the corporation." The manager of a large bank suggested that media attention brought senior managers into the political decision-making process.[49]

Although stalemate was often the consequence of an intrafirm competition to define the health issue, competing interests could also push the decision-making process forward as factions struggled until one side persuaded the CEO or board to take a position and to quiet the other side. Thus the government affairs director of a large telecommunications company lobbied for agreement on a position in order to get all parties to say the same thing. When the vice president for human resources at one company was pushed by the chief financial officer to reduce the generous plan for the firm's "highly paid, creative, neurotic workforce," the vice president decided instead to join the National Leadership Coalition because it demonstrated her action on the political front to the CFO. "It was one way of resisting the CFO's rallying cry of charging them more, so it was good internal politics."[50]

Where does the CEO enter into this tale of corporate deliberation? Our stereotypical view of the firm is that the chief executive calls the shots; and indeed, respondents in almost all of the companies endorsing employer mandates reported having sympathetic leaders. CEOs not only seemed to determine whether a supportive position could be taken, they set a standard for acceptable political activism within the firm. Thus one midwestern food produce manager explained that although the CEO was on a list of Clinton business supporters, he discouraged top management from getting involved in any political arenas.[51]

Yet benefits and human-resource managers also exercised influence on the CEOs. As already mentioned, the formulation of a policy position was

---

[48] Interview with company representative, October 27, 1992.
[49] Interviews with company representatives, October 30, 1992, January 7, 1993.
[50] Interview with company representatives, January 26, 1993.
[51] Interview with company representative, February 12, 1993.

often a bottom-up process, and human-resource managers worked to convince CEOs that a formal position was needed. Often this entailed getting CEOs involved in regional coalitions: a CEO group would be formed in conjunction with a benefits manager group. Managers often persuaded their CEOs to resign from hospital boards. Even when CEOs seemed to become strongly committed to the health issue, they were often influenced by their staff in this move. For example, the CEO of a huge grocery chain became a veritable health activist after his benefits person arranged for him to meet Henry Simmons of the National Leadership Coalition.[52]

In addition, human-resources and benefits managers who were opposed to a Clinton-style health reform could prevent their company from endorsing it even when the CEO indicated interest. When the aforementioned grocer-activist persuaded other food companies to join the National Leadership Coalition, benefits managers in several of these firms instead held to the conventional wisdom of the grocery manufacturers that health reform would be economically damaging to low-wage employers. Although these companies nominally belonged to the group, they fought against developing a company political position and refused to participate in the group's activities.[53] The resistance of these business managers was enough to sidetrack the busy CEOs' agendas (although not all issues for the company could be as easily dropped).[54] Just as it is not enough to have an active benefits manager without some support from the CEO, it is not enough to have the CEO's blessing without benefits activism.

At times activist benefits managers prevented their CEOs from rejecting comprehensive reform. For instance, one benefits manager reported that shortly before the 1992 election, President Bush asked the company's CEO to back the incremental Bush health plan. The CEO sought advice from the benefits manager, who argued that this stance could complicate the firm's relationship with the White House should Clinton be elected. The benefits manager, a supporter of play or pay, thereby pushed a very Republican company to the center on this issue.

Groups and the Road to Political Action

Group membership was also absolutely critical to firms' support for employer mandates. (See the ordered probit results in tables 3.6 and 3.7 and the discussion of the statistical findings in the appendix.) The case mate-

---

[52] Interview with company representative, January 8, 1993.

[53] Interview with company representatives, May 11, 1993, May 6, 1993, January 7, 1993.

[54] See in another venue Michael Lipsky, *Street Level Bureaucracy* (New York: Russell Sage Foundation, 1980).

rial confirms that groups were essential to the defining of health care problems and solutions for participating firms. Respondents indicated that they were often confused about health reform before their groups addressed the issue; most were followers rather than leaders in this area. They considered groups especially helpful in exposing them to new information about, and analysis of, the larger health system; therefore, it is not surprising that many came to endorse systemic solutions for the high cost of health care. Managers were very proud of being introduced to the latest trends in health care cost containment. Thus when two human-resource professionals in a large midwestern company were transferred to health benefits from other parts of the firm in order "to inject activism" into company policy, they immediately joined groups "to get up to speed on the health issue" and quickly determined that national health reform was absolutely mandatory.[55]

The solidarity effects of small-group participation also seemed to bring opposing interests closer together in the quest for health solutions, further increasing the likelihood that managers would come to share understandings with their noncorporate, fellow participants. A member of the Iowa Leadership Consortium recalls that participants were able "to leave their sacred cows at home" (they have plenty of pastures in Iowa) and the group subsequently produced a statewide play-or-pay plan:

> This has been an incredible process. To go through the process of people walking through the door who are obviously going to have conflict. Doctors talking to businessmen. Twenty to forty people sitting down together and staying focused on a complex issue for a long time. One thing that made it work is that they decided to take the sacred cows and leave them at home.[56]

One might, of course, protest that there is a chicken and egg problem in play here. Interest in a solution could cause one to join a group. Firms that join groups might be more likely to participate in other forms of political activities. This seems intuitively true, but in my case study most firms entered into groups that were established for other reasons before health reform became a national issue. Members were invited to participate by contacts in the area and joined for a variety of reasons, but once in the group they were exposed to a host of new information and their outlooks often changed accordingly.

Several kinds of groups exposed managers to the ideas of comprehensive health reform. First, regional coalitions, designed to control health costs through *market* manipulations at the community level, ironically brought many participants to consider national governmental solutions

---

[55] Interview with company representative, May 1993.
[56] Interview with company representative, March 26, 1993.

as well. Alain Enthoven developed the concept of community-based purchaser coalitions to reinstate market rationality into the health system. These coalitions, representing a large pool of corporate consumers, would negotiate cost and collect information about quality so that individuals could make better health decisions. By banding together in purchasing coalitions, firms could leverage lower health rates with their greater market power.[57]

Initially coalitions sought to alter health costs, but they gradually targeted quality of outcomes as well. Walter McClure, the Moses of quality, preached productivity in health care to his corporate following, suggesting that too many health dollars are wasted in unsuccessful treatments. If we can identify and implement successful interventions, costs will be reduced. This focus on quality was politically appealing because it suggested that the productivity of health care can be improved and costs lowered without sacrificing benefits levels. One benefits manager recalled this attraction for CEOs:

> The CEOs were in a very uncomfortable position. They were between three rocks: health care costs, . . . significant employee relations problems, and the medical people or doctor problem. . . . The CEOs did nothing about the health problem because they got beaten up any way they went. Quality gave them a way out. First, it clearly had appeal and had a chance of actually working. Second, it did not cost them anything financially. Third, it gave them a good-guy position in the community. People thought about how it would play in the papers.[58]

The coalition movement was helped enormously by the efforts of McClure disciple, Dale Shaller. Shaller brought a background in community action to the task of organizing the corporate world. Shaller believed that business must be mobilized the way that others in society are propelled to political action: within the community. As a consultant to many regional coalitions, Shaller offered his organizing skills to help employers to overcome the limits of collective action.[59]

The coalition movement received seed money from several sources. The Washington Business Group on Health helped to set up local coalitions in a number of regions, as did the Chamber of Commerce. The Robert Wood Johnson Foundation invested in the coalition movement. In 1992 the Hartford Foundation gave $2.25 million in a three-year grant to the

---

[57] Carol Cronin, "Business Wields Its Purchase Power," *Business and Health* 6, no. 1 (1988): 4–7; J. Jaeger, *Private Sector Coalitions: A Fourth Party in Health Care* (Durham, N.C.: Duke University Press, 1985).

[58] Interview with company representative, May 1993.

[59] Interview with Dale Shaller, May 6, 1993.

National Business Coalition Forum on Health, an organization that represents forty-eight member coalitions and was quite active in protecting the community approach in the legislative cycle.[60]

But the true stories of coalitions are local, just like the politics that describes them. In some communities coalitions gained a position of prominence among employers; in others the coalitions quickly dissolved. Some regional groups moved into collective purchasing arrangements; others remained informational in function. The coalition movement seemed to be strongest in the Midwest and West, perhaps because regulatory solutions were more popular in eastern states, but even within the heartland success varied greatly as did the dynamics of local business movements.

The Cleveland Health Quality Choice Coalition has been a poster child of the coalition movement with a joint purchaser-provider effort to produce outcome measurement techniques for sixty diagnostic-related groups. Hospitals are evaluated in terms of their performance in each group; employers can use this outcomes data to steer their employees to the best providers.

The Cleveland case is interesting both because of the high level of cooperation between employers and providers and because the business community took the initiative in trying to change health care delivery system. The story began with a coalition of employers called the Health Action Council of Northeast Ohio (HAC), which covered 350,000 lives and had been meeting since 1982 to try to reduce health costs. Executive Director Pat Casey remembers that participants tried the full gambit of usual interventions to restrain costs, but that nothing worked. HAC member Don Flagg, the vice president for human resources at the Nestle Corporation and "a good egg breaker," began railing against rising health costs and the hospitals' role in this escalation. Flagg aroused the ire of providers but drew considerable attention to his aggressive campaign, perhaps "presoftening" hospitals for later change.[61]

When Flagg left Nestle, he was replaced by Powell Woods, a born mediator with a peaceful, humorous manner, who ultimately left the corporate world and went to seminary school. In 1988 Woods and the Health Action Council met Walter McClure and reported being "blown away" by his philosophy. McClure had been working to develop a statewide data collection system in Pennsylvania; however, providers had stonewalled

[60] John Craig Jr., "Private Foundations' Role in Coalitions," in Jaeger, *Private Sector Coalitions;* "Rethinking the Health-Care Marketplace," obtained from the Health Action Council of Northeast Ohio 3.

[61] Interview with Pat Casey, April 1993.

the effort. Consequently, the Cleveland employers decided to limit the scope of their ambitions to the community level.[62]

Woods, Casey, and the Health Action Council set out to sell Cleveland's CEOs on a McClure approach to cost containment, armed with information and the spirit of true believers. HAC commissioned a study that found Cleveland's per capita hospital costs to be 50 percent higher than those at the Mayo Clinic. Woods persuaded his former CEO, John Morley of Reliance, to agitate at the executive level, and Morley invited the Health Action Council to present its findings to Cleveland Tomorrow, a group of fifty CEOs that had sponsored reforms since the city's near bankruptcy in the 1970s. One CEO wag remarked, "We could send our people to the Mayo Clinic with their families and still pay less." Woods remembers that the model had enormous impact on the CEOs, because it allowed them to be the "good guy on a social issue of immense importance. . . . They could be the white knights on this issue."[63]

Cleveland Tomorrow and the Health Action Council joined with the prominent small-business organizations and the local hospital and physician associations in setting up the Cleveland Health Quality Choice Coalition. Hospitals devoted eighty thousand dollars apiece to the effort and participating business came up with an additional six hundred thousand dollars. The employers decided that providers had to be involved from the beginning "so that they couldn't just say that the system stinks." Hospitals were adamant that the data on which they were to be judged had to be correct and different from Medicare's Health Care Financing Administration (HCFA) data. Hospitals also demanded that the data be provided only to employers trained to interpret them. Employers responded with a velvet glove ultimatum: either the hospitals generate acceptable data or employers would base purchasing decisions on cost. Pat Casey attributed Cleveland employers' success in negotiating with hospitals to the focus on quality over cost. Cost-based negotiations suggest zero-sum dynamics, whereas quality suggests a win-win situation. Powell Woods agreed that the logic was hard to deny:

> The CEOs could say to the hospital, "Everyone knows that these are the best hospitals in Cleveland, so isn't it time to let everyone know it. If they are not, we need to be the first to know." The hospitals couldn't disagree.[64]

But the other realpolitik ingredient in Cleveland's success was the extreme unity of the business community. The top ten companies were mem-

[62] Interview, April 1993.

[63] Interview with Pat Casey, April 1993; interview with Powell Woods, May 1993.

[64] Kathleen Kisner, "A Partnership Takes a Gamble to Measure Quality," *Business and Health* 10, no. 4 (1992): 20; interviews.

bers of the coalition, as were small-business managers. As one hospital executive put it, "These guys are all over my board."

Although the Cleveland effort to control health costs was exceptional, it was not unique. Like Ohio, Minnesota has a strongly unified business community and a coalition committed to quality of care. Minnesota has a progressive history dating back to the Democratic Farmer Labor Party; the spirit of cooperation among business managers is powerful in the state. The Business Health Care Action Group was formed by fourteen of the Twin Cities' largest firms in order to purchase collectively health benefits from a network of doctors called the GroupCare Consortium. But the group was not content to negotiate merely on price; it also decided that it wanted to play a role in changing the health care market and in improving the quality of care. Like the Cleveland effort, the group sought to ensure quality, but in this case it did so by developing clinical practice guidelines. According to Fred Hammacher of Dayton Hudson, "People don't understand the health care marketplace—it's a dumb market. . . . The mission statement of our group is to change the health care marketplace [in Minnesota] for the benefit of everyone." The group has already developed approximately forty best practices in medical interventions and hopes to complete eighty in all. Each has been developed by a subcommittee made up of business managers, physicians, and hospital representatives. As Hammacher puts it, "You need to develop them at the grass roots so that you can get ownership."[65]

St. Louis also has a well-organized business community with an activist coalition; but the balance of power between purchasers and providers of health is quite different, and early efforts to control health costs collectively failed. Hospitals and medical schools in the city are very strong, and employers were essentially outflanked. Jim Stutts of the St. Louis Area Business Health Coalition estimates that the greater metropolitan area has about 2,669 extra beds—a powerful testimony to providers' power and a different context for reform from Cleveland or Minneapolis.

Despite the presence of a seemingly omnipotent medical-industrial complex, corporate purchasers of health decided in the late 1980s to reduce costs by publishing hospital prices for selected inpatient services, called the Prospective Pricing Initiative (PPI). The effort was led by the St. Louis Area Business Health Coalition, with the backing of a CEO group called Civic Progress, representing the twenty-nine largest companies in St. Louis. St. Louis employers had been pooling claims data organized by diagnoses (DRGs) since 1983, but now they were going public

---

[65] Jon (no last name), "Power in Numbers: How Businesses Are Ganging Up to Control Health Care Costs," *Corporate Report Minnesota,* November 1992, 73; interview with Fred Hammacher, May 3, 1995.

with the prices. Employers had hoped to snag the interests of the interme-diaries who were best suited to use the data, but managed-care adminis-trators showed little interest. One administrator responded, "I've already picked my providers, and have already gotten my discounts from them." Employers took this as a sign that the current discounts meant little.

The coalition set out by surveying outpatient hospital rates and found a wide spread between the highest- and lowest-priced provider. Next the employers moved on to inpatient care, asking thirty-six hospitals to give them "real live market prices" on 250 DRGs. Although participants be-lieved that they had cultivated providers' support, on the day of delivery only three out of thirty-six hospitals complied entirely; another five of-fered partial information. The employer coalition spent the next five months trying to persuade the top hospitals to comply, and Stutts even approached the Federal Trade Commission, but the resistance was unified and immutable.

Despite the failure of the PPI initiative, St. Louis employers later reorga-nized as the St. Louis Quality Alliance and began a project to measure outcomes data in alliance with other interests. St. Louis employers also worked closely with state government to pass a health care data disclosure law in 1992. Stutts felt that regulation was a natural outcome of provid-ers' resistance to a voluntary data project:

> Prospective pricing was employers' last chance to say, "This can be done voluntarily." We did all we could do to do it voluntarily, and the providers said no. So we finally said [to state government], "Go do what you want to do." Odd bedfellows have developed in health care in Missouri. Business and labor have a lot in common on this issue. Some of our most conservative members were thrilled at state regulation for data disclosure even though it entailed a lot of government intervention.[66]

Coalitions varied in their stance toward national reform: some were intrigued by the idea of becoming a health alliance under the Clinton plan, while others feared that the federal government would destroy what regions had accomplished and "worried that the big employers could be dwarfed." Employer's relationships with government also varied across coalitions. While the Cleveland coalition had little involvement with gov-ernment, the Iowa coalition endorsed a state play-or-pay bill. Yet regard-less of their approach to health reform, almost all coalition participants reported that the movement acted as a kind of think tank for evolving corporate perspectives. The coalitions have been criticized for failing to contain costs, in part because voluntary, community-based efforts do not

[66] Interview with Jim Stutts, May 1993.

have the scope to address the structural sources of cost increases.[67] But coalitions have made a contribution to the policy process as forums in which local employers have learned about health issues. Despite the market and community orientations of the movement, many participants began to consider broader solutions to the problems of the health system, ranging from quality controls to national health reform. As Jim Stutts put it, "Working together in the group has led to more cooperation among benefits managers—the process has built trust."

A second forum for changing employers' thinking about health policy was the national policy group. The earliest group, the Washington Business Group on Health (WBGH), was developed by the Business Roundtable as a special forum to consider health questions, but its leader, Willis Goldbeck, quickly established the group as an independent body. Goldbeck wanted the group to include all the members of the Roundtable but also believed that the group had to be independent to make big business "a credible participant in national health policy" instead of simply a lobbying force in the health arena. As of 1990, 185 Fortune 500 companies belonged to WBGH.[68]

Although Goldbeck's departure in 1989 (combined with the increasing presence of provider groups in the organization) eroded the organization's capability for leadership, WBGH was an important early influence on large employers' conceptions of cost containment. Goldbeck was acknowledged by both admirers and critics to be ahead of business on most health issues and was an early advocate of national health reform. The group helped local communities set up coalitions and intervened in key political conflicts, such as opposing the Reagan administration's deregulatory efforts to phase out health planning and physician peer review.[69] WBGH's Carol Cronin remembers the process by which the group came to endorse national health reform. A committee had been set up to study cost-containment strategies, but after a few months the discussion deepened into a wide-ranging analysis of the problems of the larger health system:

> It became clearer and clearer as the discussion went on that the problem was part of a larger system and there was only so much one could do within one's own company to control costs, and they'd already tried lots of those. . . . It

---

[67] Lawrence Brown and Catherine McLaughlin, "Constraining Costs at the Community Level: A Critique," *Health Affairs* 9, no. 4 (1990): 5–28.

[68] Bergthold, *Purchasing Power in Health,* 42; Marybeth Burke, "Business Leaders Bring Their Clout to Washington," *Hospitals,* April 20, 1990, 32.

[69] Willis Goldbeck, "Health Is Not a Free Market Commodity," *Business and Health* 7, no. 7 (1989): 48; Linda Demkovich, "On Health Issues, This Business Group Is a Leader, but Is Anyone Following?" *National Journal,* June 18, 1983, 1278–80.

became clear that the system dynamic was the problem, so they changed the focus to health care reform.[70]

Two professional organizations for human resource and benefit managers have been very visible in health policy: APPWP and ERIC. The Association of Private Pension and Welfare Plans (APPWP) was formed as an educational and research organization specializing in employee benefits in 1967. Its five hundred members include human-resource managers from manufacturing companies as well as representatives of consulting and insurance companies. With the passage of the Employment Retirement Income Security Act (ERISA), which gave states the right to impose regulations on private industry plans, APPWP enlarged its lobbying function. The organization intervenes in a variety of areas in order to protect ERISA preemption prerogatives for its members. APPWP's health care task force was a center for early corporate support for overhaul of the health system. Ellen Goldstein remembers the process by which cohesion emerged between factions with very different perspectives: "We were a very disparate group but over time experienced tremendous bonding with one another."[71]

The ERISA Industry Committee (ERIC) is another professional organization for human-resource and employment benefits managers. Unlike APPWP, its one hundred participating companies include no insurers and usually constitute Fortune 100 firms. ERIC was founded in 1976 to respond to the increased regulations created under ERISA and at the behest of the Ford administration. The group was originally primarily concerned about pensions, but in recent years the focus has shifted to health benefits. ERIC became interested in exploring a comprehensive systemic approach to health reform and met repeatedly with Senator Kennedy's staff in the mid-1980s to consider what should be included in a standard benefits package.[72]

Several informal health care coalitions were also important to helping large employers understand issues. The National Leadership Coalition (NLC) was a group of large employers who got an enormous amount of early press but ultimately played a small role in the health debate. In 1985 Henry Simmons received a planning grant from the Pew Foundation to work on a public- and private-sector solution to health care and formed the initial NLC with thirty-six individual members. The group was educated by a stream of outside speakers and produced a widely circulated report entitled *For the Health of a Nation*. At this point the coalition began laying the groundwork for a broader membership by meeting with

[70] Julie Kosterlitz, "Bottom-Line Pain," *National Journal,* September 9, 1989, 2204, 2201–5.
[71] Interview with Ellen Goldstein, December 9, 1992.
[72] Interview with ERISA Industry Council.

corporate boards, labor organizations, and state legislators. The expanded National Leadership Coalition primarily consisted of business and labor groups, with some consumer members as well. The business members of the NLC largely came from an earlier coalition called American Business for Cost Containment, organized in the 1980s by Larry Atkins, formerly on the staff of Heinz. A number of companies and trade associations joined with their unions, especially in sectors where labor-management accords committed both sides to participating in the national debates over policy. To belong members had to agree with the statement of the problem, the charter, and the commitment to systemic reform and to accept a process of majority rule. Participants claimed to be willing to take tough positions; as one put it, "The coalition is prepared to have members walk away."[73]

The group rather quickly moved to develop a play-or-pay legislative proposal that endorsed a mandate and was presented in fall 1991. Staff were sanguine, and one described a "convergence of thinking since 1990 with the learning that has been taking place." Yet at this point a sizable group of the companies (including AT&T, Du Pont, Arco, Eastman Kodak, and 3M) dropped out of the coalition. In part, the exodus represented a belief that the coalition was moving in too radical a direction and that "play or pay" was in actuality a first step toward a single-payer system. Another problem was the division in interests between those companies with heavy commitments to retirees and those without. Some profitable and largely nonunion companies were drawn to health reform because they were hurt by the tax assessed on corporate earnings to cover uncompensated care, yet they had little in common with those largely unprofitable companies who wanted health reform to shift responsibility for their early retiree population.[74] The National Leadership Coalition also ran into trouble with some labor groups who were resistant to the tax on workers' income to fund the public parts of the plan or wanted a single-payer plan. The American Federation of State, County and Municipal Employees (AFSCME) resigned from the coalition when the NLC endorsed play-or-pay.[75]

Many of the firms that departed the National Leadership Coalition formed a new group ultimately called the Corporate Health Care Coali-

[73] Business participants included Bethlehem Steel, Chrysler, Dayton Hudson, Georgia-Pacific, International Paper, Meredith, Northern Telecom, Pacific Gas and Electric, Safeway, Southern California Edison, Time Warner, Westinghouse, Xerox corporations, and various unions. Interview with National Leadership Coalition representative, June 1992.

[74] Interview with National Leadership Coalition representative, June 1992; interviews with company representatives, October 30, 1992, December 9, 1992.

[75] Marybeth Burke, "Business and Labor Move Forward Via Joint Health Care Reform Plan," *Hospitals*, February 20, 1992, 53–54. For a broad discussion of labor see Marie Gottschalk, "The Missing Millions," *Journal of Health Politics, Policy, and Law*, forthcoming.

tion. ARCO's Richard Sawaya and Larry Atkins organized the group and explicitly sought to attract profitable members who had a limited commitment to early retirees. This group also supported the employer mandate but preferred a managed-competition approach to "play or pay." Of primary importance to this group was the continuation of the employer-based system and the certainty that large companies would retain their considerable buying power in the marketplace.[76]

Also important to the development of corporate conceptions of cost containment have been the health foundations. The Pew Foundation funded a number of programs to educate managers such as the corporate fellows program at Boston University. Developed by Richard Egdahl, the program brought benefits personnel together to discuss a variety of health problems. The Robert Wood Johnson and Hartford Foundations contributed to the health care coalition movement.[77]

Third, in some cases awakenings to the health problem came through participation in sectoral trade associations and labor-management forums. For instance, the American Iron and Steel Institute brought large and small companies with varying profitability and rates of unionization together in a unified industry position. The steel industry's association began in the early twentieth century as a forum for fighting labor; however, this early organization laid the groundwork for considerable cooperation (and collusion) among companies that encouraged subsequent collective action. Interests were certainly the driving motive for this later cooperation, but a history of cooperation allowed the companies to see their interests from a more collective perspective. Bethlehem Steel displayed early, avid interest in the problem of health costs and urged the American Iron and Steel Institute to set up a task force devoted to health. Later Bethlehem recruited its fellow steel companies to the National Leadership Coalition.[78]

The American Iron and Steel Institute had its nonmanufacturing counterpart in the Edison Electric Institute. Here a spirit of interfirm cooperation dated from the crisis in nuclear energy beginning in the 1970s that brought the industry group to coalesce around a new sense of purpose.[79] The group took a leadership role in health policy and later brought the gas trade association to adopt its position.

The James River Corporation played a similar role in working through the American Forest and Paper Association to educate other paper manu-

[76] These included Alcoa, ARCO, Allied Signal, Amoco, Ameritech, AT&T, Bell Atlantic, Chevron, DEC, DuPont, IBM, Kodak, MCI, Motorola, NYNEX, Southwestern Bell, U.S. West, and USX corporations. Interviews with Larry Atkins, 1992–95.

[77] Interviews; Craig, "Private Foundations' Role."

[78] Interview with steel industry representatives, June 1992.

[79] Campbell, Hollingsworth, and Lindberg, *Governance of American Economy*.

facturers about health problems. The association set up a group for human-resource vice presidents to exchange information about benefits, and respondents reported learning much about systemic problems in health care through this forum. The association has been especially important for collective contemplation because the paper sector has no industry-wide labor-management structure.[80]

Finally, labor-management groups were a source of learning about health affairs for some firms. One might posit that companies willing to work with labor unions were generally more open to government intervention, but the cases suggest that labor-market forums also fostered new modes of thinking about health care. One respondent from a large manufacturing firm remembers the labor-management wars of the middle 1980s and the subsequent move toward more consensual politics within the labor-management committee structure:

> The strikes over the issue were very emotional; management and unions were polarized, and the issue was very complex. So the company set up an informal process to educate people at each location, including union and management committees at each plant. . . . In this way we began to peel back the onion. We began to realize that the problem wasn't a labor-management problem. The things that management had done were quite logical. Rather we realized that it was a systemic problem and that the entire system needed to be changed. This took the emotion out of the issue and made us focus on what the best options were.[81]

The auto industry's interest in health reform grew out of efforts to build bridges to labor. Joseph Califano, Chrysler's chairman of the board, established a health task force that included Lee Iacocca; William Milliken, former governor of Michigan; Douglas Frazier, president of the United Auto Workers; and Jerome Holland of the American Red Cross, and was staffed by benefits manager Walter Maher. The task force informed the board that firm-level and even private-sector interventions were unlikely to contain costs without systemic change. The company subsequently sent Maher to Washington "to try to sensitize the business community, to develop coalitions, and to impress the public sector that health costs were hurting the competitiveness of private industry."[82]

Thus, the story told here portrays a core and periphery in the American business community. Companies plugged into groups exposing them to the latest trends in cost containment collectively moved toward political

---

[80] Interview with company representative, April 23, 1993.

[81] Interview with company representative, April 1993. Thus although unionization in itself was not statistically significant to firm preference, participation in labor-management networks helped some companies move toward support of national health reform.

[82] Interview with auto industry representative, June 1992.

solutions. Peripheral firms outside of these networks relied more heavily on insurers for information and, consequently, had less exposure to analyses favoring government intervention. Some respondents feared that the groups were so eager to participate in the policy debate that these groups committed themselves too quickly to comprehensive reform. These skeptics worried that the desire to participate made it harder for the business perspective to be represented. One industry representative said,

> I am also concerned that the Chamber of Commerce, NAM, and APPWP are all trying to develop a strong position and to show the administration that they can be flexible. But it is too early to put stakes in the ground. . . . In the past business groups have been viewed as, "We are opposed to everything." This was not a bad position to take in the Bush-Reagan years, when they [the Republican presidents] wanted to say this to Congress. . . . Now there is a new set of dynamics. People don't want to say no, but they may be too eager to say yes.[83]

When the Market Fails

The third institutional variable, percentage in managed-care networks, was not statistically significant. Yet prior experience with firm-level interventions did seem to have an impact in some cases, persuading some companies to turn to national solutions. As health benefits consumed a larger share of the total compensation package, benefits managers searched for ways to curb private health costs. Large firms began to self-insure, using insurance companies to administer their plans but not to bear the risk. In addition they introduced cost controls that changed the incentives of both providers and consumers in the health care marketplace.

An initial device to contain costs was the health maintenance organization, and many firms encouraged workers to join HMOs in the 1970s. HMOs (in their purest form) pay doctors' salaries; by doing away with the piecework payment of fee-for-service, the physician has no incentive to offer inappropriate care. Doctors often receive a share of the yearly profits as further incentive to restrain unnecessary intervention. HMOs seek to limit hospitalizations with preventative care, thus keeping patients healthier and restraining inpatient costs. Studies report that HMOs have lower hospitalization rates, although these may reflect relatively healthier populations. Yet for many years HMOs failed to restrain costs to companies, perhaps because too few employees joined them.[84]

---

[83] Interview with company representative, June 1993.
[84] Regina Herzlinger, "How Companies Tackle Health Care Costs," *Harvard Business Review* 63, no. 5 (1985): 108–20; Lawrence Brown, *Politics and Health Care Organization* (Washington, D.C.: Brookings Institution, 1983).

Frustrated by the continued expansion of health costs, employers then turned to a variety of techniques to limit excessive medical intervention and to ensure appropriate care. Systems of utilization review were put into place in which independent physicians randomly monitored medical decisions and identified excessive interventions. In some systems patients were required to seek prior authorization from a "patient advocate" for all but the most emergent interventions or a second opinion for planned surgical procedures. From 1983 to 1985 a sample of large companies with utilization review programs in place jumped from 17 to 45 percent. By 1990, 82 percent of a sample of large and medium-sized firms were using the technique. Utilization review initially seemed promising, yet over time doctors found ways to avoid the constraints imposed by the procedure.[85]

While some firms monitored physicians' decision making, others experimented with managed care. Preferred provider organizations (PPOs) offered special discounts to firms when employees sought treatment from the physicians in the network; yet health costs seemed to escalate just as rapidly. Despite initial enthusiasm for PPOs, only 20 percent of one sample of companies in 1991 found them to be very effective.[86]

Recently point-of-service (POS) plans have enthralled corporate payers. Halfway between HMOs and PPOs, the point-of-service plan assigns patients to a family practitioner who acts as a gatekeeper for other services and often has financial incentives to restrict inappropriate care. In 1992 Foster Higgins found nearly three-fourths of its sampled companies offering a managed-care option (either POS or HMO). Companies using managed care reported dramatic reductions in the growth rate of costs in 1993 and 1994. More recently, however, the growth rate seems to be edging up again; for example, Towers Perrin found health costs for employers up 4 percent in 1996, a modest growth rate but still above the 1995 figures.[87]

Employers also tried to alter the demand for health care by changing consumer incentives; for instance, cost shifting required workers to bear a greater share through larger premiums, deductibles, or copayments. In

[85] Robert Friedland, "Introduction and Background," in *The Changing Health Care Market,* ed. Frank McArdle (Washington, D.C.: Employee Benefit Research Institute, 1987), 15; Marc Grobman, "UR Only as Good as What You Save," *Business and Health* 9, no. 7 (1991): 21; Spencer Vibbert, "Utilization Review: A Report Card," *Business and Health* 8, no. 2 (1990): 40.

[86] Jon Gabel, Steven DiCarlo, Cynthia Sullivan, and Thomas Rice, "Employer-Sponsored Health Insurance, 1989," *Health Affairs* 9, no. 3 (1990): 161–75, 163; "The 1991 National Executive Poll on Health Care Costs and Benefits," *Business and Health* 9, no. 9 (1991): 66.

[87] Foster Higgins, "Health Care Benefits Survey; Managed Care Plans," distributed by Foster Higgins (1992), 5; "Managed Care: Employer Perspective, 1992," *Profile* (distributed by Towers Perrin), vol. 1 no. 2 (1992): 2; Towers Perrin, "1996 Health Care Cost Survey," Towers Perrin Employee Benefit Information Center, March 1996.

1991 over 80 percent of a *Business and Health* sample was seriously considering increasing the workers' share of premiums; but at the same time, only 35 percent believed that this approach would control the escalation of health costs. Many human-resource professionals resisted cost shifting because they felt personally responsible for interventions that limited employee benefits. One respondent explained, "The lack of coverage for people and cost shifting affects me personally; for example, it is very hard to tell people that they are not eligible for infertility treatments."[88]

A subtle form of cost shifting is flex benefits, in which workers are allocated a sum to pay for health and day care or, sometimes, take as ready cash. Under such plans workers have financial incentives to choose less comprehensive health coverage. The approach rests on a betting man's logic: healthy individuals use the health system less; therefore, they should pay less up front and put their money where they need it more. Quaker Oats bragged that its costs went up only 6 percent a year from 1983 until the early 1990s, a figure considerably below the industry average. But flex benefits have a dark side as well. Flex plans, like block grants, have often been used to disguise a real reduction in benefits. Another cost-saving device aimed at changing individual incentives and behavior was the wellness movement, which assumed that medical costs go down if health goes up. Hershey Foods, for instance, developed a complicated formula for rewarding exercise, nonsmoking, and weight maintenance with deductions from monthly premiums; bad behavior resulted in penalty surcharges. Some employees endorsed this approach energetically; others believed it smacked of social control.[89]

The private provision of health benefits was a learning experience for the soldiers in the health field—benefits managers, human-resource vice presidents, and government relations professionals. By the late 1980s failed firm-level efforts to stop the scandalous escalation of costs made some businesspeople consider grander solutions. Numerous respondents described their path to systemic reform as one of increasing frustration with company efforts to change provider behavior. One participant remembered the shift in his thinking from a market competition approach to a national regulatory one: "Most of us recognize that the things we did in the mid-1980s didn't really work." Another remembered being asked in a survey to identify the solution to the health crisis: "I realized at that

---

[88] "The 1991 National Executive Poll on Health Care Costs and Benefits," *Business and Health* 9, no. 9 (1991): 66; interview with company representative, December 9, 1992.

[89] Linda Stern, "What's New in Flex Benefits," *Business and Health* 9, no. 3 (1991): 14–15; Joyce Frieden, "Hershey's Newest Nonfat Product: Wellness," *Business and Health* 9, no. 12 (1991): 56–60.

moment that the only thing that would make a difference was to have a national solution."[90]

Conclusion

This chapter has analyzed the causes of variation in firms' preferences for employer mandates, an important part of the Clinton health plan. Although escalating costs made some firms desire health system restructuring, economic factors alone were insufficient to account for the changes in attitudes. Companies endorsing health reform possessed institutional structures that gave them access to new ideas about cost containment. They had a formal role for policy professionals who had contact with noncorporate policy analysts, and they participated in groups that disseminated information about the latest trends in cost controls. These mechanisms for the exchange of information brought the companies to favor comprehensive restructuring of the health system, including employer mandates as an important component.

These findings have important implications for the way that we think about political action by business. Conventional views of political mobilization suggest that corporate interests are easily recognized and that solutions are readily apparent. Yet health reform illustrates that preference formation takes place in collective organizations as policy personnel search for new solutions to a social problem. In accounting for companies' preferences, we often emphasize economic structural characteristics to the neglect of institutional factors. Yet this study suggests that among the largest companies, corporate policy capacity is vital to outcomes. Size certainly would have mattered more in a sample including smaller firms. But the story of decision making presented here offers insight into the way that size matters. It was the institutional ability to gain access to new ideas about policy that brought large companies toward government solutions.

The primacy of economic concerns to corporate managers was real. This was not a story of corporate actors engaging in altruism, choosing the public good over private interests. Rather, it was a story of business managers' struggle to locate their interests in a world of imperfect knowledge. Thus, the institutional approach adds a context for the interpretation of interests, an explanation for why problems become political issues, and a view of the corporate road to political participation.

---

[90] Interviews with company representatives, January 1993.

TABLE 3.1
Descriptive Statistics

Variable	Means	Correlation with Interest
Economic		
Annual sales	$9.38 billion	.35*
Total annual health costs	$1.56 billion	.35*
Annual health costs per worker	$3,460	.02
Net income as a percentage of sales	3.41	−.17
Percentage of workforce unionized	29	.26
Capital intensity (net sales/number of employees)	232553	.17
Percentage operating in regulated sector	26	.35*
Exports as percentage of total sales	16	−.09
Institutional		
Percentage with government affairs office in Washington, D.C.	66	.46**
Number of policy groups a member of	2.3	.49**
Percentage of workers in managed-care plan	33	.37*

* Significant at .05   **Significant at .01.

TABLE 3.2
Correlation Matrices

Variable	Interest	Health Costs	Profits	Sales	% Unionized
Interest	1.0000	.0160	−.1668	.3544*	.2645
Health costs	.0160	1.0000	.0316	−.2982	.4289**
Profits	−.1668	.0316	1.0000	−.1307	−.2530
Sales	.3544*	−.2982	−.1307	1.0000	.0106
% unionized	.2645	.4289**	−.2530	.0106	1.0000
Capital intensity	.1751	−.0928	.1459	.1076	−.1483
Regulated sector	.3535*	.4662**	.0400	.0493	.4860**
% exports	−.0954	−.2011	−.0157	.0006	−.3330*

	Capital Intensity	Regulated Sector	% Exports
Interest	.1751	.3535*	−.0954
Health costs	−.0928	.4662**	−.2011
Profits	.1459	.0400	−.0157
Sales	.1076	.0493	.0006
% unionized	−.1483	.4860**	−.3330*
Capital intensity	1.0000	−.0376	.0920
Regulated sector	−.0376	1.0000	−.4042*
% Exports	.0920	−.4042*	1.0000

	D.C. Office	Number of Groups	% Managed Care
Interest	.4645**	.4881**	.3674*
D.C. office	1.0000	.3768*	.3841*
Number of groups	.3768*	1.0000	.3176*
% managed care	.3841*	.3176*	1.0000

One-tailed significance: *−.01   **−.001

TABLE 3.3
OLS Regression Results (dependent variable = health costs per worker)

Equation	1	
	b	Beta
	(SE)	(T)
Independent-Economic		
Sales	−.29	−.29
	(.11)	(−2.54)***
Regulated sector	71.04	.31
	(30.98)	(2.29)**
% unionized	1.30	.31
	(.57)	(2.29)**
Constant	309.99	
	(22.70)	
N Adjusted R^2	.34	

** Significant beyond .05 level, two-tailed test.
***Significant beyond .01 level, two-tailed test.

TABLE 3.4
OLS Regression Results (dependent variable = supportive position on employer mandates)

	Equation 1		Equation 2	
	b (SE)	Beta (T)	b (SE)	Beta (T)
Economic Independent Variable				
Sales	.003	.165	.003	.156
	(.003)	(1.21)	(.003)	(1.201
Regulated sector	.151	.032		
	(.78)	(.194)		
Capital intensity	1.052E-06	.093	1.150789E-06	.101
	(1.42300E-06)	(.74)	(1.37220E-06)	(−.839)
Profits	−.06	−.132	−.052	−.114
	(.058)	(−1.024)	(.054)	(−.957)
Health costs	.001	.059		
	(.003)	(.386)		
% unionized	−.005	−.057		
	(.014)	(−.353)		
% exports	−.009	−.077	−.008	−.072
	(.016)	(−.570)	(.015)	(−.572)
FT1			.070	.033
			(.293)	(.24)
Institutional Independent Variable				
D.C. office	1.849	.406	1.88	.413
	(.617)	(2.996)**	(.595)	(3.16)
Number of groups	.262	.224	.248	.212
	(.177)	(1.477)	.168	(1.472)
% managed care	.012	.172	.012	.175
	(.009)	1.350	(.008)	(1.429)
Constant	2.886		3.149	
Adjusted R^2	.39		.42	
Standard error	1.68		1.64	
N	47		47	

**Significant beyond .01 level, two-tailed test.

TABLE 3.5
OLS Regression Results (dependent variable = supportive
position on employer mandates)

	b (SE)	Beta (T)
Economic Independent Variable		
Sales	.003	.127
	(.003)	(1.03)
Regulated sector	.747	.149
	(.608)	(1.23)
Profits	−.076	−.182
	(.047)	(−1.63)
Institutional Independent Variable		
D.C. office	1.266	.279
	(.597)	(2.12)**
Number of groups	.289	.237*
	(.159)	(1.806)
% managed care	.008	.115
	(.009)	.935
Constant	3.518	
	(.49)	
Adjusted R^2	.34	
Standard error	1.77	
N	56	

*Significant beyond .10 level, two-tailed test.
** Significant beyond .05 level, two-tailed test.

TABLE 3.6
Ordered Probit Results
(dependent variable = supportive position on employer mandates)

	Coefficient (Asymptotic SE)	Z (P>IzI)
Economic Independent Variable		
Sales	.002	.93
	(.002)	(.35)
Regulated sector	−.086	−.15
	(.576)	(.88)
Capital intensity	1.09E-06	1.02
	(1.07E-06)	(.31)
Profits	−.015	−.35
	(.044)	(.73)
Health costs	.003	1.30
	(.003)	(.19)
% unionized	.000	.02
	(.011)	(.98)
% exports	−.013	−.106
	(.012)	(.29)
Institutional Independent Variable		
D.C. office	1.333	2.77
	(.481)	(.006)**
Number of groups	.361	2.42
	(.149)	(.015)**
% managed care	.005	.74
	(.006)	(.46)
∧ cut 1[a]	2.101	
	(1.026)	
∧ cut 2[a]	4.028	
	(1.116)	
Pseudo R^2	.34	
N	47	

[a]For an explanation, please see note 95 to chapter 3.
**Significant beyond .01 level, two-tailed test.

TABLE 3.7
Model Estimation of Positions on Employer Mandates with Changes in Sales,
Group Membership, and Offices in Washington, D.C.

Category of support	As data are	Plus $100 in sales	Join One More Group	All without D.C. Office	All with D.C. Office
No	23%	20%	17%	42%	11%
Maybe	43%	42%	41%	45%	48%
Yes	34%	38%	42%	13%	41%

Appendix to Chapter 3

Methods

The first statistical technique used to examine the hypotheses was an OLS regression method of estimation. Regression analysis was appropriate because of the interval level quality of the dependent variable.[91] Hours of interviewing convinced me that the firms truly were distributed along an ordinal scale with interval qualities. The statistical results were supplemented and complemented by the qualitative interview evidence concerning the dynamics of political participation by the firms. This evidence provided a check and added confidence to the assessments of the importance of the independent variables in the multivariate analysis.

Second, I conducted an F-test to evaluate the relative weights of the economic variables as a group versus the institutional variables as a group. This test was motivated by a concern about a moderate degree of correlation between some of the variables in each group and a possibility of multicollinearity. I conducted a regression entering the economic variables on the first step and the institutional variables on the second step, and calculated the R-squared change and the associated F-test.

Third, as a mechanism for checking the robustness of the findings, I estimated the model using an ordered probit. The dependent variable was altered somewhat for the probit analysis. Those companies with an explicit formal position favoring mandates were coded 2. (This corresponded to value of 8 on scale 1 in chapter 3.) Those companies that had not taken a position supporting mandates but were not absolutely opposed to them were coded 1. (This corresponded to values of 4–7 on scale 1.) Those companies in which top management was opposed to mandates were coded 0.[92]

---

[91] The interviews with corporate managers suggested a rather smooth progression from a strong negative position opposing mandates, through weak rejection of or support for mandates with no formal position, to a strong positive position in favor of mandates. The distance between each point on the scale seemed approximately equal; thus the data take on many attributes of continuous data. The parameters of the quantitative regression equations resulting from the statistical calculations were consistent with the qualitative data of the interviews. Barbara G. Tabachnik and Linda S. Fidell, *Using Multivariate Statistics* (New York: Harper and Row, 1989), 7–9.

[92] Those coded as opposing mandates had not, with one exception, taken a formal public position; however, the company respondents reported that top management within the firm was uniformly opposed to the measure. The tendency for only those supporting mandates to take a formal position reflected the nature of the issue. Since mandates promised a general rather than a narrowly targeted impact, firms were less likely to develop the kinds of defensive positions protecting themselves that one finds, for example, in very specific environmental regulations.

(This corresponded to values of 1–3 on scale 1.) This coding of the dependent variable should reassure anyone concerned about the subtle distinctions in the ordering of scale 1. Those companies coded as 2 all took public official positions in support of mandates; those coded as 0 all reported that top management firmly rejected employer mandates.[93]

Some might be concerned that multicollinearity lay behind the poor performance of the economic variables; yet the variables were only moderately correlated. Percent unionization was correlated with health dollars per worker at .43 and with regulated and troubled sector at .47. Still, to protect against multicollinearity, I conducted a principal-component factor analysis with the three highly correlated economic variables: health dollars per worker, percent unionization, and regulated and troubled sectors. These variables seemed theoretically to go together as a type of firm: the regulated, heavily unionized company with generous health benefits such as one finds in the auto or steel sectors. The factor produced accounted for 66 percent of the variance and had an eigenvalue of 1.977. Yet the new variable produced by this factor (called FT1) had a T-value of only .24 in the regression equation. (See table 3.4, equation 2.)

Given the intercorrelation between variables and the small N, it seemed useful to try to reduce the number of variables in order to give fair play to the competing hypothesis. I pursued two different statistical approaches to reduce the number of variables.[94] The initial approach was to run a series of regressions, beginning with the ten independent variables and discarding them one at a time until the removal of a variable increased the standard error of the equation and decreased the adjusted R-squared. This approach delivered a model with the following variables: sales, profits, D.C. office, number of groups, and percentage in managed care. The other approach was to test the economic variables and the institutional variables independently and to select those that were statistically significant from each group for inclusion in the final equation. These regressions produced sales, regulated and troubled sectors, D.C. office, and number of groups. I then ran a regression equation including all of the variables identified in two procedures, including sales, profits, regulated and troubled sectors, D.C. office, number of groups, and percent managed care. In this more parsimonious equation (presented on table 3.5) profits approached statistical significance with a T-value of !1.63 and a probabil-

[93] The revised dependent variable had a distribution of sixteen supporting mandates, twenty-seven neither supporting nor opposing, and fourteen opposing.

[94] See also Theda Skocpol, Marjorie Abend-Wein, Christopher Howard, and Susan Goodrich Lehmann, "Women's Associations and the Enactment of Mothers' Pensions in the United States," *American Political Science Review* 87 (1993): 686–701.

ity of T at .11; yet, none of the other economic variables were close to significance.

An F-test assessing the significance of the change in R-squared across the economic-variable and institutional-variable equations gave some reassurance that the weakness of the economic factors was related to something besides multicollinearity. When the seven economic variables were run in a regression alone with the dependent variable, they explained only .13 of the adjusted R-squared.[95] The three institutional variables, entered on the second step of the regression, produced an R-squared change of .26 and an F-change of 1.99; the significance F-change was .08.

Finally, I estimated the hypotheses with an ordered probit model, which can be used to illustrate the probability of a response falling into each category of the dependent variable; one evaluates the effect of an independent variable by examining the change in probability of the response falling into each category.[96] In other words, one must imagine what would happen to the dependent variable with an incremental change in the dependent variable.

Discussion of the Statistical Findings

The OLS regression results show that none of the economic independent variables was statistically significant and only sales and profits had a T-value greater than 1 (or !1). A 1-point increase in sales produced only a .003 point increase in the firm's support for employer mandates; a 1-point decrease in profits produced only a .06 increase in support for mandates.

The D.C. office variable was by far the most robust variable and was statistically significant at the .01 level with a T-value of 3.0 in the equation with all of the variables together. A 1-point increase in the Washington government affairs office independent variable produced a 1.8-point increase in dependent variable.

---

[95] The highest adjusted R-squared using only economic variables was .20, produced when sales and regulated sector were run alone. The institutional variables run alone produced an adjusted R-squared of .35.

[96] The ordered probit model assumes a latent-variable structure of the form $y^* = XB + e$. We observe

$$y = 0 \text{ if } e < XB, y = 1 \text{ if } XB < e < XB + {}^{\wedge}, y = 2 \text{ if } XB + {}^{\wedge} < e,$$

$$\text{where } {}^{\wedge} > 0, \text{ and}$$

$$P_0 = F(XB), P_1 = F(XB + {}^{\wedge}) - F(XB), P_2 = 1 - F(XB + {}^{\wedge}).$$

The $^{\wedge}$ signifies lambda. The lambda cuts specified on table 3–6 refer to the divisions between response categories of the dependent variable. Thus cut 1 separates those opposing man-

The group membership variable became close to statistically significant in the parsimonious OLS regression equation on table 3.5, with a T-value of 1.8 and a probability of T at .08. A 1-point increase in group membership produced a .29-point increase in the dependent variable. (The moderately high correlation between the three institutional variables partly interfered with the performance of this variable: group membership was correlated with D.C. offices at .38 and with percentage in managed care at .32.)

But the ordered probit estimation of the model with its revised dependent variable found the groups variable to be statistically significant with a p-value of .01. Apart from the slightly better performance of the group membership variable, this change in measurement of the dependent variable produced findings virtually identical to those produced with the less truncated dependent variable. The revised dependent variable rather than the different method of statistical analysis was responsible for this difference in statistical significance.

The two key institutional effects held for an OLS estimation of the model of the truncated dependent variable. The OLS regression using the 3-point dependent variable produced virtually the same results as the ordered probit estimation of the model. I felt confident using the OLS method because the 3-point scale approximated a normal distribution with 16 supporting, 27 in between, and 15 opposing. In this equation, the DC office variable was statistically significant at the .01 level with a T-value of 3.0. The truncated dependent variable had exactly the same T-value as the 8-point dependent variable and was comparable to the ordered probit Z-level of 2.8. The group membership variable was also statistically significant at the .05 level with a T-value of 2.2 (comparable to the ordered probit Z-level of 2.4). None of the economic variables had a significance of T lower than .27. The adjusted R-squared of the OLS regression run with all of the variables and the truncated dependent variable was .40 (again comparable to the adjusted R-squared of .39 using the 8-point dependent variable) and the standard error of the equation was .59.

Table 3.7 illustrates the effect of changes in sales, D.C. offices and groups on the probability of supporting employer mandates. Taking the data as they are, the model predicts 23 percent opposing mandates, 43 percent in between, and 34 percent supporting mandates. With an incremental increase of $100 million in sales (very close to the standard deviation), the probability of supporting employer mandates only increases to

dates from those in between; cut 2 separates those in between from those supporting mandates. See William Greene, *Econometric Analysis* (New York: Macmillan, 1993), 672–76.

38 percent; the probability of opposing mandates only drops to 20 percent. With an incremental increase in membership of one group, the probability of supporting employer mandates increases to 42 percent; the probability of opposing mandates drops to 17 percent. If all of the firms are given D.C. offices, the probability of supporting employer mandates is 41 percent; with none of the firms having D.C. offices the probability of supporting mandates is only 13 percent. The D.C. office variable is statistically significant with a p-value of .006. Thus the ordered probit gives one a sense of the strength of the effects of the independent variables.

FOUR

ON THE BUS:

BUSINESS ORGANIZATION IN TRAINING

AND WORK-FAMILY ISSUES

ISSUES seem to capture the popular imagination in sudden and surprising ways: if this week's story of the hour is child abuse, next week's may be global warming. Business issues often also have a star-is-born quality, as managers in diverse settings simultaneously fix on the latest overnight sensation. *Total quality management, lean and mean,* and *diversity training* are but a few of the buzzwords to infiltrate corporate language in recent years.

It turns out that issues are put on the business agenda in much the same way that they gain the attention of the mass public, through the efforts of highly committed political activists. Although issues often seem propelled by natural forces, the reality is usually less instinctive and more contrived. Issues come of age through careful plotting, and core political supporters from all walks of life make use of common trade secrets. Spin doctors with MBAs frame issues in terms likely to resonate with their colleagues: social policies portrayed as props for growth are better received than those evoking images of redistribution, labor radicalism, and anti-capitalist equality.

This chapter takes up the question of how a social issue gains a significant following among managers. We may anticipate that two policies will be equally attractive to managers, yet we find that one commands far greater corporate interest and action than the other. Some social issues resonate with corporate concerns about productivity and international competition, while others are viewed with suspicion. Thus it is important to understand how issues come to managers' attention and why employers respond so differently to various initiatives in public policy.

I argue that the institutional resources of an issue's core business supporters help to account for differences in issues' appeal to the business community. One can evaluate the relative political strengths of these core supporters with the same institutional measures of corporate policy capacity that we used to analyze decision making in the firm, thus moving our discussion from the level of the firm to the level of policy. First, firms have limited resources and must decide where to concentrate their political energies; therefore, the standing within a company of *private experts* on an issue is important to its fate. In comparing issues, we should examine the strength of their advocates within the firm and the linkages between these advocates and potential sympathizers (or reference groups). Second, core activists are helped or hindered by the ideas and *policy legacies* to which the issue is linked. Activists self-consciously depict their goals and ideology in terms appealing to the interests, values, and beliefs of the individuals they wish to attract. Third, *business organization* at the level of policy influences the fortunes of the social issue. An activist group dedicated to spreading information about the issue increases its political salience for the broader business community.

This chapter compares the business networks organized around work-family and training issues and investigates how these networks politicized issues for the broader business communities. (Subsequent chapters explore how the institutional characteristics of these networks also affected the issues' chances for legislative success.) Training and work-family policies have much in common, yet the issues differ in important ways. Both are linked to productivity; both areas have grown enormously within firms in recent years. Both issues have been put on the corporate agenda through the agitation of core corporate advocates. But employment and training policy has attracted considerable business political backing at the national level; by comparison, work-family concerns have been virtually left off employers' political agenda. The major employer associations—NAM, the Business Roundtable, and the Chamber of Commerce—all promoted the School-to-Work Opportunities Partnership Act and Goals 2000. None of these organizations could be persuaded even to testify on the Child Care Block Grant legislation in 1989 (originally designed to be a much broader initiative), and they vigorously opposed the family leave act until the very end. The business press has followed training policy more closely than child care legislation. For example, a Nexis search of selected major business periodicals generated eighty-six citations when training was combined with legislation, productivity and business; but only fifteen when child care was inserted into the equation.[1]

The training issue has, at least in part, gained more business interest and commitment than work-family because its activists have greater corporate policy capacity. First, the experts on the two issues within firms have different resources. Human-resource managers with close ties to government relations departments are the stalwarts on matters of training; work-family issues are largely the domain of newcomers to the corporate structure, often women. Second, the two issues have been connected to different ideas or policy legacies: training has prospered in its link to education

---

[1] I searched five periodicals: *Business Week, Fortune, Forbes, Nation's Business,* and the *Wall Street Journal.*

reform, whereas work-family policy has been hurt by its ties to the women's movement. Finally, the organizational profiles of the two movements are quite unequal in strength. A political commitment to training evolved long ago among managers when Lyndon Johnson encouraged the formation of a corporatist-type employer association, the National Alliance of Business. No similar central group exists to organize business in the work-family realm. Thus, work-family concerns constitute a much newer issue than training, have less evolved organizational champions, and have largely been promoted by women, who in general enjoy less power both within the firm and society.

The Case for Employment and Training Policy

The central idea behind a national employment and training policy boils down to one of my father's favorite maxims: "You get what you pay for." Workers need to be trained to make high-quality, cutting-edge products. If we want U.S. companies to deliver the goods, we as a nation need to deliver the training.

Training has occupied a relatively small space in the American political landscape as compared to Western Europe; indeed, many active labor market policies have never been seriously considered in the United States. These constraints on the scope of training reflect a narrow interpretation of Keynesian ideas after World War II, early linkages made between training and welfare, and the manner in which early decisions about training policies divided constituents at later points.[2]

But a more active approach to training gained in popularity in the 1980s, when technological change altered industrial production at an exponential rate. An explosion of advanced technology rapidly changed the organization or work and created demand for a more highly skilled workforce. Simultaneously, increased international competition meant that foreign goods would overwhelm countries unable to meet the demanding new prerequisites for high-technology production.[3]

At least some soothsayers foresaw an ill-fated course for the United States, a slow slide to a low-wage economy. The preponderance of new jobs in low-wage jobs sectors seem to defend this unhappy reading. Two million manufacturing jobs have been eliminated since 1980, and the fast-

---

[2] Weir, *Politics and Jobs;* Desmond King, *Actively Seeking Work?* (Chicago: University of Chicago Press, 1995); Gary Mucciaroni, *The Political Failure of Employment Policy* (Pittsburgh: University of Pittsburgh Press, 1990); Baumer and Van Horn, *Politics of Unemployment..*

[3] William Johnston and Arnold Packer, *Workforce 2000* (Indianapolis: Hudson Institute, 1987), 32–35.

est-growing occupation in 2005 is projected to be retail clerk. Of the 13.6 million new jobs created between 1979 and 1989, 5 million paid at a rate that would put full-time workers below the poverty line for a family of four. The average weekly wage in real dollars dropped from $387 in 1979 to $335 in 1989. Between 1960 and 1985 the U.S. economy grew at only 3.1 percent per year, a laggard compared to the worldwide growth of 3.9 percent per year.[4] *America's Choice: High Skills or Low Wages* warned, "America is headed toward an economic cliff. . . . If basic changes are not made, real wages will continue to fall, especially for the majority who do not graduate from four-year colleges. . . . It is no longer possible to be a high wage, low skill nation. We have choices to make."[5]

The image of losing high-skill jobs played into the general fear of declining employment in many sectors of the economy. Migrating multinational companies have for some time sought cheaper prices for low-skilled labor in developing countries. The jury is still out on NAFTA. The Bush administration predicted a job loss of 150,000; labor unions pushed this estimate up to 600,000. The end of the cold war brought a great reduction of jobs in the military and defense industry.[6]

Readers might protest this dismal view of a low-skill economy; indeed, American universities are among the best in the world. Whereas the Japanese worry that their system of rote learning stifles creativity, we point with pride to our grand record of scientific innovation. Yet not all levels of society share in this proud tradition of Yankee ingenuity. Training for those students who are not college-bound is especially dismal, because our high schools have a strong academic bias. Over a third of young adults (ages twenty-one to twenty-five) have less than eleventh-grade reading skills.[7] What will happen to this undereducated, silent, but sizable minority? Baxter Corporation chairman Vern Loucks Jr. predicts dire consequences for a society that consistently underinvests in the education of those in the bottom tier: "The last thing that any of us in business can afford is the existence of a permanent and largely ignored or forgotten underclass. All of us fully understand the negative potential of a society where a very large minority does not participate in the successes of society as a whole."[8]

Even young Americans who finish high school or college tend to drift. As Dustin Hoffman's character in *The Graduate* discovered, there are few

---

[4] Beverly Geber, "Retrain Who to Do What?" *Training,* January 1993, 27; Johnston and Packer, *Workforce 2000,* 6.

[5] Commission on the Skills of the American Workforce, *America's Choice,* 91.

[6] Rochelle L. Stanfield, "Answer to NAFTA," *National Journal,* October 31, 1992, 2498.

[7] Office of Technology Assessment, *Worker Training,* 20.

[8] Loucks, "Business and School Reform," 466.

institutional mechanisms for easing the transition from school to work. In other countries, apprenticeship programs and other forms of private-sector off-the-job training help young adults to enter the working world. For example, 40 percent of young Americans receive additional training after high school, compared with 75 percent of German youths.[9] The community college system has increasingly become a source for post–high school technical training, and many pin high hopes for the future on this development.

Low skills also pose a problem for American manufacturers, especially when they fail to get qualified workers. In a NAM study, firms rejected five-sixths of their applicants due to inadequate skills and found one-third lacking in essential reading and writing skills. Deficiencies in workers' skills prevented 40 percent of the firms from upgrading production technology, and 37 percent from reorganizing.[10] Another study found employers reporting that 20 percent of their workers were inadequately trained. Fifty-seven percent said that the past three years had brought increases in their requirements for workers' skills. In another survey firms complained that 40 percent of their new hires needed upgrading in basic skills, as well as almost 40 percent of their current workforce.[11] Although the numbers vary, these studies all point to a need for better-trained workers.

Companies can respond to this dilemma by increasing wages to attract more competent employees, by training workers, or by moving production elsewhere. Increasing wages drives up the costs of goods; to many employers, training is a much better solution. Conceived of as an investment, training presents a way to improve the productivity of workers. A recent Census Bureau study found that investment in education now has a greater payoff for firms than investment in capital equipment: a 10 percent increase in educational attainment increases productivity by 8.6 percent, whereas a 10 percent increase in capital stock value increases it by just 3.4 percent. Motorola estimated that it got back thirty-three dollars for every one dollar spent on training.[12] In-house retraining permits firms to retain experienced workers; for example, Intel retrained six hundred

[9] Lisa M. Lynch, "Entry-Level Jobs: First Rung on the Employment Ladder or Economic Dead End?" *Journal of Labor Research* 14, no. 3 (1993): 251.

[10] Towers Perrin, produced for the National Association of Manufacturers, "Today's Dilemma: Tomorrow's Competitive Edge," November 1991, obtained from Towers Perrin.

[11] National Center on the Educational Quality of the Work Force at the University of Pennsylvania study, cited in Peter Applebome, "Employers Wary of School System," *New York Times,* February 20, 1995, A1, 13; "Skill Levels Inadequate, Survey Reveals," *Managing Office Technology* 40, no. 10 (1995): 4–45.

[12] Peter Applebome, "Study Ties Educational Gains to More Productivity Growth," *New York Times,* May 14, 1995, 22; "Training for New Technology Reaps Rewards, Says New Edition of Work in America Study," Press Release, June 12, 1991, Work in America Institute.

workers laid off in from 1990 to 1992, to avoid damaging morale and losing trust. The corporate concern about employment and training was also connected to the general awakening to the need for quality: in manufacturing, in products, and in the workforce. One observer suggested, "[Edward] Deming's message to the firm [about quality] coincided in many ways with the message of Workforce 2000 to the nation."[13]

Despite the many benefits of employment and training, there is not enough in-house training. Small firms have a difficult time managing it, and training is often the first to go when budgets get cut. There is a predilection for hiring skills rather than training existing workers, in part because devoting resources to education presents a collective-action problem: employers fear that their investments will take better jobs elsewhere. Some worry that workers with the most skills are the ones who get more training; however, a *Training* magazine survey found that the average company with over one hundred employees invested the most resources in training sales personnel and showed no gap between management and blue-collar workers.[14] In any case, our European and Japanese competitors spend two to three times as much on training as U.S. firms.[15] Christine Keen of the American Society for Human Resource Management believes that human investment is undervalued in the United States:

> In the U.S., people are viewed as costs, not investments. Payroll is a cost. Training is a cost. In contrast, new equipment is an investment. Until we convince ourselves that what we spend on people should be seen—and managed—as an investment, too, we will not come to grips with the role intellectual capital needs to play in our economy.[16]

Despite the general support for training, government policy to expand this investment in human capital draws critics from three directions. First, some question whether the projected demand for highly skilled jobs is accurate because only a small portion of companies require a high-performance workforce. Unless supply can create its own demand, training constitutes wasted effort. Projections for an increase in highly skilled jobs do not factor in the higher pay scales that would accompany the higher skills.[17] In addition, firms face enormous start-up costs in teaching funda-

---

[13] "The Changing Nature of Work," *Financial World*, June 23, 1992, 66; Arnold Packer, "The SCANS Challenge," *Employment Relations Today*, December 22, 1992, 367.

[14] Norman Bowers and Paul Swaim, "Recent Trends in Job Training," *Contemporary Economic Policy* 12 (January 1994): 79–88; Beverly Geber, "Because It's Good for You," *Training*, April 1993, 17.

[15] Lisa Starkey, "Job-Linked Literacy Programs Build Competitiveness, Says New Work in America Report," press release, Work in America Institute, Scarsdale, N.Y., April 8, 1992.

[16] "The Changing Nature of Work," *Financial World*, June 23, 1992.

[17] Lawrence Mishel and Ruy Teixeira, *The Myth of the Coming Labor Shortage* (Washington, D.C.: Economic Policy Institute, 1991), 1–3.

mental reading, writing, and arithmetic before they can move onto more advanced skills. As discussed above, company training, at least, often does little to provide the basics.

Second, some view training policy as the government's micromanagement of the firm. Without considerable government oversight, firms could simply reclassify current efforts as new training. Would, for example, working with a supervisor on the job count as training? Training policy could spawn a whole new bureaucracy devoted to making sure that the company's definition of training meets that of the government. Tom Lindsley captured the complicated aspects of a training tax: "They want it to go to line workers primarily and to new work organizations and increased productivity, whatever that means. It's one of those broad policy ideas that has a lot of validity but when you try to implement it, it runs into a maze of problems."[18]

Third, training purports to help both low-income, marginally employed persons *and* displaced workers; but these groups have different needs. This goal conflict, combined with lack of funding, reduced the effectiveness of past legislation, such as the Manpower Development and Training Act, the Comprehensive Employment and Training Act, and even the Jobs Training Partnership Act.[19] Some on the right believe that the problem of the unskilled worker stems from the pernicious influence of the welfare system rather than from inadequacies in education. Remedial work training programs designed to fill in educational gaps do little to address the deeper culture of poverty.[20] The Left also worries about who would benefit from employment and training. Would the truly disadvantaged gain skills from training designed to produce a high-wage economy? The focus on training (and individual inadequacies) neglects race, class, and other systemic inequities that are responsible for poverty.[21] Kazis and Sabonis argue that business has never followed through with the hard-core unemployed and routinely asks for more monetary incentives and less red tape for training efforts. The Jobs Training Partnership Act, passed in 1982, ostensibly to help the have-nots of society, ended up benefiting displaced workers and subsidizing firms' normal start-up costs. Thus, Japanese automobile plants asked the federal government to subsidize training costs for their well-educated new hires! Anthony Carnevale of the American

[18] Geber, "Because It's Good for You," 17.

[19] Elaine Bonner-Tompkins, "A Changing Workforce and More Job Training Programs," *CBCF Policy Review* 1, no. 2 (1994): 1–9; LaLonde, "Promise of Training Programs."

[20] Glazer, *Limits of Social Policy,* 84–85.

[21] Richard McGahey and John Jeffries, "Minorities and the Labor Market," *Social Policy* 17, no. 3 (1987): 5–11; Gordon Lafer, "The Politics of Job Training," *Politics and Society* 22, no. 3 (1994): 349–88.

Society of Training and Development characterized this dualism as a "schizophrenia in purpose."[22]

Business Mobilization for Employment and Training Policy

Despite challenges from both the Right and the Left (and divergence on significant details), employment and training policy as a societal goal enjoys enormous backing from business and from both political parties. More than any other social issue, training policy's connection to economic growth is reified in the corporate mythology. Fortune 500 executives in a 1986 survey ranked training and motivating employees number 3 in importance out of twelve issues of concern. These same CEOs ranked labor problems last; consequently, their interest in training transcended concerns about labor peace. A National Association of Manufacturing survey found 64 percent of its sample interested in "a national, business-run remedial education program."[23]

Three phenomena helped employment and training to gather such strong employer support: the ideas or policy legacies linked to the issue, the position of the policy experts (professional trainers) within the firm, and the organizational structure of the movement. First, employment and training policy has been relatively popular among employers because it has been able to piggyback on the larger corporate debate about education reform. Education enjoys a privileged position in the pantheon of American social issues because equality of opportunity places a major role in American political culture and in our identity as a classless society. Absence of class or social mobility means that hard-working individuals can move between income levels. Education is a major vehicle for bettering oneself and has always enjoyed a political legitimacy lacking in other social spheres.

Corporate interest in employment and training policy grew out of the business movement for educational reform to improve community schools. Firms invested in local schools through adopt-a-school programs but sometimes directed corporate dollars to inner-city children. For example, Chicago's Corporate/Community School was based in a very poor neighborhood. Corporate foundations also joined the movement for school reform; thus, the RJR Nabisco Foundation gave $30 million to the

[22] Richard Kazis and Peter Sabonis, "CETA and the Private Sector Imperative," *Social Policy* 10, no. 4 (1980): 7; Kirk Victor, "Helping the Haves," *National Journal,* April 14, 1990, 898.

[23] Maggie McComas, "Atop the Fortune 500: A Survey of the C.E.O.s," *Fortune,* April 28, 1986, 29; Towers Perrin, produced for the National Association of Manufacturers, "Today's Dilemma: Tomorrow's Competitive Edge," obtained from Towers Perrin, 30.

Next Century Schools program, which set out to restructure radically the education system.[24]

Perhaps the most important business effort to reform schools has been the Compact experiment. The Boston Compact, formed in 1982 to cope with the crisis in the public schools following desegregation, brought business managers from the Boston Private Industry Council and educators together to improve schools, to reduce the unemployment rate among minority youth, and to ease the school-to-work transition. In 1986 the National Alliance of Business (NAB) expanded the Compact Project to twelve cities.[25] The cities participating had mixed experiences; even in Boston early efforts at reform were disappointing. Managers were frustrated by the lack of connection between process and outcomes, and in 1988 Boston employers would sign an extension of the Compact only after educators agreed to decentralize the management and to put more emphasis on goals. But part of the problem was that many managers who do not understand the system had a short time frame and wanted immediate results, as Vern Loucks Jr. explained:

> [M]any of us are far too willing to take on part of the problem, and far too few of us are willing to tackle the whole damn thing; that is, the politics that will foster an integration of all the parts into a productive whole. Businessmen want to "get along" with the world, and so they tend to shy away from controversy. But any effective school-reform effort will be ablaze with controversy. . . . [B]usiness people want results. But what they think of as "results" are often not appropriate in the context of the schools. . . . Part of why we are so confused about results is that in our business lives, many of us are ruled by three-month reporting periods.[26]

Although school reform was often disappointing, the partnerships between business and educators did bring about much-needed changes in some settings and, more importantly, laid the institutional and ideological groundwork for business's commitment to training policy. The NAB credited groups as the essential component for success: "An institutional structure is needed at the local level to orchestrate ongoing business commitment and to build the likelihood of continuity of business involvement." The Compact groups also fostered an evolution of corporate thinking about education and training. Business professor Sandra Waddock suggests that a major impact of the Compact Project was to link education

---

[24] Loucks, "Business and School Reform," 466; Rochelle L. Stanfield, "School Business," *National Journal,* July 27, 1991, 1862.

[25] National Alliance of Business (NAB), *The Compact Project* (Washington, D.C.: National Alliance of Business, 1989), iii–vi.

[26] Loucks, "Business and School Reform," 466.

and work much more closely than they had been linked before and to create ongoing networks for the study of employment and training issues.[27] For example, the California Business Roundtable, made up of CEOs from eighty companies, produced an influential report called *Mobilizing for Competitiveness* that pushed for an Education and Economic Development Council to help small and medium-sized firms become high-skill, high-wage companies. The report advocated more employee training through the community college system and the creation of one-stop career centers. The San Diego Business Roundtable for Education testified to Congress in support of business oversight committees "to ensure that there is a structured mechanism for employer input into policy-making and planning for the school-to-work system."[28]

A second source of strength for the employment-and-training movement has been the growth of the training profession within the firm. Many large companies (especially high-technology producers who compete abroad) have experimented with in-house training programs. As training professionals have developed a secure base within their companies, they have sought to expand company commitment and resources to this issue.[29]

Some companies imported a training bias from the old country. Remmele Engineering is a tool-and-die-making company, established by German-born Fred Remmele in 1949. The German craft tradition permeated the company. In the 1960s the firm had a problem finding people with the skills to make its special equipment, and Remmele decided to open his own apprenticeship program at an off-site training center. The training center operated for eleven years until vocational schools and community colleges became more abundant, but the company still has apprentices within the company who spend between six thousand and ten thousand hours learning their trade from master mechanics. After Remmele's death, Remmele chairman Bill Saul began a crusade for training and founded the Minnesota Business Foundation for Excellence in Education. Saul dismisses the oft-heard corporate complaint that trained workers will take their skills elsewhere, saying that if all companies were doing their job, mobility would not matter: "Somehow, through various manufacturing associations and the Business Roundtable, you've got to get people interested in training skilled labor."[30]

---

[27] NAB, *The Compact Project*, v; Sandra Waddock, "Lessons from the National Alliance of Business Compact Project," *Human Relations* 46, no. 7 (1993): 849–79.

[28] "Job Training Witnesses Tell House Subcommittee Firms Should Be Involved in Job Training," *BNA Management Briefing,* March 8, 1995, n.p.; J. A. Savage, "Is California Handing Over Its Schools to Business?" *Business and Society Review,* June 22, 1994, 12.

[29] Scott and Meyer, "Rise of Training Programs," 228–54.

[30] Joseph McKenna, "Fred Remmele's Investment, Bill Saul's Crusade," *Industry Week,* November 2, 1992, 22.

Siemens Corporation, a New York–based subsidiary of a German company and a leader in the business training movement, has been offering youth apprenticeship programs based on the German model for one hundred years. When Albert Hoser (himself an apprenticeship graduate) became chairman of the U.S. company in 1990, he realized that the firm's workers lacked many skills and set out to develop comprehensive training programs. Each of the company units imposes a self-tax to create a training pool, used to upgrade the skills of existing workers, to run the youth apprenticeship programs, and to develop industry skill standards. In the first year of the Lake Mary, Florida, apprenticeship program, for example, students spend twenty hours a week in class at Seminole Community College and twenty hours on the shop floor. The second year consists entirely of on-site training, while the final half year finds students finishing course work. Siemens provides these students with a stipend and college tuition and actually prefers training high school graduates to college graduates because it is less expensive. According to Siemens's John Tobin, these training programs prepare workers better for the manufacturing needs of the company, give them a head start in life, and solve the mismatch between the supply of, and demand for, labor in the firm's rural operating locations.[31]

Some companies link training to corporate responsibility and embrace the social goal of hiring the hard-core unemployed; for example, Aetna made a commitment to fill 6 percent of its entry-level positions from Hartford's inner city. Community groups screen applicants for Aetna, rejecting the two-thirds that lack sixth-grade reading skills. Those who make the first cut spend six months improving their skills and learning to adapt to corporate culture; at the end Aetna hires about a third and offers an additional four months of training.[32]

Professional trainers are at the forefront of the training movement both within the company and in the political arena. Driven by a blend of professional concern about the issue and career building within the firm, the human-resource pros have been leaders in the quest for the high-skilled workforce. Lesley Grady, executive director of the Atlanta Partnership of Business and Education, pointed to the critical role of human-resource activism: "Unless you have a very enlightened CEO, most of these programs are driven by an energetic, visionary human-resources person."[33] Anthony Carnevale of the American Society for Training and Development recognized the training profession's link to public policy when he

[31] Interview with John Tobin, May 20, 1996.

[32] Amanda Bennett, "The New Work Force: Aetna Schools New Hires in Basic Workplace Skills," *Wall Street Journal,* April 13, 1995, sec. 2, p. 1.

[33] Marie Powers, "Atlanta's Dirty Little Secret: Functional Illiteracy Is a Devastating Plague on the Business Community," *Business Atlanta,* March 1991, 26.

called the training payroll tax proposed by Clinton a "full employment act for trainers" and calculated that firms would spend $221.4 billion more if a mandate were passed. *Employment Relations Today* boasted that greater attention to employment and training "establishes a new role for HR professionals both within and outside their firm."[34]

Finally, a strong organizational base has enhanced training's fortunes as a political issue among large employers. At the core is a multisector, broad-based association devoted to human-resource development called the National Alliance of Business. NAB's auspicious origins, broad scope, and twenty-five-year history of activism helped to develop considerable employer commitment and consensus in this area of policy. This quasi-corporatist business group was set up by Lyndon Johnson to cut unemployment among minority youth and to secure urban peace. Riots during the summer of 1966 concentrated the administration's attention on the problems of the inner city, and a task force chaired by George Schultz (then dean of the University of Chicago School of Business) recommended targeting manpower programs to inner-city areas and creating a national business council to bring business into the effort. Because there were insufficient funds for a major new government program, LBJ aide Joe Califano instead developed the Job Opportunities in the Business Sector (JOBS) program to contract with private industry for training and jobs. The new program assumed that business would not simply participate from philanthropic impulses; rather, the program had to appear profitable.[35]

The administration set up the National Alliance of Businessmen to encourage employers to participate in JOBS. William Zisch, formerly president of Aerojet General, was hired as a special assistant at Commerce to serve as a liaison between private industry and government. The administration constructed a tight organizational plan for managing its corporate allies. Howard Samuels was to become an "operating officer" of the Commerce Department and was to personally supervise the entire operation. Samuels was to keep central control of the test program in Washington, D.C., but deals with business participants were to be made locally. The hope was to find local representatives "entrenched in the local establishment [to] make sure our salesman have access to the right clubs and other pathways where their quarry might be found." Although the National Alliance of Businessmen was ostensibly a private organization, the admin-

---

[34] Geber, "Because It's Good for You," 17; Packer, "The SCANS Challenge," 367.

[35] Memorandum to files from James Gaither, "The National Alliance of Businessmen," November 15, 1968, LBJ Library, Legislative History, National Alliance of Businessmen, "Background Summary"; memorandum to LBJ from Califano, January 12, 1968, LBJ Library, Legislative History, National Alliance of Businessmen, "Weekly Progress Reports to the President on the Test Program."

istration realized that these local agents could not simply work freelance on their own initiative, that they couldn't be "part-timers, businessmen on loan, or retired executives."[36] The White House needed to supervise its operation.

The National Alliance of Business conducted a huge jobs campaign for the administration. CEOs from 750 large companies attended a White House luncheon to kick off a massive public-relations campaign, and meetings were held with twelve thousand employers to urge them to participate. Private sources contributed $15 million to the NAB campaign, so that the government only had to come up with five hundred thousand dollars. Advertising agencies, TV stations, and publishers offered services. In one participating city, thirty-two business managers ran a phone bank for two days and secured pledges for forty-seven hundred youth.[37]

NAB also helped the administration develop legislative backing and legitimacy for its conception of an interventionist state. The administration asked permission to publish the names of firms that had made jobs commitments as a means of legitimating the program. Later, NAB tried to make inroads among small employers with a "small-business buddy system." NAB recruited the National Association of Manufacturers, the Chamber of Commerce, and community groups to the effort.[38] NAB also supported the administration in Congress. Califano made the point that "Critical to the success of the NAB program is the full funding of the fiscal 1969 OEO [Office of Economic Opportunity] appropriation. . . . If the Senate reduces the OEO appropriation by an amount anywhere near the $300 million cut made by the House, it would be extremely difficult to provide the funds needed for the Alliance." Five days later NAB wrote a letter requesting the Senate Appropriations Committee to grant Johnson's requests.[39]

NAB made stirring claims about its contributions to solving unemployment. By December 1968, six hundred private firms had contracted to

[36] Memorandum to files from James Gaither, "The National Alliance of Businessmen"; memorandum to James Gaither, "Expanding the Test Program," December 11, 1967, Legislative History, National Alliance of Businessmen, "Background on Further Development of Jobs Program and NAB."

[37] Memorandum to LBJ from National Alliance of Businessmen, "Progress Report on the JOBS Campaign," LBJ, WHCF EX FG816, "8/1/68."

[38] Memorandum from Califano to LBJ, "Status of Major New Program Initiatives," November 17, 1967, Legislative History, National Alliance of Businessmen, "Weekly Progress Report to the President on the Test Program"; letter from Leo Beebe to LBJ, April 25, 1968, attached to memo to LBJ from Califano, April 26, 1968, LBJ Library, WHCF EX FG 816 "3/6/68–7/31/68."

[39] Memorandum to LBJ from Califano, July 11, 1968, LBJ, WHCF EX FG816, "3/6/68–7/31/68"; letter to Lister Hill from NAB chairmen, July 16, 1968, WHCF EX FG816, "3/6/68–7/31/68."

provide jobs and training and had loaned the government 526 managers to help with the program. The private sector had hired 118,000 hard-core unemployed, and 92,000 were still on the job, in school, or in the armed forces. NAB claimed that the effort for each individual would add ten thousand dollars per year to the GNP, increase purchasing power by thirty-four hundred dollars, and cut government welfare payments $1,308 per person per year.[40]

Others were less sanguine about the program's ultimate contribution. As the unemployment rate increased, hard-to-employ persons had to compete with others for scarce jobs. Firms tended to underinvest in the training of special-needs workers, and companies' commitment to the program declined over time.[41] In the early years urban riots prompted many business managers to back mechanisms for social control; yet as urban unrest declined, corporate commitment dropped off accordingly. Participating firms tired of the effort when the Nixon administration showed rather less interest in its success.

Yet Johnson's efforts to form a partnership with business in training established an institutional legacy of business organization that has generated support from employers down to the present day. As the country seemed to lose interest in the fortunes of the inner city, the NAB also shifted gears, expanding its focus to dislocated workers at risk from international competition. The Jobs Training Partnership Act of 1982 was the turning point for this new organizational purpose. The group's current mission is "a concern with the quality of the workforce: spelling out skill standards and bringing business to the table to support and bring about changes that are necessary." As former NAB president William Kolberg explained, "Now that we are debating what the workforce system should be, we are much more concerned about white-collar and blue-collar workers and about the availability of training. . . . [Since 1982] we have felt that society had an important mission to give aid to these workers even if they are not poor."[42]

Despite its shift in goals, the group continues to operate in the neocorporatist mode established by the Johnson administration. Both government and the thirty-five hundred corporate sponsors contribute to the funding of the group. The organization's niche is the workforce, and it tries to attract members by explaining that "there is a new workforce agenda with an important bottom line significance." For five thousand

[40] Memorandum from Jim Gaither to LBJ, December 19, 1968, LBJ, WHCF EX FG816 "8/1/68—"; memorandum to LBJ from Califano, October 31, 1968, LBJ, WHCF EX FG816, "8/1/68."

[41] Otto Davis, Peter Doyle, Myron Joseph, John Niles, Wayne Perry, "An Empirical Study of the NAB-JOBS Program," *Public Policy* 21, no. 2 (1973): 235–62.

[42] Interview with William Kolberg, April 19, 1995.

dollars a year firms can join the policymaking enterprise, attend national conferences, and participate in thirty to forty advisory bodies working on a variety of workplace issues. Although the day-to-day issues have changed, the organization has enjoyed a close relationship with every administration since LBJ's.[43]

This structure of partnership has had considerable impact on the development of the employment and training issue. Because NAB is a meeting ground between business and government, it acts as a forum for introducing new ideas to the business world. The association enjoys a privileged position as a government-sanctioned group with greater access to decision makers in the public sphere. Initially, the members of the organization must themselves become comfortable with the technical concepts of employment and training. Kolberg remembered that many of the ideas put forth by the influential study *America's Choice* were initially greeted with skepticism by the members of NAB: "We don't get rapid change; rather, we have to convince companies that this contributes to the bottom line and is a much more productive way of training and bringing young people into the enterprise."[44]

As NAB members accept new ideas, the organization starts to spread them to the larger business community in order "to promote change on the private side." NAB sees itself as on the frontier and strives to be "proactive, not just reactive": "After we identify more effective ways to do business and become convinced about these innovations as an organization, then we become empowered, get money from foundations, and work closely with other organizations." Despite its changing fortunes, the group organized managers whenever related policy issues arose and, by its very existence, established a precedent for a public-private partnership in training policy.[45]

Business-oriented think tanks have also helped to educate managers about training issues. Jobs for the Future (JFF) is a Boston-based nonprofit organization that conducts research and offers technical assistance to firms and to governments on training workers. JFF was formed in the early 1980s by Arthur White to analyze training needs and to offer resources largely at the state level. But by the late 1980s President Hilary Pennington concluded that the organization could best contribute by specializing in youth apprenticeships (where the United States is woefully inadequate) and by expanding the policy focus to the national level as well. JFF's Benchmark Communities Initiative offers community-wide school-to-work transition programs to students in five cities. Together

[43] Interview with Kolberg.
[44] Interview with Kolberg.
[45] Interview with Kolberg.

with the Hitachi Foundation, the organization is investigating the changing relationship between companies and communities in providing "em-
ployability security" in the new competitive era. The organization has
also worked with the National Alliance of Business to disseminate industry-specific tools for developing school-to-work programs.[46]

Another important source of information about employment and training is the Work in America Institute, led by Jerome Rosow, former assistant secretary of labor under Richard Nixon and an architect of the Family Assistance Plan. The institute was founded in 1975 and, according to
Rosow, was one of the first small organizations to recognize the connection between productivity and "quality of working life" issues. The institute is a membership organization, with about sixty corporations and
twelve labor unions paying twenty-five thousand dollars a year to belong;
for their fees, members are exposed to "the most advanced ideas in managing work" and given the opportunity to visit high-skill/high-perfor-
mance factories. The institute has a small think tank that conducts national policy studies and offers two roundtable meetings each year,
presenting in-depth case studies of cutting-edge corporate strategies to
organize human resources in a way that maximizes competitiveness.[47]

The institute has recently sponsored policy studies in job-linked literacy, work and parenting, high-commitment management, and strategic
relationships between human-resource managers and union leaders. The
job-linked literacy study explored how to provide basic skills for entry-
level workers and to meet technological requirements in a constantly
changing economy. The project generated detailed case studies of industry
efforts to enhance skills; for example, new hires from disadvantaged back-
grounds who completed a course in skills development at the Boston Federal Reserve Bank were shown to advance nearly as quickly as their better-
educated peers and to stay with the firm longer than those who had not
received training.[48] The project also offered "networking opportunities"
by creating a forum for companies offering job-linked literacy programs
to come together and discuss their experiences.

[46] Interview with Richard Kazis, May 1996; Jobs for the Future, "Accomplishments and
Current Projects," obtained from the organization.
[47] The institute's tax-exempt status prohibits lobbying (interview with Jerome Rosow,
June 6, 1995).
[48] Jeannette Hargroves, "The Basic Skills Crisis," in *Job-Linked Literacy*, ed. Jerome
Rosow and Robert Zager, National Policy Study, Work in America Institute (Scarsdale,
N.Y.: Work in America Institute, 1991). Sponsors include Alcoa Foundation, the Ford Foun-
dation, General Electric Foundation, the Hewlett Foundation, the Boeing Company, Chemical Bank, Eastman Kodak Company, Exxon Corporation, and the United States Postal
Service.

Foundations have also helped to involve employers in training, especially at the local level. For example, the Annie E. Casey Foundation, established by the United Parcel Service, funded a major project to improve job opportunities in low-income areas. Casey's project in Milwaukee is of interest as an example of local business activism in the face of conservative attack. Casey promised to donate $5.1 million over eight years if local business leaders could generate $2.6 million; the deal was heartily endorsed by the Greater Milwaukee Committee, a group of business leaders directed by Robert Milbourne. Two journalists (funded by the conservative Bradley Foundation) attacked the project, denounced the Coalition for a Sustainable Milwaukee that was chosen to administer the program, and ridiculed the corporate contributors: "Like a gullible spinster who loans Lothario her credit card, the Milwaukee corporations appear to be doing it in order to be loved." Milbourne retaliated in print, "I think a more accurate description is that *The Wall Street Journal* is gullible," and all of the business participants remained committed to the project.[49] The Casey Foundation's board members, many from the corporate world, also closed ranks around the program.

The Case for Work-Family Policy

Like gourmet takeout and home-shopping networks, corporate attention to the work-family nexus is a sign of the times. Demographic changes in employment have put work-family policies on the business agenda. Working mothers made up only 22 percent of the labor force in 1950, but claimed 65 percent of the labor force by 1987. Married working women now fund on average 41 percent of their families' total income, and there are more single-parent households headed by women than ever before.[50]

Female executives (in particular) have urged their companies to accommodate these dramatic gender changes in the composition of the workforce with a variety of family-oriented policies such as parental leaves and help with child care. Parenting children has been shown to restrain female career advancements.[51] Sixty percent of one group of professional women

[49] Daniel McGroarty and Cameron Humphries, "Milwaukee's Gullible Corporate Doners," *Wall Street Journal,* August 22, 1995, A11; "Who's Calling Whom Gullible," *Milwaukee Journal Sentinel,* August 26, 1995.

[50] Julie Kosterlitz, "Family Cries," *National Journal,* April 16, 1988, 994; Tamar Lewin, "Women Are Becoming Equal Providers," *New York Times,* May 11, 1995, A27.

[51] William Bielby and James Baron, "Organizations, Technology, and Worker Attachment to the Firm," in *Research in Social Stratification and Mobility,* ed. Donald Treiman and Robert Robinson, (Greenwich, Conn.: JAI Press, 1983), 2:77–113.

considered the effect on family life to be very important in deciding to take a job.[52]

Work-family policy makes the same claims about human capital investment as employment and training. Concerns about potential labor shortages have caused managers to think about investing in the future workforce. Mothers with children and good child care could fill the labor gaps. Thus, 55 percent of a Fortune 1000 sample favored work-family policies to offset potential future labor shortages.[53] A business manager noted,

> An increasing percentage of American workers require child care in order to be employed and constitute a larger share of the workforce. . . . In the long run, progressive and effective child care will increase the strength and depth of ability of American industry since:
>
> Employees will be able to devote 100 percent on the job attention to business issues
> The children will be in a safer environment more conducive to intellectual and healthy physical development
> Business will reap the benefits of increased productivity and reduced absenteeism by a more dedicated work force.[54]

Work-family policies claim to increase productivity on the assumption that happy parents make happy workers. As Carol Sladek of Towers Perrin put it, "Companies that are perceived as being family-friendly realize that it's good for that company's bottom line." New mothers in firms with flexible leave policies and health care expressed greater satisfaction, had lower levels of absenteeism, took less time off during pregnancy, and were more likely to return to their jobs.[55] Aetna's Denise Cichon believes that quality day care curbs absenteeism: "The better the quality of care, the less likely it is to have a breakdown in care." The Child Care Action Campaign explains,

[57] Galinsky, Bond, and Friedman, *The Changing Workforce,* 17; see also Marlene Piturro and Sarah S. Mahoney, "Managing Diversity," *Executive Female,* May 1991, 45.

[53] Ellen Galinsky and Dana Friedman, *Education before School* (New York: Scholastic, 1993), 17. See also Committee for Economic Development, *Children in Need* (New York: Committee for Economic Development, 1987), 4; Barbara Reisman, Amy Moore, and Karen Fitzgerald, *Child Care: The Bottom Line* (Washington, D.C.: Child Care Action Campaign, 1988), 61.

[54] Gene Beaudet, "How Managers Reacted to Two of NAM's Big-Four Issues," *Metalworking News,* April 23, 1990, 15.

[55] Fran Hawthorne, "Why Family Leave Shouldn't Scare Employers," *Institutional Investor,* March 1993, 31; James T. Bond, "The Impact of Childbearing on Employment," in Friedman, Galinsky, and Plowden, *Parental Leave and Productivity;* Hal Morgan and Kerry Tucker, *Companies That Care* (New York: Fireside Book, 1991).

It is hard to be productive on the job when you are distracted by worries about your loved ones. Repeat the scenario day after day, year after year, and you have a sure recipe for poor work performance, family problems, and stress. . . . Companies that provide child care benefits see a reduction in tardiness, absenteeism, and job turnover, all of which save them money. Employees can pay closer attention to their work, and productivity improves.[56]

Work-family policies claim both to reduce turnover and to allow parents greater flexibility in managing the dual demands of work and child-rearing. Turnover is enormously expensive for a company, as hiring new workers may cost as much as 93 percent of a yearly salary. Merck estimated that a six-month parental leave policy actually saved twelve thousand dollars per employee by eliminating turnover costs. Aetna calculated saving $2 million in 1991 by not having to hire and train replacement workers, because 91 percent of its workers return after taking a family leave.[57] A 1989 General Accounting Office study found that employers only replace about one-third of their absent workers; the only real cost of the family leave is the continuation of health insurance. The Families and Work Institute calculated that it costs 75 to 150 percent of an employee's salary to replace him or her, but only 32 percent to grant the worker a leave.[58]

Employers' interest in adequate child care also reflects concerns about integrating children into mainstream society. The Committee for Economic Development worried that "the United States is creating a permanent underclass of young people for whom poverty and despair are life's daily companions." One-fifth of the nation's children live in poverty; 10 percent are chemically addicted at birth, and 25 percent never receive high school diplomas. Data suggest that children in good early-education programs are less likely later to be put into special-education programs, less likely to become juvenile delinquents, and more likely to finish high school.[59]

Employers have also been concerned about the quality of available child care services. Forty percent of center-based day care staff on average

[56] Interview with Denice Cichon, fall 1995; "A Message to Working Parents from the Child Care Action Campaign," Child Care Action Campaign, obtained from organization.

[57] Margaret Meiers, "Down with the Wait-and-See Approach," *Management Review,* January 1989, 15; Michael Verespej, "Clinton's First Legislative Child; Will Family Leave Trigger More Government Mandates?" *Industry Week,* March 1, 1993, 57.

[58] Linda Parham, "Family Leave Policy Discussed in PW Roundtable," *Pension World,* December 1990, 14; Friedman, Galinsky, and Plowden, *Parental Leave and Productivity,* chaps. 4 and 5, iii.

[59] Committee for Economic Development, *Children in Need,* 2; Galinsky and Friedman, *Education before School,* 1, 73–74.

leave in the course of a year; 62 percent of in-house workers leave their places of employment. On average parents search for five weeks for acceptable day care. In 1987 licensed day care centers could serve only 2.5 million children; yet 10.5 million kids under the age of six had working mothers.[60]

All of these factors have led to a paradigm shift in corporate thinking about child care. In this light the Chamber of Commerce's *Nation's Business* pointed out that times and attitudes have changed since Richard Nixon vetoed child care legislation in 1971. The current debate is not whether government should play a role, but what that role should be: "Child-care legislation is once again before Congress, and no doubt critics will echo Nixon's concerns about the federal government's proper role. Time, however, appears to have wrought change in political attitudes toward a government role in child care."[61]

Family policy designed to help children has often gained wider acceptance by the American public than other social interventions because of the battle over abortion. Conservatives opposing abortion often find it hard to reject policies that would help mothers choose to carry their fetuses to term. Representative Henry Hyde (R-Ill.) explained that child-oriented policy "is usually an effective weapon against conservatives who don't buy into the liberal welfare agenda. If you don't believe in an increase in benefits, you're called anti-children, anti-poor."[62]

Despite this ideological constraint, work-family policies have their share of critics. Social conservatives worry that child benefits encourage moms to go to work instead of staying at home where they belong. Barbara Reisman suggests that there is a "cultural ambivalence that has yet to be resolved over the proper role between family care and other care."[63]

Opponents of government support for day care have also questioned whether proponents have been too quick to dismiss possible ill effects on children. While early studies of day care concluded that maternal care continued to be superior for the youngest children, more recent analyses have claimed that both types of care are equally advantageous. Critics believe that these latter claims are designed to support mothers' interests over those of children and suggest that studies "proving" the long-term

---

[60] Ellen Galinsky and Diane Hughes, "The Fortune Magazine Child Care Study," obtained from industry sources; Galinsky and Friedman, *Education before School,* 39; Ellen Galinsky, "Child Care and Productivity," prepared for the Child Care Action Campaign, March 1988, 3.

[61] Roger Thompson, "Caring for the Children," *Nation's Business,* May 1988, 18.

[62] Julie Kosterlitz, "Not Just Kid Stuff," *National Journal,* November 19, 1988, 2934.

[63] Interview with Barbara Reisman, June 6, 1995; see also Julie Kosterlitz, "Society's Child Care," *National Journal,* May 6, 1989, 1108.

beneficial effect of day care on children provides a rationale for govern-ment intervention.[64]

Critics on the right resist all new entitlements, even for worthy causes. When Orrin Hatch (R-UT) proposed a broad child-care initiative in 1988, members of his own party complained that this left the door open for a new government program that could mushroom into a multibillion-dollar endeavor. According to the American Enterprise Institute's Douglas Besh-arov, "Hatch is just 'Me too, but cheaper,' which is the traditional Repub-lican response to new Democratic social programs."[65] The new politics of budget deficits adds another obstacle to new social programs. As William Roper, deputy assistant for policy development, said, "I appreciate peo-ple's enthusiasm [over child care], but I think it's shortsighted to finesse the implementation of the Gramm-Rudman [balanced-budget act]. . . . I mean, come on, either we have a national problem with the budget deficit or we don't."[66] A corporate manager echoed this complaint:

> We must not let the camel get his nose under the tent on this one. Federal control and/or regulation of how children must be cared for will be another of the boondoggles that our country is so great at creating. Also, anything done that penalizes families that elect to have mother stay home and care for the children is, by design if not by intent, antifamily and will further weaken the family structure, which has taken such a tremendous beating in the last few decades. We should be supporting bills which will encourage one parent to devote full time to nurturing and caring for the family needs.[67]

Detractors offered the argument that requiring employers to expand benefits in one area would increase unemployment and reduce benefits in others. For example, the costs of providing health care to those on leave might be burdensome to firms.

The Left has been divided over whether advocates should limit child care to the public sector. Ellen Galinsky has raised important questions about school-based day care centers: because they are part-time programs in the school, they are not open during school holidays and can interrupt the flow of parents' work. In addition, any preschool program must be sure to help children to learn in developmentally appropriate ways; school programs must not trade pen and paper for experiential learning.[68]

---

[64] Arleen Leibowitz, "Child Care: Private Cost or Public Responsibility?" in *Individual and Social Responsibility,* ed. Victor Fuchs (Chicago: University of Chicago Press, 1996); Gill, "Day Care or Parental Care?"

[65] Thompson, "Caring for the Children," 18.

[66] Kosterlitz, "Society's Child Care," 1108.

[67] Beaudet, "How Managers Reacted," 15.

[68] Ellen Galinsky, "Business Competitive Policies and Family Life," obtained from the Work and Family Institute.

Business Mobilization for Work-Family Policy

Work-family issues, like employment and training policy, gained business's attention through the efforts of energetic corporate activists, often found among human-resource professionals. As with training, the connection to productivity and economic growth was a big part of the issue's attraction to corporate sponsors. But the work-family issue generated more limited political appeal because it was associated with the women's movement, because of the professional position of its corporate sponsors within the firm, and because it lacked a business policy group devoted to making it a political issue.

First, work-family policy is very much linked in the corporate mind to women's concerns. This has been a source of support, in that increased sensitivity to family issues was undoubtedly connected to the growth of women within the firm. In 1987 almost 40 percent of managerial and administrative positions were held by women. Women in higher-status occupations are more likely to back "feminist" positions or women's rights.[69] Not surprisingly, firms with a higher proportion of female workers are significantly more likely to offer a range of work-family benefits.[70]

But the issue's connection to women also has kept it marginalized. The flip side of the issue's special appeal to women is that it has less relevance for men who resist the changes in gender roles over the past two decades. For instance, the gender gap influenced the corporate response to the Family and Medical Leave Act: the American Management Association found that 56 percent of the female managers in its sample approved of the FMLA, but only 37 percent of the males expressed satisfaction with the act. One manager remembers producing a report on child care for a prominent business organization and encountering an uncomfortable silence. When she inquired about this discomfort, one member of her audience explained that he was not even sure that women should work.[71]

Second, corporate child care benefits exploded within the firm during the 1980s, but the new private experts on policy have not been well positioned to push the issue politically. Consequently, big firms have been quite inactive in the realm of national policy. Benefits have grown steadily. The Conference Board estimated that only 110 firms provided child care bene-

---

[69] Margaret Meiers, "Shaping an Effective Parental-Leave Policy," *Training and Development Journal* 43, no. 1 (1989): 46; Ethel Klein, *Gender Politics* (Cambridge: Harvard University Press, 1984), 108–9.

[70] Jerry Goodstein, "Institutional Pressures and Strategic Responsiveness," *Academy of Management Journal* 37, no. 2 (1994): 376.

[71] "Fax Feedback for FMLA," *Management Review,* November 1993, 5; interview with industry representative, September 1995.

fits in 1978, but over 7,000 firms did so in the early 1990s. Family leave policies have grown as well during this period: a Towers Perrin survey in March 1993 found that 69 percent of their sample firms offered leaves and that the same percentage subsidized health coverage. Over 90 percent said that their current administrative costs were not onerous, and 97 percent said that the programs had satisfied the managers' goals of keeping employees, boosting morale, and increasing loyalty to the company.[72]

Initially, companies decided that lack of information was the problem and developed resource and referral services. Aetna was an early innovator, creating a new program in 1983 to ease the move to a new office facility outside its Hartford operations. Later the company joined a group called the Connecticut Consortium for Child Care that worked with United Way to provide a statewide database of child care providers. A few companies offered on-site day care centers for their employees' children.[73]

Many companies soon discovered that resource and referral services were insufficient because their communities lacked high-quality child care; therefore, companies shifted their attention to improving community resources. Some entered into public-private partnerships with state agencies to develop child care infrastructure; for example, in Maryland government, business and labor leaders developed a network of community Child Care Resource Centers to give technical assistance to providers, to help parents find child care, and to facilitate community planning in this area.[74] Companies created funds to improve quality in local child care centers by seeking accreditation from the National Association for the Education of Young Children (NAEYC). Aetna's Denise Cichon explained, "The accreditation process looks at quality and goes beyond the licensing of many states whose standards are abysmal. What the accreditation attempts to do is to demonstrate that by complying with the accreditation you have higher quality child care and to set a standard that is beyond licensing and regulation. To maintain economic viability you need to provide quality child care."[75]

AT&T was a leader in business efforts to improve community child care resources. A convergence of affirmative action, union pressures, women's career options, and a grassroots group called Working Parents Support Network put child care on the AT&T agenda. Although a corporate task force was formed in 1986, serious action came only in 1989 in contract

[72] Mercedes Erickson, "The Benefits Trailblazers," *Direct,* March 1993, 40; Towers Perrin, "Family and Medical Leave Programs: Before and After the New Federal Law," May 1993, 1–5.

[73] Interview with company representative, fall 1995.

[74] Child Care Action Campaign, "Making the Connections," 1990, obtained from organization, 22–23.

[75] Interview with Denise Cichon, Aetna, June 8, 1995.

negotiations with the Communications Workers of America and the American Brotherhood of Electrical Workers. AT&T's Deb Stahl said that the labor contract precipitated much more corporate attention to this area, and in 1990 the company did "state-of-the-art programs across the board," including resource and referral, adoption assistance, reimbursement accounts, family leave, and the family care development fund.[76]

The family care development fund, perhaps the most creative of the initiatives, consisted of monies for community child and elder care. Provider organizations were eligible for funds if they satisfied both community and AT&T needs. AT&T tried purchasing slots, but quickly determined that their workers had diverse needs and that buying slots did nothing to improve the general quality of community care. The funds have "strings attached," in that the company asks that preference be given to their employees. But the company has done much to improve services in its business locales. The fund has topped $25 million, and the firm just promised another $15 million, contributing to six hundred projects in twenty states. Minigrants of up to three hundred dollars are given to employee-nominated programs for quality improvement, training, and NAEYC accreditation. Larger grants have gone to expand supply in a community: these typically are forty thousand dollars but have been up to one hundred thousand dollars.[77]

In 1992 the community development movement received a big boost with the formation of the American Business Collaboration, a consortium of companies committed to improving community child and elder care. The American Business Collaboration grew out of a meeting of companies in April 1991 hosted by IBM to explore collective efforts in child care. The sentiment of the group—and what later became its motto—was "we can accomplish more by working together than by working alone." After the initial session thirteen companies agreed to act as "champions" for the project, committing to recruiting other members and to pledging necessary funds. Today 156 companies and other organizations participate in the group and contribute $27 million to 355 dependent-care programs in forty-five communities.[78]

The group quickly determined that efforts to expand child care had to go beyond the direct needs of the individual firms; real improvement in this area demanded a commitment to the community. Thus the object quickly became to improve quality in the communities where employees live. For example, large employers in Dallas were appalled by Texas state

---

[76] Telephone interview with Deb Stahl, July 6, 1995.

[77] Interview with Deb Stahl.

[78] "The American Business Collaboration for Quality Dependent Care, Questions and Answers," provided by Deb Stahl, AT&T.

law allowing two adults to care for twelve babies, and set out to improve the quality of infant care in the community. The employers decided to help a local child care organization to meet the accreditation standards of the NAEYC. Initially skeptical of the plan, the provider anticipated that parents would be unwilling to bear the extra costs of additional teachers. But within six months the center was fully enrolled, and the provider later added staff to its other Dallas operations.[79]

Given the considerable activism of child care advocates in communities, why have these private experts on policy not pushed harder to put their concerns on the national policy agenda? One key problem has been that those running these new programs have been disproportionately newcomers, female, and at odds with the relative old-timers in human-resources and government affairs departments. Work-family experts are often new to the company and new to human-resource departments; their issues are viewed with skepticism by their longer-tenured peers. Traditional human-resource, benefits, and government affairs managers are often reluctant to share their scarce political resources with the new work-family advocates. One respondent explained that while "benefits people are quite linked into public policy," the work-family newcomers have, as a whole, had less exposure. Management professors Teresa Joyce Covin and Christina Brush found evidence of this marginal treatment of work-family issues by traditional human-resource managers. A random sample of Georgia state members of the Society for Human Resource Management revealed that managers had little interest in expanding the corporate or government role in the work-family area. Female managers, not surprisingly, were significantly more likely to push work-family concerns than were male managers.[80]

One work-family manager recalls being brought in as director of workforce partnering at a large corporation after top management acted on a task force recommendation to start a new division in child care. Although her division was part of the human-resources department, she became locked in a battle with the benefits people. Her antagonistic colleagues would not accept child care resource and referral as a benefit and refused to help her put it in place. She later addressed the Conference Board's

---

[79] Work/Family Directions, "American Business Collaboration for Quality Dependent Care, 1994 Annual Report," obtained from industry source.

[80] Teresa Joyce Covin and Christina Brush, "Attitudes toward Work-Family Issues," *Review of Business* 15, no. 2 (1993): 25–27. Women are quite often assigned marginal tasks within the firm. Susan Hardesty and Nehama Jacobs, *Success and Betrayal* (New York: Franklin Watts, 1986), 48–49. As Skocpol, Paula, and others have pointed out, women historically pursued a private strategy for political gain when their lack of suffrage prevented a more public strategy. It is ironic that these corporate women have once again been pushed in this direction.

Benefits Council and encountered a similar attitude: "It was a very confrontational meeting. There were no women on the Benefits Council." She remembers, "In most companies there was a divide between benefits people and the new work-family professionals. The benefits people didn't get it. If they had been on top of things, the work-family field would not have developed."[81]

Finally, the area of work-family issues is less politically organized than employment and training. In particular, work-family policy does not have a single-issue business group, such as the National Alliance of Business. This vacuum has been partially filled by outside consultants who offer technical expertise to the business world, helping clients to develop benefits, to work with outside suppliers, and to develop community child care resources. But these consultants generally do not offer assistance in political action.

Work/Family Directions is the preeminent child care consulting company. The firm started in 1983 when IBM wanted to provide child care benefits to its employees and asked Glenn Morgan and Faith Rodgers at Wheatlock College to help them in this endeavor. IBM did not want to develop on-site child care facilities, in part because it wanted to treat all workers equitably and not simply to meet the needs of those at the largest plants. Rodgers and Morgan created for IBM a resource and referral system for securing information about openings from local agencies and for monitoring the standards of care. This early effort led to the development of Work/Family Directions, initially under the auspices of Wheatlock but later established as a separate agency. Over the years the agency has added eldercare, adoption, and school issues to its list of services. It works very much like employee assistance plans, offering telephone advice and referrals on the practical problems under its jurisdiction.[82]

Work/Family Directions was quite involved in the development of the American Business Collaborative, described previously. From the beginning Morgan and Rogers believed strongly that development of resources was integral to delivery of adequate child care and over time convinced their corporate clients to invest in community development. By providing feedback on employees' attitudes about their options, the consultants demonstrated to the companies that resources were woefully inadequate in many locales. Morgan and Rogers argued to employers that better child care was necessary for business, rather than for charitable purposes. The vast disparity in available options violated firms' mandate for equity. Although early leaders such as AT&T and IBM established individual funds,

---

[81] Interview with industry participant.
[82] Interview with Glenn and Hal Morgan, June 19, 1996.

after a few years managers realized that they could not do much alone in each of their operating communities and set out to build a collaborative effort among large employers. Work/Family Directions is now the agent for the American Business Collaborative.[83]

Another consulting company, the Families and Work Institute, offers corporate and government customers a variety of services related to work-family issues. The institute encourages firms to make decisions based on data rather than on assumptions; therefore, it strives to project an image of neutrality and includes a strong research component in its operations. Ellen Galinsky, codirector of the institute and former president of the National Association for the Education of Young Children, is often called in to assist with community disputes in child care. She believes that negotiated outcomes are often the most successful and brings stakeholders to the table in order to talk about the issues at hand. For example, in 1994 newly elected New York mayor Rudy Giuliani was considering changing city contributions to child care from a direct funding system to a voucher system. Immediately child care advocates protested the idea, and business managers supported it. The Families and Work Institute sponsored a project that brought together city administrators, child care advocates, and business managers to look at five cities that have switched from direct funding to vouchers. The working group designed a questionnaire and interviewed program administrators in the other cities. The study showed that the voucher system had not proven to be cost-effective in other settings, and the city decided to abandon the plan. Galinsky believes that the decision would surely have generated greater conflict had opposing interests not jointly investigated other cities' experiences.[84]

A few general business groups have studied work-family concerns; however, the major umbrella associations have largely neglected this area of public policy, except to work against the Family and Medical Leave Act (discussed in chapter 7). The Conference Board established a Work and Family Council in 1984 with the help of the Families and Work Institute's Dana Friedman. Many of the companies that later became the champions in the American Business Collaboration began thinking about the issue in the Conference Board study group.

The Committee for Economic Development (CED) also investigated needs for child care and published an influential report in September 1987 titled *Children in Need*. The CED study argued that future demands for a skilled workforce meant that society had more reason than ever to invest in its children. Current corporate investments in education, such as

[83] Interview with Glenn and Hal Morgan, May 28, 1996.
[84] Interview with Ellen Galinsky, May 3, 1995.

"adopt-a-school programs" usually did little to help children in poverty. Instead the business community should work toward the goal of intervening with at-risk children early in the preschool years, when such education seems to make the biggest difference.[85]

Not surprisingly, the CED investigation grew out of a concern with education, the impetus coming from Brad Butler, CEO of Proctor and Gamble. Butler was shocked to confront the vast difference between Japanese high school graduates newly hired by his company and their U.S. counterparts. He convinced his peers at CED that it was both in business and collective interests to uncover the causes of this disparity; this led to a CED project subcommittee on the problems of secondary education chaired by Butler. As the committee began collecting data, participants realized that the problem went much deeper than secondary education; entrants were not prepared to learn. Investigating ever earlier stages of schooling, they ultimately traced the pathologies back to early child development. Scott Fosler, formerly at CED, now president of the National Academy of Public Administration, remembers:

> The thing that was fascinating was that it was initiated by a clear recognition that it was a problem for business but bigger than any one firm could do anything about. We then set about to do a rational research project to figure out what the problem was. Brad Butler was very conservative, but was committed to following the facts where they lead you. We just continued following the facts.[86]

Finally, an advocacy organization, the Child Care Action Campaign, has worked to present the connection between work-family issues and productivity to employers and to the media. For example, CCAC sponsored a widely covered conference in 1988 called "Child Care: The Bottom Line." Testifying in 1994, Chairman Richard Stolley presented the group's perspective:

> American business leaders are very powerful, and the policies they urge upon governments or institute themselves can make a real difference for families and thus for children. . . . The cold reality is that business is quick to react to problems that affect the balance sheet, but right now too few companies and corporate leaders recognize the price they are paying for our national failure to care for and educate our children.[87]

[85] Committee for Economic Development, *Children in Need,* 3, 9, 65, 21.

[86] Interview with Scott Fosler, spring 1996.

[87] Richard Stolley, "Child Care for Working Families: True Welfare Reform," statement before the U.S. Senate Committee on Labor and Human Resources Subcommittee on Children, Family, Drugs and Alcoholism, February 24, 1994.

Conclusion

This chapter tells the story of emerging business activism in employment and training and work-family policies. In each case a core group of company managers worked to make their concern a political issue within the broader business community. In both cases these private experts on policy linked social policies (at the company or national levels) to productivity arguments.

But business politics in these two areas of policy look quite different. Training activists pursued a national policy agenda and, as we will see in chapter 6, were solidly behind the training acts passed during Clinton's first few years in office. By comparison child care activists eschewed a national political strategy, preferring instead to develop resources privately or at the community level.

To some extent these very different policy profiles may reflect the relative ages of these issues: child care is a newer issue that has become relevant with the massive movement of women into the workforce in the past twenty years. Training has an older history, although it has recently gained in political salience with the rise of global competition. One might also insist that training is closer to a firm's bottom line, although many work-family proponents would undoubtedly disagree and retaliate with productivity arguments about adequate child care and family leave.

But in addition to these factors, the intrafirm position of the pri experts on policy, the appeal of the ideas or policy legacies, and the poli level groups devoted to the issue influenced the issues' relative success gaining wider corporate attention. Profound differences in the reference ideas, activists, and group profiles distinguished the two issues. Employment and training flourished through its close connection to popular education reform; by comparison, child care was closely linked to less acceptable feminist theory and to enhancing the role of women within the firm. Training within companies has largely fallen under the jurisdiction of human-resource departments; these departments have traditionally enjoyed a close relationship with government affairs departments. Child care resources have largely been developed by newcomers to the corporate structure (and often women), brought in by CEOs to establish new initiatives in previously undeveloped areas. The organizational commitment to training dates back to the 1960s, when the Johnson administration established the National Alliance of Businessmen, a quasi-corporatist group that brought business and government together in a quest for jobs. Child care has no comparable organizational structure to engage in political conflict.

FIVE

THE LEAST-COMMON-DENOMINATOR
BUSINESS COMMUNITY:
CORPORATE ENGAGEMENT
WITH HEALTH POLICY

T HE PORTRAIT of many large employers as interested in policies to increase human capital investment does not mesh with the political positions usually taken by major business associations. If many large employers accept the high-performance workplace logic, why have they not become more involved in enacting corresponding policies? Like Sherlock Holmes, we are puzzled by the dog that did not bark in the night.

Chapters 5 through 7 investigate how variations in core activists' institutional profiles, or corporate policy capacity, have influenced business's engagement with key legislative initiatives in health, training, and work-family policy. Previous chapters suggested that group organization, policy legacies, and private expertise in policy are important in putting social issues on the business agenda and attracting support from individual firms. Yet it is easier to express concern for abstract problems than to make a commitment to specific legislative proposals; therefore, corporate behavior at the point of legislation may be quite different from that at the agenda-building stage.[1] In the following chapters I argue that the growth of private expertise, the pattern of organization, and the policy legacies in an area also matter to whether managers organize to support legislative initiatives.

The general pattern of business organization in the United States predisposes employers toward negative or neutral stands on collective social goods for two reasons. First, umbrella business associations compete with one another for members and are unable to generate common positions on issues that might alienate a segment of their constituency. The proliferation of interest groups, each with its own particular agenda, means that the many voices that speak for employers seldom say the same thing. Interests that might find common ground in other settings are often di-

---

[1] John Kingdon, *Agendas, Alternatives, and Public Policies* (New York: Harper Collins, 1984).

vided by narrow, sectoral splits in the United States. Even the broad
multisector groups that bring many interests in under one umbrella fail
to advance collective, corporate social concerns. Because these umbrella
groups vie with one another for prestige and members, they tend to ignore
activists of any ilk within their ranks. Decision making in these umbrella
groups usually entails a least-common-denominator politics; in an effort
to offend no one, groups search for neutral positions and seldom move
beyond empty platitudes. Thus, the general pattern of American business
organization creates a bias toward inaction at the level of national policy
and diminishes the expression of support for human capital investment
initiatives.

Second, the legacies of private social provision by large firms contribute
to the difficulty of securing agreement on collective social goals, because
employers (with diverse starting points) seek to protect their existing programs and jurisdictions. Because employers have developed their own social programs in part to compensate for the lack of broader public plans,
they will consider reforms threatening their own offerings in only the most
limited circumstances. This compounds the problem of finding a collective
business position, as participants often begin negotiations with very different vested interests.

These organizational features add up to a big-business community that
seems incapable and unable to move quickly to take action on modern
policy issues. Anxious to protect their own prerogatives, business groups,
industries, and firms are reluctant to relinquish power for the sake of
larger concerns. American business organization brings to mind Isaiah
Berlin's two freedoms: "freedom from" versus "freedom to."[2] Excessive
concern about the first kind of freedom can limit possibilities for the second. Thus, U.S. business managers, in their rush to protect themselves
from collective coercion, may lose opportunities for satisfying collective
needs. By contrast, European business managers might sympathize with
John McCrae's timeless search for home: "Freedom's just another word
for nothing left to lose."

Nowhere are the legacies of the private employer-based systems and
limited organizational capacity of business more apparent than in the case
of national health reform, and this chapter begins the comparison of areas
of social policy with this story. Reams of paper (indeed entire forests) have been
devoted to accounting for the demise of national health reform. Some
analysts have argued that health reform was simply bad public policy
that would require an entirely new and untried bureaucracy.[3] Some have
argued that the public was divided between the dominant reform propos-

[2] Isaiah Berlin, *Four Essays on Liberty* (New York: Oxford University Press, 1969).

[3] Lawrence Brown and Ted Marmor, "The Clinton Reform Plan's Administrative Structure," *Journal of Health Politics, Policy, and Law* 19, no. 1 (1994): 193–200.

als, that politicians insufficiently listened to true public opinion, that ideology worked against a broad new government proposal, and that budgetary decision-making processes worked against reform legislation.[4] Some blame a hostile press for misrepresenting the Clinton plan.[5] Others locate failure in the institutional structure of government, arguing that government institutional structures gave excessive power to interest groups.[6] One wonders if the fate of health reform was overdetermined.

This chapter explores a more narrow question: given the substantial early business interest in national health reform, why did corporate support vanish at the point of legislation? That health reform died may not be surprising, but the struggle within the business community challenges conventional thinking. Scholars as varied as William Domhoff and Kevin Phillips have emphasized the power of large employers in matters of public policy, but in this case large employers lost to small-business managers.[7] Of course, business managers acted in this case as consumer interests rather than as producer interests, which tend to be harder to organize.[8] But the numerous and geographically scattered small-business managers were more highly mobilized in the health case than were large employers, even though interest group theory suggests that dispersed interests should be more difficult to organize.[9] Granted, the devil often lurks in details, and support for a specific proposal was bound to be less than that for broad concepts, but one wonders why large employers could not work with the administration to negotiate compromises and to get what they

---

[4] Mollyann Brodie, "The Public's Contribution to Congressional Gridlock on Health Care Reform," *Journal of Health Politics, Policy and Law* 20, no. 2 (1995): 403–10; Lawrence Jacobs and Robert Shapiro, "The Politicization of Public Opinion," in Weir, *Social Divide;* Joseph White, "The Horses and the Jumps," *Journal of Health Politics, Policy, and Law* 20, no. 2 (1995): 373–83.

[5] Theda Skocpol, *Boomerang* (New York: W. W. Norton, 1996); Tom Hamburger, Ted Marmor, and Jon Meacham, "What the Death of Health Reform Teaches Us about the Press," *Washington Monthly,* November 1994, 35–41.

[6] Mark Peterson, "The Politics of Health Care Policy," in Weir, *New Democrats;* Sven Steinmo and Jon Watts, "It's the Institutions, Stupid!" *Journal of Health Politics, Policy, and Law* 20, no. 2 (1995): 329–72.

[7] William Domhoff, *Who Rules America?* (Englewood Cliffs, N.J.: Prentice-Hall, 1967); Kevin Phillips, *Post-Conservative America* (New York: Vintage, 1983); Edward Herman, *Corporate Control, Corporate Power* (New York: Cambridge University Press, 1981); Maurice Zeitlin, *American Society, Inc.* (Chicago: Rand-McNally, 1973). Pluralists agree that big business enjoys superior power but believe that this (1) depends on the extent of mobilization and (2) can be partially offset by mobilized citizen groups. Jeff Berry, *The Interest Group Society* (Boston: Scott Foresman, 1989). But none of these would account for why large employers, especially when in considerable agreement with many consumer interests, fail to make an impact on public policy.

[8] Wilson, *The Politics of Regulation.*

[9] Olson, *Logic of Collective Action.*

wanted from government. If antistate ideology were the main obstacle to business support for health reform, why did so many managers initially support the concept?

I suggest that the corporate policy capacity of the health policy business network explains this quick disappearance and also contributed to the litany of troubles leading to the reform measure's downfall.[10] The policy legacies of the employer-based system created dilemmas for policymakers. Employers were interested in health reform because private firm-level solutions had failed, but they were unwilling to deviate too far from the status quo. They demanded that they retain benefits accorded to them under the current employer-based system, even when these benefits detracted from the collective goal of cost containment. The reform proposal's goals of controlling costs and expanding access came into conflict with large employers' desire to protect their interests in the current job-based system.

In addition the lack of an encompassing business organization devoted to health meant that no group could translate general corporate anxiety into specific legislation. Perennially weak and fragmented umbrella organizations catered to strong, vocal minority objections, and the proreform employers lost internal policy battles within these groups.

The business-related strategies of political leaders from both parties also worked against comprehensive health reform. As the process became deeply politicized, the Republicans sought to frame the measure in ideological terms as an expansion of big government. The Clintons' ideological language of class warfare, aimed at mass mobilization, also made it difficult for policy experts within the firm to frame health reform as a technical fix for economic growth.

National Health Reform: The Legacy of Private Provision

The period preceding the attempted legislation of national health reform saw tremendous growth in the private sector's health expertise, as companies across the country struggled to contain their costs. Yet at the point of legislation big-business participants were not significant players. In retrospect, one Senate staffer expressed amazement that big business was so invisible: "They were a big part of why we tackled this problem, and then they started backtracking."

As described in chapter 3, considerable private policy expertise had developed in health, and employers became quite knowledgeable about

---

[10] Dynamics similar to big business's incapacities plagued the physicians as well (Wilson, "Interest Groups").

the problems of the system. Yet the other two components of corporate policy capacity, policy legacies and group organization, worked against large-employer support for health reform.

The Clinton administration designed its proposal with the legacies of the employer-based system in mind, a move that single-payer advocates believed fatally flawed the plan.[11] First, by organizing reform around market correctives, the administration offered a solution consistent with our general ideological bent toward private-sector intervention. Recognizing the "don't reform my plan" syndrome, they were careful not to deviate from the employer-based system. The proposal allowed large employers with over five thousand employees to form their own health care alliances and to opt out of the public system.

Second, managed competition was politically appealing because it matched developments in the private sector. Health alliances on the purchaser side were to be quasi-public entities to negotiate rates with providers. Alain Enthoven's work inspired both the health care alliances and the business coalition movement; consequently, accepting the concept of health care alliances should have been an easy step for former coalition participants since many had become sensitized to the issues of health financing through their participation in regional coalitions.[12]

The accountable health plans on the provider side also had much in common with current business practices. The accountable health plans, designed to move users away from fee-for-service arrangements and toward managed-care networks, looked a lot like the point-of-service plans already serving many corporate clients. A Foster Higgins study found three-fourths of the firms already offering point-of-service plans.[13]

Third, the big insurers' vested interests in the system added to the political feasibility of managed competition. The big five insurers were the primary organizers of managed-care networks for corporate purchasers and hoped to administer the new Clinton system. Alternatively, small and medium-sized insurers, represented by the Health Insurance Association of America, opposed managed competition even while favoring the more radical mandates and community-rating proposals.[14]

Fourth, the administration financed the plan with employer mandates over tax revenues (although Blendon found that 66 percent of Americans would tolerate a small tax increase targeted for health care).[15] Employer mandates seemed in advance not to be an especially big change for the

---

[11] Hamburger, Marmor, and Meacham, "What Death Teaches Us."

[12] See Bergthold's excellent discussion of this in *Purchasing Power in Health*.

[13] Foster Higgins, 1992, 5.

[14] Interviews, September 1992.

[15] Robert Blendon, "The Public's View of the Future of Health Care," *Journal of the American Medical Association* 259, no. 24 (1988): 3587–93.

large employers, as many already provided health benefits. A defined-benefits package with tax caps on employee deductions might help firms to curb their health commitments to unions and could force others in the industry to provide comparable levels of health benefits.

Finally, the Clintons' proposal protected the jobs of the enormous private-sector bureaucracy already in place. Company benefits managers, consultants, and insurance administrators were drawn to system rationalization, but not at the expense of their own livelihood. Thus, where a single-payer arrangement and the virtual end of the employer-based system would be a big leap for business, managed competition was a small step from the status quo. One benefits manager explained:

> With significantly rapidly increasing costs, if someone said, "Turn the management of the benefits system over to us," I would have more of a willingness to say, "Be my guest." You now hear a lot of executives say, "We are not in the business of medical care." . . . But I'd also want to see what kind of job opportunities there are out there before phasing out the employer-based system.[16]

If health reform enjoyed widespread acceptance among many big-business managers, why did its proponents ultimately fail to do more to gain its legislation? An easy answer was that managers feared economic aspects of the bill, especially when presented with the devilish details. By failing to provide an adequate financing scheme for a large benefits package, the Clintons gained the mistrust of their business supporters. Managers considered the minimum benefits package excessive and worried about losing control over their plans and being transformed into "check writers." They doubted that health reform could be achieved without a tax hike, and some worried that the cost-control mechanisms in the president's plan were excessively weak.[17] Many feared that mandated benefits would create a new burden on small business and precipitate a loss of jobs.[18]

The details of the administration's health alliances prompted widespread concern: because only firms with at least five thousand employees were permitted to opt out of the public plan, managers worried that few cou'   de the public pool. Because the public alliances were to span   ns, companies feared losing their current considerable pur-   age over providers. A Foster Higgins model predicted that   s would find it economical to continue to operate their own

---

.ew with company representative, April 1993.

ichard Smith, "Getting Business Support for Health Care Reform," *Washington ost*, June 13, 1994, A18.

[18] Wilensky argues that mandates would increase the hourly cost for workers receiving the minimum wage by up to eighty cents. Gail Wilensky, "The Real Price of Mandating Health Benefits," *Business and Health* 7, no. 3 (1989): 32.

plans or would find appealing the option of forming a corporate alliance. Large employers were adamant that the legislation have equal application across states; yet it became increasingly apparent that states would have much flexibility to experiment with financing mechanisms. Managed competition also got slammed for eliminating choice. One lobbyist told a staffer that "a business's right to choose their own health insurance is as important as a woman's right to choose." The female congressional aide reported feeling physically ill at this comment.[19]

During the legislative process, the bill gave ever larger subsidies to small business and placed heavier burdens on large firms; yet many large employers were initially drawn to reform as a mechanism to end the substantial cost shifting from small companies. Many anticipated that a cross-subsidization scheme would have big companies contribute to coverage for the uninsured, but they believed that the final bill went too far.

Finally, business managers, like many policy analysts, believed that Clinton's proposal was excessively complicated and, despite claims to the contrary, created a new federal bureaucracy. Richard Smith of APPWP put it, "Bill Clinton gave mandates a bad name."

> The fundamental strategic mistake was creating a bill of issues that nobody has ever heard of. If you look at how American politics works, you would quickly realize that to pass a law that mandates that employers would provide insurance, you would need a president fully focused on it. But that's not what they did. They decided that they had to address all of the issues under the sun. If they had not attempted to centralize all decisions and centralize benefits design, they could have left it to the real world.[20]

Economic concerns about the health reform bill were very real, yet they take us only so far in understanding the movement of employers away from health reform. The initial proposal was much closer to large employers' preferences than the final outcome; one wonders why big business was not more influential in protecting its turf. Why did not large employers make the bill meet their interests?

Health Care and the Limits of Business Organization

The disappointing big-business showing was also related to the limits of business organization. Although business groups helped to make health reform a top political issue, they were unable to get business consensus

[19] Jeannie Mandelker and Steven Findlay, "Truth in Numbers," *Business and Health* 12, no. 1 (1994): 25; interview with aide, summer 1994.

[20] Interview with Richard Smith, summer 1994.

for a specific legislative proposal. During the agenda-setting stage the health issue benefited from the dynamism of the Washington Business Group on Health, but by 1990 it had lost its activist edge, dulled in great part by the organization's decision to admit insurers as voting members.[21] None of the umbrella associations ultimately endorsed the reform legislation: each was crippled by divisions within its ranks.

The experience within the National Association of Manufacturers exemplified how difficult it was for umbrella organizations with a minority representation of health care providers to exert leadership in health care reform. The NAM members are big losers in the cost-shifting game: 99 percent offered benefits in 1988, and a NAM-commissioned Foster Higgins study found health care costs increasing 30 percent on average in 1989. These costs represented 37.2 percent of employers' profits.[22]

NAM investigated health reform in a white paper entitled "Meeting the Health Care Crisis," cosponsored with the Washington Business Group on Health a symposium to consider legislative issues, and formed a health care task force to develop a NAM policy. Some of the task force companies (GE, Allied Signal, and Motorola) were drawn to a managed-care approach; others (Southern California Edison and Chrysler) favored regulation. Ultimately the task force supported a play-or-pay plan much like that of the National Leadership Coalition's. The NAM newsletter was to brag that "NAM policy initiatives will help maintain the association's continuing key role in the health debate, broadly representing the business community."[23]

The NAM board debated the task force recommendations from February until October 1991. The association's tax task force, which viewed play or pay as a corporate tax, opposed the recommendations; providers and insurers also lobbied hard against health care reform. Finally, in October the board voted down the task force proposal and instead endorsed a set of principles that were essentially a reiteration of long-standing policy. One task force member complained:

> Last September NAM received the Lewin report claiming that $11.5 billion has been cost-shifted onto its members. NAM should have been outraged, but has done nothing with that. Isn't there some responsibility of the leadership to rattle chains, rather than giving in to Aetna and the pharmaceuticals?[24]

---

[21] Bergthold, *Purchasing Power in Health*.

[22] Donna DiBlase, "Group Health Bills Equal a Third of Profits," *Business Insurance,* May 29, 1989, 37–38.

[23] Jerry Geisel, "NAM Proposes Plan to Contain Health Costs," *Business Insurance,* May 29, 1989, 39; "NAM Board Considers Health Reform Policy," *Employee Benefits Newsline* (NAM, Washington, D.C.), October 1990.

[24] Industry representative, June 1992; company representative, June 1992.

After this incident, the health reform contingent commissioned another Foster Higgens survey of NAM members on health care issues. Insiders hoped that solid member support would move the board toward comprehensive health reform. The study showed 55 percent of the members favoring a play-or-pay approach (complete with employer mandates) as part of overall system reform.[25] A NAM survey in the late summer of 1993 found a clear majority of its members backing mandates and health alliances for firms with over five hundred employees.[26]

The Clinton administration hoped to gain NAM support and met with the association a number of times throughout 1993. NAM tried to remain open to the variety of health proposals on the legislative table and gave the president kudos for putting the issue on the congressional agenda. According to Ira Magaziner, Jerry Jasinowski, president of NAM, was one of the first individuals to see the draft in the summer of 1993. An informal deal was struck: Jasinowski agreed to a resolution that he would take before the board; the administration would fix five issues troubling to large employers. In reference to a September 1993 press release praising the Clinton plan, Jasinowski wrote, "I avoided any mention of mandates in order to imply that they may be a cost that business has to pay to get comprehensive reform; and to signal that mandates are not likely to be a top priority concern to manufacturers."[27] The administration believed that with NAM and the Chamber of Commerce on board and the Business Roundtable divided between its insurer constituents and large employer purchasers of health care, it might be able to push through a reform package.

But renewed efforts to push NAM toward supporting a comprehensive health reform were stymied by providers and fast-food magnates on the board. Opponents circulated a letter to members in advance of the February 1994 board meeting. The Clinton administration's promise to assume some of the costs of early retiree coverage also divided the supporters of comprehensive reform within the organization. NAM staff reported going into the board meeting having "good things to say about the Clinton bill" and watching the board do an 180-degree turn.[28]

The Chamber also worked closely with the Clinton administration in the early days of health reform. Chamber vice president William Archey hoped for business and government to work together to improve U.S. competitiveness and tried to change the Chamber's direction. Archey worked with the Chamber's Health and Employee Benefits Committee to

[25] Industry representative, June 1992; Foster Higgins/NAM, "Employer Cost-Shifting Expenditures," November 1992.

[26] Unpublished survey provided by the administration.

[27] "Administration Health Care Plan," memorandum to Magaziner from Jerry Jasinowski, September 15, 1993.

[28] Interview with NAM staffers.

endorse a 50 percent employer mandate, managed competition, and a standardized benefits package. Robert Patricelli, the chair of the Chamber's task force on health care, told Ira Magaziner that the Chamber would back universal coverage "if there is an appropriate government subsidy mechanism to assist low-wage workers and their employers." To this end the administration agreed to adopt its small-business discount schedule for health reform; in return, the Chamber testified in favor of the administration.[29] Yet, as is discussed below, the Chamber reversed its position on reform.[30]

The Business Roundtable did not even get as far as NAM and the Chamber, because its health care task force was controlled by insurers from the beginning. At one point the Roundtable seemed close to considering a universal-access bill, but General Mills and the insurers began a campaign to dissuade CEOs from this option.[31]

ERIC also endured considerable internal struggle over health reform. The organization's task force on health care strongly favored a play-or-pay proposal, but the board objected to the employer mandate provision and instead issued a set of broad, unspecific principles. Although members of the group agreed that the weaknesses of the health system were "structural, not superficial" and that reform would require "a coordinated, comprehensive public policy," deep divisions split the organization, and it was unable to resolve the question of mandates.[32]

Some groups did manage to support the broad outlines of a comprehensive health reform bill, but these groups tended to be limited in scope and membership. The Corporate Health Care Forum endorsed an employer mandate in principle, as did the APPWP (which has many health consultants among its membership); both groups believed that the mandate was a necessary bitter pill for systemic change. The group self-consciously tried to begin with what it wanted from the health care system rather than to start with the various proposals. Said one participant:

> We began with a blank sheet. In fact, this might have made it easier for our group to get a position. We didn't have to go through the NAM experience— trying to take a position and then getting it rejected. Instead we began with a clean slate—it was easier to move toward consensus.[33]

---

[29] "Follow-up to March 8, 1993 Meeting," memorandum to Ira Magaziner from Robert Patricelli, March 18, 1993.

[30] Interview with Chamber of Commerce staff, May 24, 1994.

[31] Letter to [name blacked out] from H. Atwater Jr. (chair and CEO, General Mills), December 2, 1993, obtained from White House sources.

[32] Director Mark Ugoretz said that no clear position had been taken by the task force, but other participants disagreed (interviews with participants, April 1993). The ERISA Industry Committee, "Interim Policy Statement on Health Care System Reform," obtained from ERIC, approved by board December 12, 1991, 14, 22–24.

[33] APPWP company participant.

The National Leadership Coalition also tried to overcome the stalemates that limit umbrella organizations with an important organizational rule: in order to belong to the coalition, firms had to endorse the plan. But many companies left the coalition because they preferred a different option or believed the coalition's position to be too radical. Others believed that the leadership had a preset agenda: play or pay was the group's choice from the beginning, and employers' input was an exercise in legitimation.[34]

The business community tried during the summer to come up with a final business position. Early in the summer NAM began holding meetings to explore common ground; the APPWP organized another forum called the City Club meetings. Yet these meetings had limited success. Only when legislators considered curbing ERISA waivers (which allowed self-insured employers to avoid state regulations) did the business community unite in protest.[35]

Small-Business Activism

Just as big business was weakly organized, small business and the forces opposing reform were well organized. The major small-business associations joined forces with small insurers and providers to fight the trend toward comprehensive national reform.

Many small employers believed strongly about the problems of the health system. In 1991 57 percent of the National Small Business United members surveyed ranked the costs and availability of health insurance as the number one problem facing business. Eighty-three percent had changed insurance carriers during the past five years, primarily due to costs.[36]

But many small-business also opposed the comprehensive reform approach on both ideal and material grounds. They favored reforms to help small buy group health insurance but opposed employer mandates any small firms currently do not offer insurance. For example two somewhat contradictory goals: one was to tear down component of health reform, employer mandates; the other age the reform process to move forward so that its con ve better access to health insurance. As one respondent lenge was how to tear down a mandate but

---

[34] Interviews with participants, September 1992 through May 1993.

[35] ERISA regulates s and preempts them from having to comply with state regulations.

[36] National Small Business United, "Small Business Outlook and Attitudes," conducted by the Gallup Organization, 1991, 4–5, obtained from the organization.

build up a consensus bill."[37] These somewhat contradictory goals left the association in a difficult position, but killing the employer mandate became the all-consuming goal. Even the multitude of subsidies offered to small companies as the process unfolded failed to convert the leadership, because it was convinced that employer mandates would create a new entitlement.

In the early days small-business ideology was less fixed than it seemed in retrospect; small-business groups had limited experience with health reform, and set out to educate themselves about the issue. Big business ignored small business in the early stages, believing that cost shifting came from small firms, so the interests must be quite different. In contrast providers, insurers, and miscellaneous Republicans actively courted the small-business community.[38]

The small-business community was also not nearly as unified in its vision as might appear from the outside, but it constantly worked to overcome natural divisions. For instance, the early alliance between small insurers and small business came under considerable stress when the Health Insurance Association of America (HIAA) endorsed employer mandates. As a sort of preemptive warning, the National Federation of Independent Business "sent a strong signal to HIAA that if they supported mandates, we'd support premium caps." NFIB had conflicting attitudes about premium caps and was silent on the issue for a long time. On the one hand, many in the association rejected price controls on principle; in addition, they did not want to alienate their partners in the for-profit provider community, such as Pam Baily and Michael Bromberg. On the other hand, their membership polls showed some support for premium caps. The small-business association also rationalized that potential mandates required guarantees that costs would not exceed a specific amount.

NFIB's chief lobbyist John Motley and HIAA's president Bill Graddison met in early 1994 to prevent a fissure. Motley asked if there was any way that HIAA could change its position on mandates. Graddison said that there was not, but that mandates would not be the association's chief priority. An uneasy truce followed, which ended when HIAA tried to make a secret deal with Dan Rostenkowski. NFIB tentatively decided that if the Ways and Means Committee endorsed a mandate, the association would urge the Republicans to vote for premium caps.[39]

Despite the occasional internal rifts within the small-business lobby, its powerful lobbying capabilities profoundly damaged the reform effort. A turning point in the legislative history was when small-business opposi-

---

[37] Interview with NFIB staffer, November 15, 1994.

[38] Interviews with many from small-business community in the fall of 1991 and the spring of 1992.

[39] Interviews with participants, fall 1994.

tion prevented the Energy and Commerce Committee from producing a bill. The committee's chair, John Dingell (D-Mich.), was highly motivated to enact reform, as his father had been a sponsor of national health reform in 1943. But the committee was rich with representatives from rural and southern areas, helpful to the chair in his conservative positions on environmental regulation but obstructive when it came to his more liberal views about health care. The conservative Democrats were worried about getting "BTUed," as when Clinton moved away from the energy tax in the stimulus package that he had earlier urged conservative Democrats in the House to back. Jim Slattery (D-Kans.) was running for governor and wanted to maintain good relations with the small businessmen in his state.

Dingell made many concessions to the conservative Democrats: making alliances voluntary in order to allow insurers to stay in business, introducing community rating slowly, and exempting small businesses from mandates. He promised legislators that he would not publicly identify supporters of the plan before he had lined up all of the votes. The Democratic leadership worried about pressures on conservative members during Easter recess, but ultimately believed that all but Slattery had made a firm commitment. Shortly before the break, Dingell's staff leaked a compromise plan to the press "in order to show the members that there was movement on some issues that were giving them heartburn. The expressed purpose of the leak was to let the legislators on the fence know that headway was being made."[40]

The leak backfired when the opposition mobilized against Clinton and the compromise plan. The Republicans and their small-business allies targeted Slattery and other conservative Democrats to keep the committee from passing a bill. NFIB sent action alerts to all of its members in the ten districts with swing legislators and faxes to about 10 percent of its members. The organization contacted all eight thousand members in the state of Kansas and, as part of the Coalition on Jobs and Health Care, held a press conference the day before Slattery was to appear with President Clinton in Topeka. NFIB also produced action alerts in a series of moderate Republicans' districts as a kind of preventative measure. The association compiled the list from the Republicans who had voted for the family leave act. Meanwhile Pizza Hut, headquartered in Topeka, wrote to all of the local Chambers of Commerce in Kansas. Dennis Hastert (R-Ill.) worked closely with a group to resist the mandate that included the National Restaurant Association, J. C. Penney, and Pepsico among others. The National Restaurant Association developed a formula for members to evaluate the economic impact of mandates on their enterprises. Hastert also arranged for the restaurateurs to fax their legislators en masse from

[40] Interview, staffer, November 15, 1994.

a national meeting in Chicago. One participant recalls that the object of these activities was to convey to legislators that the Dingell compromise was unacceptable:

> We wanted to create an atmosphere for the Slatterys of the world where they thought that they were doing a backroom deal on the Dingell plan that was quite new, and then they had small businessmen in their districts come up and say, "Vote no on Dingell."[41]

Ultimately Slattery reversed his position on the mandate, even though his natural inclinations led him to support his former mentor, John Dingell. NFIB was especially thrilled with Slattery's about-face. In early March he had told a group of NFIB representatives that he was going to endorse a mandate and that there was no way out of it. One participant said that the legislator was defiant about backing mandates: "He was very bold, it was a brave performance."[42]

The Health Insurance Association of America also exercised considerable political muscle during the legislative process. Composed largely of small and medium-sized insurers, the association's primary target was the managed-competition proposal, and its most dramatic contribution to the debate was the Harry and Louise ads. Although the $12 million ads were actually shown only in Washington and a few other cities, the television networks picked them up as newsworthy and aired them for free as nightly news.[43]

The activism of small business and corresponding inability of the big business to endorse the parts of the proposal it favored made the administration and Congress less willing to take seriously big-business objections to other aspects of reform. Politicians wanted active help in getting votes in exchange for attention to corporate concerns. As it became more apparent that big-business groups were incapacitated by minority opposition, legislators granted concessions to try to buy off the better-organized small-business groups. The bill increasingly benefited small-business interests; for example, legislators gradually expanded the size of firms to be excluded from a mandate. A Wyatt study showed that under a partial mandate (exempting firms of less than one hundred employees), large employers would cover 14.7 million more individuals than they would under

---

[41] The Coalition on Jobs included NFIB, National Retail Federation, National Restaurant Association, and the Pepsico, General Mills, and J. C. Penney corporations. Interviews with business participants and congressional staffers, 1994–95.

[42] Interview with industry representative, fall 1994.

[43] Catherine Manegold, "Using TV to Create Skewed Window on Nation," *New York Times,* July 17, 1994, 16. The Democratic National Committee retaliated in kind with a $250,000 spoof on Harry and Louise; again the networks offered them to a nationwide audience on the evening news.

a full mandate.[44] By the end of the legislative cycle the bill that initially attracted big business because it could reduce cost shifting was shifting more costs than ever.

Big Business and the Clinton Administration

Business reformers also blamed the Clinton administration for the inability to rally corporate support for health reform. The administration failed to put together a broad, centrist coalition in favor of health reform: a puzzling fact since it designed the proposal to appeal to large employers. Business managers believed that the administration neglected them, refused to take seriously their concerns, and created a needlessly complex plan. They believed that the Clintons confused campaigning and governing by rewarding loyalists and excluding others and thus limited its policy coalition. Employers believed that the administration's Office of Public Liaison (OPL) restricted the access of prior enemies in order to protect the privilege of its allies. In fact the OPL warned against ending up "wasting a huge amount of staff time 'receiving input' that would not accomplish very much toward actually building the coalition that will help us pass health care reform."[45] As one trade association representative put it, "Outreach to them means access to those who have been with them from the beginning and shutting out everyone else." Business managers also were alienated by the procedures of the administration's task force to develop a health plan, which seemed to signal official exclusion. Whereas Lyndon Johnson had used a task force to build consensus and to pursue a centrist politics of inclusion, the Clintons seemed to use it to keep out special interests. Many employers believed that the exclusionist image of the task force worked against their selling the Clinton plan to their business groups.[46]

The administration counters that it vigorously courted business managers in the early days of reform, but acknowledges that its ability to mobilize large employers was compromised at times by competing priorities. Secular changes in American policymaking have made business mobilization by Democrats more difficult. First, presidents are much more vulnerable to shifts in public opinion, after years of "going public" and cultivat-

[44] The Wyatt Company, prepared for Association of Private Pension and Welfare Plans, "Unintended Consequences of Excluding Small Firms from an Employer Mandate," Washington, D.C., May 1994.

[45] "Office of Public Liaison Plan for Health Care Reform Campaign," memorandum to Mrs. Clinton from Alexis Herman and Mike Lux, February 5, 1993.

[46] Interviews with industry respondents, spring and summer 1994.

ing a mass power base.[47] The Clinton administration was caught in a vise-grip between rallying the mass public with a populist attack on insurers and providers and working behind the scenes with its business supporters. It opted for populism partly because it likes stories of good and evil, a lesson learned in Clinton's unsuccessful bid for reelection in 1980. In the area of health care the administration decided that doctors were too powerful to be the villains, but that drug companies and insurers were perfect for the part.[48] Populist attacks on drug and insurance companies may be deserved in many cases, but the language of heroes and villains elicits emotional, ideological responses that distort the larger picture. The attack turned the debate from technical fixes to ideological class conflict. This undercut the ability of policy experts within the business community to portray the issue in technocratic terms that had a better chance of attracting corporate adherents.

The shift from emphasizing cost containment to access as the major goal of health reform also grew out of a desire to rally mass support, but again alienated corporate backers. Business managers were drawn to health reform in the first place because they believed that total overhaul of the system was necessary to curb costs; consequently, corporate supporters responded best to the administration's plan when the problem was framed in this way. Stan Greenberg argued, however, that mass mobilization depended on framing the issue as one of access; people were inclined to disbelieve that the government could really curb costs:

> *The dominant goal should be health care security:* that people will have health insurance and that they will never lose it, never. . . . Health care security has much more power than the cost argument, and it is much more believable: people think we can deliver on security; they are not sure we can deliver on cost control. There is also an emotion in security (lacking in cost) that empowers our rationale for bold changes.[49]

Second, the administration was torn between conflicting demands from Congress in an era of decentralized decision making when each committee has become a legislation-generating operation. No one disputes the complexity of the Clinton plan, but the administration suggests that congressional needs were partly to blame. Congressional Democrats wanted a bill that would close the ranks of the party in a top-down fashion: nothing short of a complete presidential plan could unify diverse factions. Thus

---

[47] Kernell, *Going Public;* Jeffrey Tulis, *The Rhetorical Presidency* (Princeton: Princeton University Press, 1987).

[48] See also Bob Woodward, *The Agenda* (New York: Simon and Schuster, 1994), 110, 147.

[49] "The Health Care Joint Session Speech," memorandum to Ira Magaziner from Stan Greenberg, obtained from White House sources, 2.

the Clinton magnum opus was partly designed to unite fragmented congressional Democrats. At the same time, legislators wanted to be the dealmakers and resented the negotiations by the administration at the proposal-development stage. In the fall of 1993 congressional leaders told the administration that it could not make any more deals with special interests, and in October the Clintons began "to shut down the process."[50]

This process of negotiation and then withdrawal damaged the administration's credibility with business allies. Employers had repeatedly pointed out provisions troubling to them; yet after promises to the contrary, the Clintons seemed uninterested in adjusting the bill to these very real corporate concerns. The administration tried to overcome the limits on its deal making by showing business managers a set of "end game scenarios" that outlined reform compromises acceptable to the president and addressing the corporate concerns.[51] Although this behind-the-scenes strategy may have had impact with business managers close to the administration, it did nothing to assuage the fears of those who could judge the Clinton plan only by its public manifestation. NAM's Jerry Jasinowski told Magaziner, "I have a problem with some of my members. They're afraid that you're rope-a-doping me." Others told the administration, "[Corporate opponents] say that you're going to roll us and that you won't be flexible. If you made some of the changes that you yourselves admit, even if you don't change employer mandates or benefits, it gives us something to work with."[52]

Real economic concerns combined with the seeming inflexibility of the administration transformed the business view of managed competition from a private-sector solution to a first step toward a single-payer system. Firms were willing to back employer mandates and system reform only if they could opt out of the public system and continue to provide health benefits for their own employees. Yet the size of the alliances and conditions governing company opt-out options made managed competition seem increasingly all-embracing. One manager noted, "I might be willing to support a single-payer system, but I'd like to check out the job options first."[53]

Third, the fiscal climate of health reform severely limited both its potential for legislation and its business backing. The zero-sum budgetary cli-

[50] Interviews with Ira Magaziner, July and September 1993.

[51] The most business-oriented end game scenario showed phased-in universal coverage, possibly voluntary alliances of one hundred or under, less stringent triggered premium caps, a smaller benefits package, lower Medicare and Medicaid cuts, and a cut in the 1 percent corporate assessment. "Passing Health Reform: Policy and Congressional Summary," December 17, 1993, but first draft had been developed in August 1993, 10–14, obtained from the White House.

[52] Interview with Magaziner, September 1993.

[53] Interview with company representative, January 1993.

mate of late-twentieth-century America made all new social programs dubious. More specifically to health reform, the constraints imposed on the administration by the Congressional Budget Office (CBO) prevented early concessions to business allies. A major sticking point for employers was the acceptable size of firms for opting out of the health alliances, set at five thousand employees. The administration says that it wanted to lower this to five hundred, but the CBO indicated reluctance to score a bill with a lower figure.[54]

Fourth, the growing intrusion of the Fourth Estate in modern politics limited coalitions with both congressional and corporate allies. Media concerns guided development of the original proposal: the administration was careful to avoid the T-word (read taxes). Fear of the media also delimited contacts to the outside world. There was early talk of "detailed briefings to the health care press perhaps two or three times every week" and even allowing the media to attend sessions of the task force. But Clinton's media advisers wanted a more secretive approach, fearing that interaction with the press would distract decision makers, shift attention away from the budget, and make controlling the message difficult. The concern about leaks greatly diminished the administration's sharing of ideas and strategy with congressional allies.[55]

The Republican Countermobilization

The Republican mobilization effort far surpassed the Democratic one. Of course, the Republicans had an easier task: opposing is always easier than endorsing, and the business groups sympathetic to the Republican position were much better organized. (The major reform-oriented lobby, the Jay Rockefeller-initiated Health Care Reform Project, was severely underfunded. The group's organizer Robert Clopak estimates that they spent about $3 million while the NFIB, the HIAA, and the health care industry spent over $100 million.)[56]

The issue became a vehicle for intense partisan conflict when Republican pollster Bill McInturff told House Speaker Newt Gingrich that health reform's defeat could lead to a Republican House.[57] Republicans could

[54] Theodore Marmor and Jerry Mashaw, "The State as the Guarantor of Social Welfare," in *Professions, Health Care, and the State*, ed. Patricia Day, D. M. Fox, Robert Maxwell, and Ellie Scrivens (New York: Blackwell, 1995); Magaziner, interview, July 1993.

[55] "Health Care Press Strategy," memorandum to George Stephanopoulos and Bob Boorstin from Magaziner, February 4, 1993; interview with Magaziner, September 1995.

[56] Interview, fall 1994; Darrell West, *The Sound of Money* (New York: W.W. Norton, 1998).

[57] Robin Toner, "Pollsters See a Silent Storm That Swept Away Democrats," *New York Times,* November 16, 1994, A14.

not entirely deny the health crisis—too many middle-class Americans were concerned about their own health benefits. But the party argued that only marginal adjustments were necessary, adopting a stance that acknowledged the crisis but rejected a solution of crisis proportions. This made for considerable ambivalence and vacillation. Torn between his moderate inclinations and his presidential ambitions, Bob Dole first agreed that there was a crisis and then joined voices with William Kristol, chairman of the Project for the Republican Future, and the Republican Right in denying the health crisis.[58] Public opinion seemed ill disposed toward the skeptics, and Dole acknowledged the crisis in the spring of 1994 but flipped again during the summer. Dole's position on the employer mandates also moved from supporting universal coverage as a goal to opting instead for individual mandates. Finally, he rejected all mandates.[59] Most Washington observers concluded that conservative Republicans were determined to block any bill with a Democratic label, even centrist efforts. Giving credence to this theory was William Kristol's advice to the Republican Right:

> The fate of health care reform is now out of the hands of Bill and Hillary Clinton. . . . Acting Presidents Mitchell and Gephardt will unveil a new Democratic health care bill. . . . the actual details of this not-quite-universal-coverage bill don't matter. *Sight unseen, Republicans should oppose it.* Those stray Republicans who delude themselves by believing that there is still a "mainstream" middle solution are merely pawns in a Democratic game. . . . Our enemy is no longer Clinton, it is Congress.[60]

The Republicans dramatically pressured business to reject reform, threatening retaliation in future areas of policy. The conservative Republican leadership, organized through the office of Newt Gingrich, tried to direct business toward incremental alternatives, to frame the health debate in larger terms, and to draw on its historical relations with individual companies. The message to business was that health reform was "a new entitlement" and "a whole package," and that firms should not sell out for individual benefits:

> "If you want our help in killing the Clinton plan, don't do separate deals on other things." Again and again we were trying to lay out the big picture for

---

[58] Adam Clymer, "G.O.P. Line Gels on Idea of No Real Health Crisis," *New York Times,* January 27, 1994, 16.

[59] Robert Pear, "G.O.P. Promises Help on Medical Care," *New York Times,* September 16, 1993, 21; Adam Clymer, "Dole Gathering Broad Backing for a G.O.P. Health Care Plan," *New York Times,* June 30, 1994, A1, B10.

[60] "Health Care: Why Congress in Now More Dangerous Than Clinton," memorandum to Republican Leaders from William Kristol, Project for the Republican Future, July 26, 1994; see also Julie Kosterlitz, "Brinksmanship," *National Journal,* July 9, 1994, 1648.

them. "Maybe you can accept the deal right now, but think about what can be done to you in ten years."[61]

In the spring of 1994 the Republicans put intense political pressure on major business associations and firms. Shortly before the Business Roundtable vote, Gingrich argued to two dozen CEOs that "their interests were best promoted by being principled rather than going for short-term deals." Ameritech, a long-time supporter of health reform, planned to sponsor a presentation by President Clinton. Republican congressmen on the House Energy and Commerce Committee told the company that if it backed the president, it would be punished in other regulatory areas under the committee's jurisdiction. Caterpillar and several telecommunications companies received similar threats. CEOs were told, "If you are going to come back and ask for help in future areas, you should know that it's not in your interests" to support mandates.[62]

Congressional Republicans can take much of the credit for the dramatic policy reversal at the Chamber of Commerce. Its position on health greatly angered conservative congressional Republicans. The Conservative Opportunity Society in the House demanded a meeting with Chamber president Richard Lesher and Archey, and "read them the riot act." At the meeting Jim Bunning (R-Ky.) gave a speech against big government, big labor, and big business. (One participant wondered if he realized that all of the big Fortune companies were in the Chamber.) John Boehner (R-Ohio and chairman of the group) sent letters on congressional letterhead to Chamber constituents saying that they should cancel their membership. Dick Armey (R-Tex.) asked for an opportunity to offer the Republican view to the board before the Chamber took any action. Meanwhile the National Federation of Independent Business initiated a membership drive against the Chamber, and the Chamber reversed itself.[63]

The Republicans received considerable help from small business in their efforts to organize opposition to reform. On the House side Billy Pitts (an aide for Robert Michel [R-Ill.]) ran a Monday morning meeting of congressional aides on the key committees and business representatives from the Health Care Equity Action League and the major small-business associations. This group was at times joined by people like Deborah Steelman, health czar from the Bush administration, to get briefed on the issues. Each week Pitts would identify the issue of the week, and the group would "brainstorm on strategies, line up key amendments to focus on, and make sure that everyone was pulling in one direction." Participants would identify "who was gettable and who wasn't" and discuss "what kinds of pressures to bring to bear in the districts." A big topic of conver-

[61] Interview with congressional staff in leadership role, fall 1994.
[62] Interview with congressional staffer in leadership position.
[63] Interview with Chamber of Commerce staff, May 1994.

sation was "when to put the plug on reform so that it didn't look like the Republicans had pulled the plug."[64]

This tight lobbying organization was helpful to the Republican leadership in disciplining members of its own party. To illustrate, the leadership worried that Dingell would be able to get Fred Upton (R-Mich.) to endorse the president's bill in Energy and Commerce. NFIB did a big preemptive strike against Upton to keep the legislator in line. Some participants spent time persuading Fred Grandy, on Ways and Means, that the Cooper bill would not pass.

Paul Coverdell (R-Ga.) and Bob Packwood (R-Ore.) led a similar group to keep moderate senators in line. Coverdell feared that a minimalist bill would snowball, and business groups reported that they were under tremendous pressure from Coverdell "to blast the Chafee bill" that included compromises between the Democratic and Republican perspectives. Coverdell argued to business participants that no bill was better than a bill legislated under the Democratic leadership. Lobbyists generally agreed that the Republicans came to this conclusion before most of the business community.[65]

By the end of the legislative cycle, some of the business representatives who were strongly opposed to the Clinton plan and employer mandates believed that the conservative Republicans had gone too far in blocking any kind of health reform. For example, some business groups offered encouraging words about a centrist, bipartisan effort; the next day Republicans retaliated through an editorial attack in the *Wall Street Journal*. One lobbyist said, "Now we are getting hit from the right and the left. . . . The Republicans want to kill the thing without leaving fingerprints. But we still want health reform."[66]

Conclusion

Corporate managers at times favor policies that promote human capital investment; yet it is extremely difficult for them to translate this support into political action. Umbrella organizations are seemingly incapable of taking action for broad, collective, but controversial concerns. Even when a majority of their members favor a position, the groups fear alienating strongly held minority sentiments.

[64] The group included NFIB, Pam Bailey, Restaurateurs, Retailers, NAW, and HIAA among others; interview with participating lobbyist, summer 1994.

[65] Interview with participating lobbyists, summer 1994.

[66] Interview with participating lobbyist, summer 1994.

Legacies of private social provision create patterns of vested interests that make it difficult for managers to agree about new initiatives. Private provision of benefits tends to increase the understanding and salience of an issue within business; therefore, government legislation is often likely to occur in areas where business has gone before. But at the same time private provision limits the possibilities for reform: private policy professionals develop an institutional commitment to their private systems that prevents their support of public programs. Years of least-common-denominator business politics have etched a system of social provision that is fragmented, heavily private, and likely to retain its disjointed form.

Large employers have also been comparatively hostile to social initiatives because their umbrella organizations are not set up to organize for collective social concerns. Large portions of the business community may endorse human capital investment policies, but the peak associations almost never join in this support. Umbrella organizations are seemingly incapable of acting for collective concerns: even when a majority of their members favor certain positions they must cater to more strongly held minority sentiments.

The defeat of health reform reflected the inherent difficulty of organizing business for social initiatives. Repeated surveys found a majority large employers favoring major components of the Clinton health Yet by early 1994, the major trade associations that initially favore ton's efforts backed away from earlier commitments. Meanwhi reform's opponents (especially among small-business and provider groups) commandeered an ever larger leadership role in the defeat of the plan. Big businesses' policy capacity faltered at the point of translating general corporate anxiety into specific legislation.

SIX

UNITED WE STAND:

CORPORATE ENGAGEMENT WITH

TRAINING POLICY

AMERICAN BUSINESS, with its entrenched factions, at times is reminiscent of the Balkans, yet corporate dissension is not a constant. Although employer associations experience general difficulty in imposing order on their members' demands, managers seem to find common ground in some areas of policy. The occasional truce brings moments of respite, when business factions suspend their turf battles to attend to common interests. Fragmentation in the business community, like ethnic affiliation, may indicate the fault lines of antagonism; however, this general pattern tells us little about the ebb and flow of conflict.

Whence come these moments of relative unity, when employers pursue common goals? To some extent corporate coalescence represents the quirky accidents of fate that often seem essential to success: leadership, environmental urgency, and a greater willingness of participants to come together for the sake of action.

But collective business political activism also reflects the corporate policy capacity within a policy area. Some areas have greater policy capacity than others and deviate from the least-common-denominator politics generally prevalent among American business. A critical component is the presence of policy-level organizations that help employers to formulate a political position and to advance that position during legislative episodes. These policy-level associations may dominate the issue, resemble peak associations within their narrow field, and enjoy formal or informal recognition as the legitimate representatives for their concerns. The usual least-common-denominator politics of business becomes most vivid when suspended by these policy-level groups.

Help in organizing business can come from surprising quarters, in the form of political leadership. At times presidents and other political leaders set out to bring together diverse parts of the business community to support legislative programs. In some cases these coalitions have been institutionalized into enduring business organizations with a broad reach and a commitment to making things happen. Politicians can thereby unify factions that would otherwise remain disparate; these political interventions can overcome much of the fragmentation within the corporate community. When presidents initiate broad business mobilizations, corporate preferences may look very different than when business is left to its own devices. Politicians may be able to persuade their business allies to restrain their narrow concerns for larger goals, thus potentially shifting the debate to a higher level.

This chapter considers how policy-level institutional arrangements partially overcome the least-common-denominator politics syndrome in the area of employment and training. A unique business group, the National Alliance of Business, has worked to unify employers in support of successive employment and training initiatives since the 1960s. NAB's raison d'etre is to foster a business-government partnership in this area, and its sponsorship of an ongoing dialogue between government leaders and diverse business groups has produced a corporate cohesion unheard of in other areas of social policy.

In part because of this strong business support, Democrats and Republicans in recent years have engaged in a high level of cooperation in training initiatives. The two phenomena are mutually reinforcing. Bipartisan efforts have reinforced business unity, which has made for easier bipartisan cooperation on this issue even during periods of heightened party conflict in other domains. Thus NAM's Phyllis Eisen bragged that the bipartisan cooperation demonstrated in training legislation in the contentious year of 1995 reflected the substantial agreement in the business community. Even when the Goals 2000 legislation became caught up in turf wars between the two parties in the House of Representatives, corporate allies intervened to push the process forward.

This is not to say that managers endorsed all aspects of the administration's training agenda. Business involvement with the legislation narrowed its scope; for example, largely in deference to corporate objections, Clinton's advisers abandoned a proposal for a sweeping 1.5 percent training mandate even before the new president was sworn into office. Many disadvantaged workers continue to lack opportunities for training. In addition, generalizations about policies affecting human capital investment to be drawn from the employment and training case must be tempered by certain realpolitik observations. With its fewer vested economic interests, training policy may be easier to enact than, for instance, health reform.

In addition, even when big-business managers have a great deal of interest in a human capital investment issue, their activism tends to be limited. For example, although large employers intervened in the programmatic design of initiatives to promote training, they did little to influence the appropriations process when Republicans sought to cut funding for employment and training after the 1994 elections. Thus, the case of employment and training is at once a lesson in the general constraints on business activism in human capital investment policy and in the special circumstances under which these constraints can be partially overcome.

Policy Legacies in Employment and Training

The field of employment and training, like the field of health care, saw an enormous growth in the private sector's expertise in policy during the 1970s and 1980s. Yet in contrast to health, the other dimensions of corporate policy capacity, policy legacies and business organization, were conducive to employers' support for employment and training policies. First, managers were drawn to the Clinton training bills because they were able to connect these pieces of legislation (with the administration's help) to legacies of education reform, bipartisan commissions, and efforts of prior presidents. Second, a central business group, the National Alliance of Business, worked hard to keep employers fully supportive of the training initiatives.

The Clinton initiatives built on ideas generated by bipartisan studies of training and economic growth and on legacies of efforts in education reform. As Weir has argued, employment maintenance policy in the United States (especially for marginal workers) has historically been viewed with suspicion by the business community; consequently, the links between training and employment work against corporate backing for training policy. By the end of the sixties, training was more often defined as an aid to income maintenance than as a spur to economic growth.[1] Yet to the extent that training could be reframed as a necessary component of productivity and as an offshoot of education, it could enjoy a better reception in the corporate mind.

A series of important bipartisan commissions during the 1980s with participation from both business and labor helped to redefine training, from a matter of income maintenance to a matter of growth. These reports drew corporate attention to the relationship between the quality of the workforce and competitiveness, and pushed training to the top of the business agenda. Reagan Labor secretary William Brock commissioned a study from the Hudson Institute to examine changes in the economy. The resulting publication of *Workforce 2000* in 1985 "alerted the human resource community to the need for more skills if this nation is to remain competitive." Elizabeth Dole then established the Secretary's Commission on Achieving Necessary Skills (with representation from business, labor, and education) to define required workplace skills.[2] George Bush came to

---

[1] Weir, *Politics and Jobs.*
[2] Packer, "The SCANS Challenge," 367.

power as the self-avowed education president and, promising a kinder, gentler approach to social policy, sought to fulfill campaign promises with investigations into both education and training. The business-appointed, bipartisan Commission on the Skills of the American Workforce (chaired by Ira Magaziner, Ray Marshall, and William Brock) issued the influential report *America's Choice: High Skills or Low Wages,* which recommended many of the training policies legislated during the Clinton years.[3]

The Bush administration sought the blessing of governors and business managers for its education and training agendas. The famous Governor's Conference in Charlottesville, Virginia, in September 1989 was to education reform what the first Earth Day was to the environmental movement: a highly visible commitment to a set of political principles. States have an incentive to keep their tax bases low because they compete for companies; therefore, many governors believed that improvement in education required a national commitment to maintain a level playing field.

Governors had cooperated closely with local employers in their efforts to update schools at the state level; consequently, the administration's overtures to employers followed naturally from this well-established governor-business connection. For instance, Governor Richard Riley (later Clinton's secretary of education) received much business encouragement to improve schools in South Carolina. Governor Richard Celeste reformed Ohio's educational system with the help of Procter and Gamble's chair, Owen Butler.[4]

Three months prior to the governor's conference President Bush met with major employer organizations and challenged them to join the campaign for education and training reforms. The president asked executives to make three shifts in their thinking about education and training. First, companies should develop long-term strategies for education reform, rather than acting as one-time partners through, for example, adopt-a-school programs. Corporate leaders should take responsibility within their communities for helping schools to train the workforce of the future.

Second, greater attention needed to be paid to *results* of schooling, and business could help to make this happen. The decentralized nature of the educational system makes it difficult to assess outcomes in any meaningful way, because grades vary across regions, schools, and even teachers. Business leaders were urged to support national standards of student performance that would allow for broader comparisons.

Third, the administration encouraged business to identify for itself a ten-year strategy, taking into account the need for "lifelong learning" as well as education reform. The White House believed that education

[3] Commission on the Skills of the American Workforce, *America's Choice.*
[4] Stanfield, "School Business," 1862.

should extend beyond the kindergarten through high school core years, and should include Head Start, adult literacy, and issues of workforce preparedness.[5]

Simultaneously, the authors of *America's Choice* began making the rounds in the business community, urging managers to endorse the principles of their report. Ira Magaziner met with NAB, NAM, and the Chamber of Commerce. Former commission staffer Mark Tucker of the National Center on Education and the Economy organized a discussion group of Washington national organizations from business, labor, and education. Tucker remembers that this was the first time anyone had organized a group that brought together the three sectors.[6]

This new education and training message met with considerable enthusiasm from business. Managers hoped that this was an opportunity for congressional action toward national systemic reform and endorsed voluntary standards. John Acorn of IBM and the Business Roundtable agreed to coordinate the development of a ten-year plan. The Bush administration hoped that the Roundtable would present its plan at *Fortune*'s Second Education Summit in 1989, but business participants had been confused about the dates and were not prepared. After this setback, the coalition began to organize in earnest, and in 1990 the Roundtable produced a ten-year plan for educational reform. A participant recalled:

> There was a consensus point in the business community, namely that there should be a shift in focus in education from inputs to results. At a *Fortune* magazine education summit it surfaced that 96 percent of businesses were involved in education reform, but none thought that they were making any difference. . . . Education, like business, needed accountability standards and measurements.[7]

Managers also believed that the federal jobs training system did not work, because it was meant to be part of a safety-net, not to promote competitiveness. Bill Clinton's rising fortunes in the election polls heightened the Roundtable's attention to training because many believed that if he were elected, action on training would follow. In addition participating CEOs believed that NAFTA required a federal system of investments in human capital for upgrading the workforce, or in the words of the Roundtable at that time, "reengineering the federal workforce program."[8] Under the leadership of Lawrence Perlman, CEO of Ceridan, the Roundtable Working Group on Workforce Development prepared a document recommending consolidation of current retraining programs, partner-

---

[5] Interview with Rae Nelson, Chamber of Commerce, May 9, 1995.
[6] Telephone interview with Mark Tucker, June 1996.
[7] Interview with Rae Nelson, May 9, 1995.
[8] Interview with Jim O'Connell, May 1996.

ships between business and schools for school-to-work transitions, and tax incentives for continuous training and development. Although Perlman described himself as "a card-carrying free marketeer," he urged corporate activism in this "transition from the Industrial Age to the Information Age." Perlman expressed concern that the worker of today will not have access to the jobs of the future, as dislocation accompanies economic transformation. In addition, a workforce increasingly composed of women and people of color who have not formerly been labor-market participants may have special needs. Perlman reported that

> the Business Roundtable has called for companies, unions, schools and government to form partnerships to develop training programs that help both workers and companies. The aim is to help people get decent-paying jobs, at the same time creating a flexible, skilled workforce that helps companies be competitive. The Business Roundtable wants American business to see training costs as an investment in human capital, not unlike our investments in research and development and plant and equipment.[9]

In April 1990 the Chamber of Commerce began its own Center for Workforce Preparedness "to launch a national grassroots education reform campaign" and "to ensure that U.S. workers are prepared with the knowledge, skills and attitudes to compete and succeed in the global economy of the 21st century." Toward these ends, the Center generated materials for local business managers to use for community education, held monthly town meetings with the Department of Education via satellite, and sponsored meetings with the Small Business Administration to explore regional employment and training needs.[10]

The National Association of Manufacturers started a joint project with the Department of Labor to encourage manufacturers "to create a high performance work environment by investing . . . in human resources." This Work Force Readiness Project held a series of focus groups for executives and workers to identify the key issues, concerns, and goals of worker retraining. Among the "eleven key findings" were that "Training Is the Highest Investment" and that "Strengthening Manufacturing Should Be National Policy."[11] NAM's Michael Baroody was to declare that a "cultural revolution" in employer attitudes had taken place and that none "of the management people defended the old way of doing [things]."[12]

---

[9] Lawrence Perlman, "Training, Equity, and Power," *Corporate Board,* January 1995, beginning 1.

[10] Center for Workforce Preparation, "Overview," April 20, 1995, obtained from the Chamber of Commerce.

[11] National Association of Manufacturers, Department of Labor, "Work Force Readiness," June 1992, obtained from National Association of Manufacturers, 5; National Association of Manufacturers, Department of Labor, "Workforce Readiness: How to Meet Our Greatest Competitive Challenge," December 1992, 8–9.

[12] Rochelle L. Stanfield, "Quest for Quality," *National Journal,* August 8, 1992, 1832.

During the Bush administration legislators introduced bills establishing training programs that were supported by both labor and business. For example, in 1991 Dick Gephardt (D-Mo.) and Ralph Regula (R-Ohio) proposed the High Skills, Competitive Workforce Act, creating school-to-work transition programs and education standards to measure skills, and drawing from the 1990 report, *America's Choice: High Skills or Low Wages*. Senator Edward Kennedy (D-Mass.) introduced similar legislation in the Senate. The Bush administration seemed sympathetic, and Bush secretary of education Lamar Alexander worked on a bill that included national education standards, a move that John Jennings compared to Nixon's opening China.[13] William Ford (House Committee on Education and Labor chair and D-Mich.) noted, "This is the first time we've had anybody with the status of [education secretary] sending up specific proposals for us to react to. That means we have a better chance of the Administration being a participant in the final product, and that's essential."[14] But the president's reform ultimately set up a state-of-the-art school in each congressional district and allocated federal monies to private schools (a concession to advocates of choice); both measures alienated Democrats. Meanwhile the Democratic bills set up standards for schools as well as for students—called opportunity-to-learn standards. The battle lines between the two camps previewed much of the tension to come, and the process reached a stalemate.

Business Organization in Employment and Training

Training policy was also helped politically by a high degree of business organization, with the National Alliance of Business (NAB) generating much corporate cooperation and activism. During the Bush years, NAB organized a multiassociation group called the Business Coalition for Education Reform. NAB and the Roundtable cochaired the group, composed of eleven national business associations, including the Committee for Economic Development, the NAM, the Chamber of Commerce, and the American Business Conference. As we see in the case studies to follow, the Business Coalition for Education Reform and its successor, the Workforce Development Coalition, provided core corporate support for the Clinton initiatives.

NAB's organizational characteristics help it to avoid some of the problems of other groups, and it has struggled to overcome the narrow focus in other areas of policy. Because it is a policymaking body funded by

---

[13] John Jennings, ed., *National Issues in Education* (Washington, D.C.: Institute for Educational Leadership, 1993), x.

[14] Rochelle L. Stanfield, "Back to Basics," *National Journal*, June 29, 1991, 1626.

grants as well as by dues, not a "bottom-line membership association," it is less fearful of minority objections. Indeed, the organization fears that it would whither away were it to lose its capacity to take substantive policy stands. The NAB leadership struggles to bring other business groups along by forming coalitions and by taking the lead in offering corporate positions on the issues of the day. NAB frequently drafts letters and provides them to coalition members such as the Chamber or the Roundtable to disseminate to their companies. So that positions are not blackballed by minority interests, NAB hands out letters at coalition meetings saying, "Here's where we think we are, and we will take comments."[15] The organization does not try to reach consensus among all members and avoids taking votes; rather it tries to accommodate as many objections as it can without threatening its capacity to take a position.

Politician's Strategies and Corporate Participation

Finally, business support for employment and training legislation was enhanced by strategic choices by politicians on both sides of the partisan aisle. Lyndon Johnson's original decision to create NAB as a quasi-corporatist organization established an important business group and the groundwork for public-private partnership. Unlike the health care reform, training policy did not become an arena for partisan competition. In part because they perceived considerable corporate demand for training legislation, both parties pursued the issue in a fairly cooperative, nonpartisan manner at least until after the 1994 elections.

Perhaps the most important strategic choice for training's political viability was Clinton's decision to build on the policy legacies of the past. When Clinton was elected in 1992, business managers worried that he would feel political pressure to differentiate himself from his predecessor despite the considerable enthusiasm already in place for Education 2000 and school-to-work initiatives. But President Clinton identified employment and training as an area of bipartisan concerns, and he cultivated existing support. The administration endorsed the 70 to 80 percent of the policy initiatives that enjoyed broad support and steered clear of conflict-ridden issues like the training mandate. Clinton's prior involvement as the "education governor" reinforced an unwillingness to break ranks with the old regime. Shortly after the election the National Center on Education and the Economy (the think tank formed by the America's Choice team) organized a two-day meeting to identify the critical propo-

---

[15] Interview with William Kolberg, April 19, 1995.

nents of a framework for national training; twelve persons present became members of the Clinton transition team.[16]

The Clinton administration proposed three major pieces of training legislation, all drawing from prior proposals: the Goals 2000 Act, the School-to-Work Opportunities Partnership Act, and the Workforce Security Act, commonly referred to as the Reemployment Act. Goals 2000 was developed during the Governors' 1989 Education Summit. The concept of a school-to-work transition, imported from countries like Denmark and Germany, had been on policymakers' agendas since the early 1980s. Two of the three bills passed; large employers supported and greatly influenced all three pieces of legislation.

Training bills also benefited from a spirit of cooperation between executive departments. Education and labor secretaries Richard Riley and Robert Reich avoided pernicious turf wars, appearing together at press conferences, congressional hearings, and the odd convention to generate enthusiasm for the bills. William Ford (D-Mich.) commented on the secretaries' joint testimony at the Committee on Education and Labor, "Your counterparts never appeared together. In fact, for many years, there was a question of whether they even talked to each other."[17] This unprecedented cooperation between departments known for their boundary disputes added to the ease with which the initiatives were passed into law.

The Clinton administration also quietly slipped into the already-existing institutional channels of cooperation with business. One manager, working on both training and health, reported that the administration's training people were much more interested in business opinion than those running the health care debate.[18] Labor secretary Robert Reich sought to include business managers with a message of "partnership between business and government," and although many corporate leaders feared Reich's reputation as a wild man of labor, the secretary gained much good will in the area of training. Reich courted business managers with a high-wage, high-skill gospel and urged them to view workers as assets rather than costs, to integrate technology and work, and to pursue "the high-road strategy" of labor-management cooperation. The secretary explained that

> no competitor can replicate the advantages of a highly motivated and well-trained workforce. A workforce that is empowered to make decisions about ways to improve productivity and satisfy customers, that is loyal and willing to go the extra mile to ensure that customers are truly satisfied.[19]

[16] Interview with Mark Tucker, June 3, 1996.
[17] Rochelle L. Stanfield, "Team Players," *National Journal,* November 13, 1993, 2723.
[18] Interview with industry respondent, May 1995.
[19] Stephanie Overman, "Labor Secretary Preaches Cooperation," *HR Magazine,* November 1993, 42.

In an interview with the *Wall Street Journal,* Reich set out methods of persuading industry to join the administration's campaign. He asked Lawrence Katz in the Department of Labor to determine whether companies with progressive human-resource policies actually did better financially. He planned to publicize companies with high levels of investment in training as paragons in the field, and to point out that the department's partnership training budget would disproportionately benefit training-oriented companies. Secretary Reich also reached out to human-resource professionals and asked them to educate their CEOs about the positive link between labor-management cooperation and productivity.[20] The business community continued to work with the new administration as if no change in political leadership had occurred. The Chamber continued its satellite meetings on education, but simply shifted partners from the Bush administration's Lamar Alexander to Richard Riley, Clinton's education secretary. A manager recalls:

> Business managers felt that Clinton was very sympathetic to their concerns; they had known the new president from his governor's days and felt that he shared their lifelong-learning agenda. Riley, like Lamar Alexander, had been a governor, so each governor had made a major commitment to work with the business communities in their states. These policies had been proposed in Congress for four years; a lot of communities had invested in the 2000 agenda. Communities responded to national political and business leadership.[21]

Small-business groups immediately distanced themselves from the overtures of the new administration. NFIB's president Jack Faris criticized Reich for describing the 360,000 new jobs created in February 1993 as being of low quality, and suggested that Reich "visit Main Street" to learn about job creation. Reich persisted in trying to reach out to small business, inviting Faris to breakfast, but the organization continued to be hostile.[22] Yet large employers had an organizational forum that did not cater to a small-business membership.

Business Mobilization for Training Policy

As the following cases reveal, the administration's overtures to large employers greatly improved the political fortunes of the training initiatives. Business allies were very involved with the initiatives (unlike health reform), defending the bills from ideological assault and lobbying vigorously for successful legislation.

---

[20] Geber, "Because It's Good for You," 17; Overman, "Labor Secretary Preaches Cooperation," 42.

[21] Interview with Rae Nelson, May 9, 1995.

[22] Kirk Victor, "Swing Time," *National Journal,* June 12, 1993, 1402.

Goals 2000 Act

The Goals 2000 bill had a big purpose and a little budget. On a symbolic level, it could claim to establish a national framework for education and to shift the evaluation of schools from measures of process to measures of outcome. The central feature of the bill was to make education meet standards of competency; in other words, schools would be judged by the knowledge and skills their students attained. The act set up several national boards to create standards for excellence and was to provide a framework for later education initiatives. Thus, despite a limited budget, Goals 2000 signified a break with two hundred years of local control over schooling.[23]

The part of Goals 2000 relevant to training was a National Skills Standards Board (made up of industry, labor, and government representatives) that together with relevant industry groups would specify skills needed for occupational clusters and standards for measuring student performance in mastering those skills. Although the bill emphasized voluntarism and state flexibility as much as possible, it required "every state to get into the business of setting standards."[24] The emphasis on standards came from the belief that nationally recognized credentials were necessary for establishing skill competencies.

Although the Goals 2000 Act enjoyed considerable bipartisan support, the initiative was nonetheless attacked from both the left and the right. One issue of contention was a proposal by liberal Democrats on the House Education and Labor Committee to establish opportunity-to-learn standards. The Left worried that economically disadvantaged children might be less able to satisfy national performance standards than kids from wealthier school districts and wanted to equalize the educational environment in which students learn. As John Jennings, chief education counsel to the House Committee on Education and Labor put it, "Once you open the door to national standards, you've raised to the national level whether kids are adequately being taught."[25] Education proponents had opposed including potentially controversial national skills standards in the Goals 2000 bill, but ultimately the skills board was easily accepted compared to the more contentious opportunity-to-learn standards.

Liberal Democrats on the Committee on Education and Labor resisted Goals 2000 for political reasons because they wanted the first educational

---

[23] Jennifer O'Day, in Jennings, *National Issues in Education,* 99; Jennings, *National Issues in Education,* 187–88.

[24] Anne Lewis, "Education Officials, Critics Pleased with New Programs, Standards," *Baltimore Sun,* January 15, 1995, 8; Baily, Burtless, and Litan, *Growth with Equity,* 126.

[25] Rochelle L. Stanfield, "Learning Curve," *National Journal,* July 3, 1993, 1688.

initiative to be a revision of the Elementary and Secondary Education Act. The Democrats were baffled by the president's desire for strong bipartisanship and believed that he spent too much time working with business, the governors, and the Republicans. At one point a rumor raced through the Democratic committee that Secretary Riley was considering shifting focus from the liberals to southern Democrats and Republicans. The administration could not understand why the House Democrats made amendments on provisions that the administration had already altered in response to their criticisms. Animosity toward Goals 2000 also stemmed from the Bush years, when a National Education Goals Panel was set up to develop reform items. Legislators joined governors and executive branch officials on the panel, but were not given voting rights. Education legislators were irritated by this slam and consequently felt no "ownership" of the process.[26]

Conservatives opposed both voluntary and mandatory opportunity-to-learn standards as "a typical, big-government response to local problems," in the words of Congressman John Boehner (R-Ohio). The Right also objected to the national boards created by Goals 2000. Boehner argued that the largely private National Education Goals Panel signified a new part of the federal government and warned, "Although given specific and limited powers, history shows that these agencies, once established, become everlasting, money-draining, authoritarian nightmares." The Heritage Foundation predicted that the National Education Standards and Improvement Council would "function like a giant, national school board" and increase "the bureaucracy which is smothering public education."[27]

The president wanted the standards to be voluntary, worrying that mandatory standards would constitute unfunded mandates and break the bipartisan deal. Although the House Committee on Education and Labor marked up a bill with mandatory standards, the Senate version was much closer to the president's conception. According to a high-ranking administration official, the president "pulled out all the stops" during the conference committee and wrote a letter to the House committee urging them to adopt the Senate language. "This letter produced an explosion on the House side, and it looked as if [committee chair] Ford would walk away from the table." But the president also implied that the House members could get what they wanted in the reauthorization of the

[26] Dale Kildee, "Enacting Goals 2000," in Jennings, *National Issues in Education*, 28–38; Carroll Campbell Jr., "The Governors and the National Education Goals," in Jennings, *National Issues in Education*, 83; interview with staff, February 20, 1996.

[27] John Boehner, "The Unmaking of School Reform," in Jennings, *National Issues in Education*, 53, 52; Allyson Tucker, "Goals 2000: Stifling Grass Roots Education Reform," *Heritage Foundation Reports*, no. 182, July 14, 1993.

Elementary and Secondary Education Act, and the liberal Democrats were persuaded to wait.[28]

Corporate allies played a major role in shaping and passing the Goals 2000 bill throughout the legislative process. First, business activists had considerable input on key provisions of the act. Michael Cohen of the Department of Education remembered that the bill was "an easy sell" to business; the administration simply made the pitch that "our agenda is your agenda." Nonetheless, the corporate community had certain concerns. The business coalition fought to have the National Skills 2000 Board led by a business chairperson, arguing that corporate leadership would both enhance the quality of the skill standards and lend legitimacy to the exercise. As Michael Baroody of the NAM testified, "If [the board is] going to be credible to American industry, it has to be led by industry."[29] Business friends of Goals 2000 also argued that industry be given maximum input into directing training funds, because labor market needs were constantly changing.[30]

On the issue of performance standards for both students and schools, the business coalition saw itself as taking a center stance between the mandatory standards favored by the Left and the rejection of all standards by the Right. NAB wrote a letter to the editor of the *Washington Post,* urging the House Democrats to move away from prescriptive standards and to stick with the version that received broad bipartisan support. Ultimately, the House Democrats came up with a compromise along the lines of that offered by big business: model opportunity-to-learn standards would be developed at the federal level, but state adoption of these standards would not be mandatory.[31] Business fears were assuaged, but the governors, also determined to maximize local control, did not believe that this compromise went far enough and ultimately refused to endorse the bill.[32]

Second, business allies had an ideological impact. Administration representatives remember that business participants were very helpful in "keeping the proposal in the center of the political spectrum rather than going to the left." One participant recalls justifying student performance standards to critics on the left: "It fell to the coalition to show that even the least advantaged children can learn if they have the right curriculum and that benchmarks were necessary to estimate educational progress. . . .

---

[28] Interview with a high-ranking administration official, April 1996.

[29] Interview with Mike Cohen, July 15, 1996; *BNA Daily Labor Report,* May 19, 1993.

[30] Interview with Bob Jones, May 6, 1997.

[31] William Kolberg, "Goals 2000: Many Reservations," *Washington Post,* September 11, 1993, A20; "School Reform on a Tightrope," *Washington Post,* March 1, 1994, A18.

[32] Campbell, "Governors and Goals."

The business managers had to convince the left that they were not trying to penalize poor children."[33]

The coalition also defended both skills and student performance standards to the Right, arguing for a system that emphasized local control within a national framework. Thus the boards would not themselves develop standards but would oversee local efforts. NAB's Robert Jones made the argument that skill standards should not even be considered a government policy and worked hard to educate conservatives to this end. Another problem was how to deal with the sizable contingent in the business community who believed that choice was the generic answer to the ills of American education. Michelle Cahn of Xerox remembers, "Critics wondered why the business coalition wasn't giving choice a more central forum. The majority view on the coalition was that choice was only one small part of the problems and shouldn't be at the centerpiece of public initiatives. The coalition leadership worked hard to persuade the choice contingent to focus on other issues."[34]

Finally, the coalition intervened at key points to keep the legislative process moving forward. The Department of Education met on a regular basis to discuss legislative strategy with a small group of sympathetic associations, including the Business Coalition for Education Reform, the National Alliance of Business, the Business Roundtable, the National Association of Manufacturers, and the Chamber of Commerce. Michael Cohen remembers that the administration did not have to organize the group, since it came already organized. The business participants helped the department with vote counts "to figure out where were the people who needed to be visited." Targeting moderate Republicans and Democrats, business representatives visited legislators, wrote letters, and urged their CEOs to write letters (especially to legislators from states with significant number of the CEOs' employees). In addition, this unified business endorsement gave legislators added confidence in the political viability of the bill. Cohen recounted, "The mere fact that the business community was virtually unanimously supportive made it easier for moderate Republicans to vote for it when there were partisan efforts on the other side. So you didn't need to have many incidents of business button-holing Congress."[35]

The Department of Labor also organized corporate backing for the skills standards board. The department was initially surprised that skills standards were put into the Goals 2000 bill and sent to the Education Subcommittee in the House Committee on Education and Labor. Staffers

[33] Interview with administration official, July 1996.
[34] Interview with Bob Jones, May 6, 1997; interview with Michelle Cahn, May 1995.
[35] Interview with Mike Cohen, July 15, 1996.

had been used to talking to a community in which a consensus had developed about skills standards; suddenly the legislation was sent to a committee that did not understand the issues or share the language. The Department of Labor asked members of the business community to explain the issues to the members and to their aides. For example, NAB staff took CEOs such as James Houghton of Corning to meet with countless legislators, and one staffer recalls, "When members saw that this was being overseen by business, they could back off their ideological stance." A committee staffer remembers that these contacts were extremely helpful in moving the process forward: "The debate came over the national standards board. Some conservatives thought that this was a bad idea because it signaled too much government intervention, but business helped people see that in fact the board was quite permissive and that business had a bigger role in the process. Business leaders helped to assuage Republican concerns on this matter and helped them to see that it was a good idea."[36] Phyllis Eisen at NAM believes that business support is what kept Goals 2000 moving forward:

> Goals 2000 passed because business supported it. The question on the table was, "Do we need another government program?" The business community said, "We have no choice but to back it."[37]

The School-to-Work Opportunities Partnership Act

The second major employment and training initiative of the Clinton administration, the School-to-Work Opportunities Partnership Act, created a national apprenticeship program with a budget of $300 million for fiscal year 1995. The program consisted of three parts: an education component in the schools, work-based training, and a linkage system to connect these two usually disparate parts of a graduating senior's life. The federal government would provide national guidelines, development grants, and implementation grants; but the bill allowed for considerable flexibility at the state and local level. In fact, the legislation built on existing regional efforts such as Wisconsin's printing and graphics program and Boston's courses to train teenagers in the health and financial sectors. The bill's sponsors characterized the program as seed money, comparing themselves to venture capitalists who sought to spark entrepreneurial activity but refrained from heavy-handed management. President Clinton said of the act's administrators:

> They will sort of operate like venture capitalists. They will provide seed money to States, set the goals and the standards, give waivers to communities

---

[36] Interview with congressional staffer, February 20, 1996.
[37] Interview with Phyllis Eisen, February 1996.

to give them more flexibility. . . . The school-to-work legislation will enable our Nation for the first time to create the kind of partnership that we so desperately need between schools, businesses, labor, and communities, so that we can connect our people to the real world. That's why the Business Roundtable, the National Association of Manufacturers, the United States Chamber of Commerce, the National Alliance of Business, the AFL-CIO [support it.][38]

The linkage component of school-to-work was essential to fostering cooperation between business and educators. Studies of successful state and local programs highlighted the importance of an intermediary institution to bridge the separate realms and to bring participants to identify their mutual interests. The Labor Department's Leslie Loble recalled,

> One thing that was obvious was the gap between business and education. Business would say, "We want to do this but we don't want to get into a big bureaucratic process. Educators don't understand us. We're very nervous about this partnership." Educators would say, "Business doesn't understand what education is all about. We don't want to just give the latest skill. Business doesn't understand us." It was almost identical language.[39]

The administration believed that the success of school-to-work legislation required congressional ownership of the legislation, especially because the concept lay outside the realm of American experience. Rejecting the magnum opus model used in health reform, the administration sent a mere twenty-five-page school-to-work bill to the Hill. An official explained, "We did not view it as, 'We have the answers, we can create a perfect program,' and we did not do pilot programs and then announce that this was what to do nationally."[40] Instead the administration left room for legislators' involvement in the bill and for state and local variation.

The Labor Department's strategy with school-to-work legislation was twofold: to keep the process bipartisan and to reach out to business. It pursued bipartisanship by meeting with interested parties and developing as much consensus as possible before sending the bill to the Hill. Thus, according to Loble, "The public exposure was more on the issues inherent to it [the act], rather than saying it's a Clinton bill."[41] There was a sacrifice involved in this strategy—the department could not use the legislation to

---

[38] Ron Scherer, "School-to-Work Programs Raise Youths' Job Prospects," *Christian Science Monitor,* August 26, 1993, 9; "Remarks at the Opportunity Skyway School-to-Work Program in Georgetown, Delaware," *Public Papers of the Presidents,* September 3, 1993, 29 Weekly Comp. Pres. Doc. 1685.

[39] Interview with Leslie Loble, February 22, 1996.

[40] Interview with Leslie Loble, February 22, 1996.

[41] Interview with Leslie Loble, February 22, 1996.

develop a high profile either for the secretary or for the president. But the sacrifice was worthwhile.

The department ran an extensive outreach to business, including meetings with coalitions, one-on-one sessions with concerned parties, and small-group encounters. NAB's Tom Lindsley met approximately once a week with the administration on Goals 2000 and school-to-work legislation. According to Loble, the purpose of these meetings was not only to secure legitimation for the bill but to improve the quality of the legislation. Business managers told the Department of Labor that they were spending a fortune on recruiting and training workers, only to lose them to other employers. One company composed a list of "disconnects" between company training needs and available talent. Another interviewed two hundred people for a yellow pages designer and found only five qualified candidates.[42]

Business had been increasingly open to school-to-work partnerships, although Kolberg recalled that the NAB board was initially skeptical. Companies said, "We've been involved in our business for one hundred years. In order for you to ask us to change the way we train young people, you have to prove to us that this new model is cost-effective."[43] Over time managers learned about the concept through trips to Denmark and Germany and through group study of school-to-work programs, so that when the legislation was introduced, there was virtually no opposition.

Despite general philosophical agreement with the act, the employers drove home certain demands. Perhaps most important was their desire to have a large ratio of business participants to representatives from labor and education on the local boards that would set up the programs. Managers wanted to do more in school-to-work programs than "to rubber stamp a plan. . . . We had to have business there at the inception—taking a critical role in the plan." As Phyllis Eisen of NAM put it, "This bill will be made or broken on the involvement of business." Ultimately business was the first group mentioned in the bill's list of participants in the local partnerships. Corporate leaders insisted that the national act only minimally specify state directives to allow for flexibility; but while managers pushed for greater local flexibility, many also wanted the grants to be contingent on stronger national requirements for local business involvement.[44] A participant remembered, "We wanted the involvement of business to be the number one item on this list [of criteria making localities

---

[42] Firms included Siemens, Ceridan, Bell South, Kodak, Thom McCann, American Express, Wilbert, and Ford as well as the major business associations; interview with Tom Lindsley; interview with industry respondent, February 1996.

[43] Interview with William Kolberg, April 19, 1995.

[44] Interview with industry participant, winter 1996; Rochelle L. Stanfield, "Maybe Bipartisanship Isn't Dead Yet," *National Journal*, August 21, 1993, 2090.

eligible for the grants]. I felt that they should say, 'If you don't have business lined up, you won't get any money.' " This position was criticized by organized labor as too prescriptive.[45]

A high-ranking official in the Department of Labor remembers that these concessions were generally easy to make; the department found managers to be natural allies in the school-to-work transition project. Both hoped that local companies would lead the effort to devise training programs, and both demanded a universal program rather than an effort for remedial populations. The School-to-Work Opportunities Partnership Act was enthusiastically endorsed by the NAB, the NAM, the Business Roundtable, and the Chamber of Commerce. As Rae Nelson of the Chamber of Commerce put it, "We feel we're being listened to; we're being consulted."[46] Coalition participants advertised their support to the broader business community because, as NAM's Phyllis Eisen explained, "The resistance to change in the business community is enormous. We have to move aggressively ahead."[47]

Ironically, the Department of Labor shared less common ground with its usual ally, labor. Unions feared that a federal initiative to improve the skills of the workforce could displace unionized workers and wanted to retain control over the training system. They viewed school-to-work as a potential threat to their own youth apprenticeship programs.[48]

After the School-to-Work Opportunities Partnership Act was passed, the Department of Labor organized an advisory business group called the School-to-Work National Employer Leadership Council (NELC). The council "proselytizes" to other firms about the benefits of in-house training, strives to raise corporate consciousness, and asks companies to make commitments to training slots. One person reported that "Reich talked to business and committed one person and tried to get them to commit another," and another felt that the NELC "is ideally suited to the goal of bringing in other companies, especially suppliers and customers." The council also represents a mechanism to solve the classic problem in training where one company hires workers already trained by another. As a vice president for human resources explained, "The main reason that we're in NELC is because other companies steal away our employees."[49]

[45] Interview with company representative, winter 1996.

[46] Interview with Labor Department official, January 3, 1996; "Business, Labor in 1994 Both See Areas for Cooperation with Clinton Administration" *BNA Daily Labor Report,* February 4, 1994.

[47] "Government Officials, Industry Urge . . . ," *BNA Daily Labor Report,* December 13, 1993.

[48] Interview with Labor Department official, January 3, 1996.

[49] Interview with Labor Department official, January 3, 1996; interviews with industry respondents, winter 1996.

The Workforce Security Act

Clinton's third training bill, the Workforce Security Act, consolidated programs for unemployment, training, and dislocated workers and created one-stop retraining/employment centers offering benefits, counseling, and training. Appropriations for fiscal year 1995 were to be $1.7 billion, with $1.5 billion going into a comprehensive training program and $250 million going into the development of the one-stop career centers. The original reemployment concept would radically redesign the entire training system, consolidating 150 separate training programs into a single streamlined process, but ultimately programs targeted for consolidation were much less numerous. The plan's creators recommended "profiling" early those unemployed persons who have difficulty getting new jobs due to outdated skills and quickly moving these persons into a training program, saving the government considerable money in unemployment benefits. Labor Department advocates also wanted to create a long-term training system with income supports for individuals undergoing fundamental change in their skills and to pay for this system by extending the 0.2 percent Federal Unemployment Tax Act (FUTA) tax that business had been paying for many years. Because the FUTA tax would not be phased out in any case, the administration reasoned, why not "set up a situation where you can make sure that it is extended for the right reason."[50]

Reemployment was introduced with great fanfare and with support from business and labor. As the Labor Department's Ann Lewis put it, "We had everyone there from Jeff Faux to John Breaux." The White House organized a large multisector business group that met on a regular basis throughout the legislative process. The Business Coalition for Education Reform reconstituted itself as the Business Coalition for Workforce Development and worked closely to shape the bill and to push for its passage. NAM president Jerry Jasinowski endorsed the broad goals of the Reemployment Act upon its release: "The general thrust of the Workforce Security Act is clearly a positive one. Without question, the U.S. needs a reemployment system to address current structural unemployment and position the U.S. to use its most valuable resources, its workers, to remain competitive."[51]

But the initial enthusiasm with which reemployment was greeted belied the contentious nature of aspects of the bill. Consolidation tends to alien-

---

[50] "DOL Strips Retraining Income Support from Proposed Version of Reemployment Act," *BNA Daily Labor Report,* March 4, 1994; interview with Labor Department official, January 3, 1996.

[51] Interview with Ann Lewis, January 3, 1996; "NAM Provides Feedback on Workforce Security Act," *Briefing* (NAM newsletter), February 7, 1994, 7.

ate congressional sponsors of existing programs. While many of the existing programs were entitlement programs, the new one-stop centers were to be financed with discretionary funds, and proponents of training were reluctant to give up the security of the entitlement structure for the sake of consolidation. Organized labor especially resisted the Reemployment Act's assault on existing programs and fought to keep separate the Trade Adjustment Assistance Program and to ensure adequate reemployment assistance for long-term training.[52] Labor objected to the original bill's proposal for a competitive bidding process to award the service-delivery contracts for the one-stop career centers, because it feared the proliferation of for-profit training agencies. (Ultimately the Department of Labor abandoned its competitive model.) Union leaders wanted the Reemployment Act to strengthen the 1988 Worker Adjustment and Retraining Notification Act (WARN), but business threatened that changes in WARN would "immediately break down the open debate on this bill currently taking place within the business community."[53] Labor Department insiders believed that organized labor was "constitutionally suspicious" of Doug Ross, the point man on the Reemployment Act, who came from the Democratic Leadership Council. One official explained: "The split between the New Democrats and Old Democrats . . . affected the Reemployment Act. The wholesale redesign of jobs training—empowering people to make decisions—all of this was an anathema to the labor movement. There was too much parochialism around individual training programs, so real reform was not palatable to labor."[54] The Reemployment Act was also hampered by the fact that the real constituents—those without work or whose jobs were threatened—had different interests from workers with well-paying union jobs. As one Labor Department official explained, the Reemployment Act was not a high priority for organized labor: "It was extremely hard to organize the base constituency. The real constituency was insecure workers. We can't communicate with an anxious working class. So we had to go to proxies—business and unions. It wasn't their highest priority. There was no pull from society. It was like trying to push spaghetti through a keyhole."[55]

The business community had its share of concerns and objections. Employers wanted a dominant role on the workforce investment boards

[52] Interview with Labor Department official, January 3, 1996; "Ways and Means Panel Hears Testimony on Reform of Extended Jobless Pay Program," *BNA Daily Labor Report,* March 9, 1994, A45.

[53] "Administration May Move Away from Promoting Competition among Providers of Job Training," *BNA Daily Labor Report,* June 9, 1994; WARN required companies with over one hundred employees to notify their workers in advance of a large layoff.

[54] Interview with Labor Department official, January 3, 1996.

[55] Interview with Labor Department official, January 4, 1996.

created by the legislation. Managers worried that the administration's proposal to extend unemployment benefits to individuals in training contained insufficient safeguards: individuals could stay on unemployment insurance longer and run the trust funds dry. NAB was sympathetic to the administration's desire to extend benefits during training and raised with coalition members ideas about reforming the unemployment system, but Chamber of Commerce and NAM participants were skeptical that their boards would consider changes in unemployment insurance deductions because these represented a predictable tax liability. A NAB staff person complained, "We have been pushing this debate to bring it into the twenty-first century, but NAM and the Chamber don't want to rock the boat." The administration ultimately abandoned the extended income support for dislocated workers.[56]

Some within the business community also worried about the financing of the proposal, although others believed that this was not a widespread concern because "the tax would never go away." NAB raised the issue of the FUTA tax in the coalition. The Business Roundtable and the representatives from the companies recognized that the tax would not be repealed in any case, so that it made sense to earmark it for training as long as there were written guarantees that if the trust fund's solvency were threatened, the FUTA tax would be reapplied to its original purpose. As one manager put it, "Since we're already paying it, we don't want to lose sleep over it. So there wasn't much big-business opposition. People tried to rustle people up on it, but big business was not that worried."[57]

The FUTA tax ran into trouble, however, from NFIB, the Chamber, and NAM. NAM's training advocates were quite sympathetic to extension of the tax, but were unable to secure the organization's endorsement because the tax fell under the jurisdiction of the NAM's tax committee. In testimony in the House, NAM "commended the Administration for recognizing the need for a more integrated approach" but urged Congress to undertake even greater consolidation of the various government training programs and to drop the 0.2 percent surcharge.[58] Because the reemployment tax was never reported out of committee, business never had to take a final stand on extending the FUTA tax.

Ultimately the bill died when the House Committee on Education and Labor failed to report it out of committee. According to a top congressional aide, "Ford didn't sign on, in part because of union concerns and

---

[56] Interview with industry representative, winter 1996; "DOL Strips Retraining Income."

[57] Interview with company representative, winter 1996.

[58] National Association of Manufacturers, "NAM Testifies on Reemployment Act," *Briefing,* June 20, 1994, 3.

in part because Ford just didn't like the bill. He thought that it smelled Republican."[59] Some also believed that the Reemployment Act fell victim to the broader transformations taking place in the political climate. The disagreements that developed over health reform care seemed to penetrate other spheres of public policy, and managers became less willing to take risks in training policy: the "bloodbath" at the Chamber of Commerce "had a chilling effect on every business representative in town." At the same time the administration expressed anger with large employers for their performance during the health debate.

> As the administration and business relations on health care deteriorated, it was harder to do reemployment. NAM wasn't invited when the president [signed the school-to-work initiative]. The administration said, "If you're not with us on this [health], you're not with us on anything." They thought that this was momentary discipline, but in the long term it lost a fruitful relationship.[60]

The Training Mandate

The story of Clinton and training policy is incomplete without reference to the 1.5 percent employer mandate for training, proposed by Clinton during his campaign for president as a mechanism for overcoming the obstacles to voluntary training within firms but dropped before the new president assumed office. The training mandate was part of the president's two-pronged approach for solving the economic ills of the nation: a $31 billion stimulus package for the short term and employment and training for skill development for the long term.[61]

Oddly, a Reagan Labor Department task force seriously considered an employment and training payroll tax similar to the one later endorsed by the Clinton administration. *Forbes* noted, "In the real world, unfortunately, it is hard for a major company, which usually already gives generous benefits, to oppose such legislation without appearing to be the worst kind of Scrooge."[62] George Bush proposed a training tax credit instead of the mandate.

Why did the president abandon the mandate so quickly? According to Rae Nelson of the Chamber of Commerce, the business community told Robert Reich that proposing the mandate "would be suicide." NAB's Kolberg remarked, "Although some firms thought that the economics were not a problem, the ideology worked against it—the idea of federal

---

[59] Interview with congressional staffer, winter 1996.
[60] Interview with industry representatives, winter 1996.
[61] Aaron Bernstein with Paul Magnusson, "How Much Good Will Training Do?" *Business Week*, February 22, 1993, 76.
[62] Novack and Banks, "Put Up the Price," 32.

bureaucrats getting involved." The administration feared that the business community would not go along with both health care and training mandates.[63]

NAB tried to sell a training tax credit to the administration and to the Ways and Means Committee, but found no interest in part because no provision had been made for offsetting revenue. After the training mandate was dropped, NAB and the Department of Labor worked on a voluntary training drive called "Investing in People" until the November 1994 election changed the political landscape in Washington. NAB members believed that small firms especially failed to grasp the need for training, and they hoped to enlighten their smaller brethren with testimonials from companies like MCI and Motorola who could demonstrate the payoffs from training. Others believed that this private training drive never "had legs" because it would not appeal to small business: "There is a natural constituency for this within big business—big business tends to be 'centrist, to the left,' while small business is conservative."[64]

Employment and Training Policy after the 1994 Election

After the 1994 election there was much consternation in the big-business community that the gains made in employment and training would be lost in the new conservative Republican climate. NAB's Kolberg was to warn, "I thought that this [the bipartisan initiatives passed in the early Clinton years] was the direction that we were going in, but now the populist Congress is starting to question these ideas. Populist Republicanism discards all of these arrangements, and we are back to the pure market again."[65] The Republican Right criticized the Clinton acts as excessively bureaucratic and intrusive, describing the National Skills Standards Board as a brave new government program and school-to-work as an attack on parents' control over their children's educational decisions. Groups such as the Heritage Foundation proposed shutting down the Department of Labor altogether, and to rewrite radically the labor laws of the land:

> Today's labor market conditions and labor-management relations have changed since most of America's major labor laws were passed. Workers are demanding more flexible hours, working conditions, and compensation packages than current laws' and regulations allow. It is time for Congress to reform the administration and enforcement of America's labor laws.[66]

[63] Interview with Rae Nelson, May 9, 1995; Geber, "Because It's Good for You," 17.

[64] Interviews with NAB representatives and with company representatives, 1995–96.

[65] Interview with Kolberg, April 19, 1995.

[66] Mark Wilson and Rebecca Lukens, "How to Close Down the Department of Labor," *Heritage Foundation Reports,* October 19, 1995, 1.

This frightened big business, which wanted to preserve the bipartisan gains of the Bush and Clinton efforts. One participant expressed amazement at the rhetoric of the Christian Right's attack on the initiatives: "Workforce development is a capitalist plot? It's frightening. In the area of school-to-work there is a tremendous mischaracterization. They don't understand that we are trying to give kids more choices rather than less."[67]

But congressional Republicans ultimately backed away from this rhetoric, and training programs fared somewhat better than other social policies, in part due to support from large employers. Education and training policies were not immune from the Republicans' knife: the new majority cut funding for training enormously and sought to zero out the Goals 2000 program. But the training initiatives were at least somewhat protected by the long-term consensus surrounding the policy debate and by the protests of large employers.

The main thrust of the Republican agenda was to consolidate employment and training programs and to devolve control over these programs to the states. The House Consolidated and Reformed Education, Employment, and Rehabilitation Systems (CAREERS) Act merged programs into four block grants tied to target groups (such as youth development) and set up mandatory local workforce development boards. In a concession to the far Right the House bill allowed states to reject the skill standards created by Goals 2000. The Senate version had one appropriation, but monies were to be functionally earmarked: 25 percent for one-stop service delivery centers, 25 percent for education activities, and 50 percent for state discretionary use. Funds for school-to-work partnerships would come out of the discretionary funds. The mandatory local workforce development boards were thrown out in committee in the Senate.[68]

The GOP plan shared many features with the Clinton's proposed Reemployment Act, but Republicans went much farther: where the administration would consolidate six programs, both the House and Senate Republican plans would consolidate over ninety. To some extent the GOP's broader consolidation reflected governors' greater power in the new political atmosphere, but consolidation also fit with the larger aims of the new majority. As one aide put it, "The moving force on the act was not the

---

[67] Interview with business participant, May 1996.

[68] "Start Getting Ready for Workforce Block Grants Now," *Educating for Employment,* December 1995; "Senate Labor and Human Resources Committee Summary of Major Provisions Work Force Development Act of 1995, *BNA Daily Labor Report,* June 15, 1995. The workforce development boards split Republicans and drew endorsements from a strange coalition of liberal and conservative interests. House Republicans supported the local boards because congressional districts are at the local level and because the boards represent further devolution of power downward. Edward Kennedy and other Democrats believed that the boards created an institutional structure for an opportunity for dialogue. Business favored the local boards because they gave employers majority control.

explicit goal of consolidation, but rather the more implicit goal of passing power to the states."[69]

Despite the general agreement on consolidation (with considerable corporate support), the two parties differed over several provisions, with large employers often sympathetic to the Democratic positions. First, the Republicans sought to greatly reduce training expenditures: proposed financing for fiscal year 1996 in the House and Senate bills was as much as 45 percent lower than it would have been under the status quo. Phil Gramm wanted to cut the Labor Department's Employment and Training Administration by 75 percent, but ultimately it decreased by a third. Large employers were quite concerned about the vast cuts in spending levels, protesting, "It is unrealistic to assume that states and localities could successfully implement the delivery systems anticipated in pending legislation if the recommended fiscal year 1996 levels—well below those recommended in reform legislation—are finally approved."[70] Yet the employers did little to prevent spending reductions because they focused their attention on the programmatic rather than appropriations committees in Congress.[71]

Second, Democrats had problems with the block grant approach because many of the current training programs were entitlements (or guarantees to certain individuals); this status would be forfeited by consolidation into block grants. Those sympathetic to labor resisted consolidating programs because they did not want these programs to lose their entitlement status. Others worried that new, innovative programs would be lost in the block grants. For example, one administration official worried that the House Republican's plan to lump school-to-work programs in with other programs would fold the recent innovation into the less effective vocational-education program.

> From a public management point of view, vocational education had no legitimacy. The business community was quite skeptical. You have huge problems with entrenchment. Some voc ed programs are fancy names for dry cleaning. So from a public management point of view, the school-to-work program was a catalyst to turn resources over to new people so that the same old people no longer control the dollars.[72]

Business managers agreed that the block grant consolidation could draw funds away from the school-to-work program. The Business Roundtable

[69] Interview with congressional aide, February 1996.

[70] Deborah Billings, "Training Reform High Priority on Congressional Labor Agenda, *BNA Daily Labor Report,* January 5, 1996.

[71] Interview with industry representative, winter 1996.

[72] Interview with Labor Department official, spring 1996.

circulated a set of principles that argued for retaining school-to-work as a separate program. Siemens circulated flow charts to demonstrate to other firms that youths continued to have choice in school-to-work programs. As one manager explained:

> All agree that flexibility is a good thing—so in theory the block grants seem like a good idea. But people also feel mixed about them. . . . Now many in the big-business community are concerned that the Republicans will fold school-to-work money in with the block grants. They are concerned that it will get lost in the process.[73]

Third, both Democrats and the employers' coalition objected to the inclusion of the Senate Workforce Development Act in the welfare reform bill. Senator Bob Dole wanted to merge workforce development with welfare because he lacked a training component in the welfare bill. The Democrats and the business community strongly objected to the linking. The administration warned that including training in welfare could greatly cut the allocation of funds for upgrading the skills of workers. Reich worried that under the Republican system, the states could use training money "for almost anything related to jobs, including welfare, but also possibly for efforts to attract companies and jobs from other states."[74]

Business managers agreed that attaching workforce development to welfare reform could target training to welfare recipients and neglect the larger aims of the legislation. Anthony Carnevale of the Committee for Economic Development, summed it up succinctly: putting training in welfare would result in a "great sucking sound" as funds earmarked for training fled to other purposes. NAB's Tom Lindsley explained:

> Welfare pushed people off the rolls without training. So NAB was concerned that the governors, recognizing the huge expanse of welfare, would just use training as a tool to get welfare off the rolls and would make training into a residual program. It could have the effect of undermining completely the Workforce Development Act and shoving resources toward just serving the welfare program.[75]

The National Alliance of Business wrote letters and lobbied, and the Democrats threatened to filibuster if workforce development remained

---

[73] In its "Principles for Reform of Job Training Programs," the Business Roundtable referred to its 1993 statement, "Workforce Training and Development for U.S. Competitiveness," August 1993, obtained from industry sources; interview with company representative, May 1996.

[74] Interview with Labor Department official, spring 1996.

[75] Deborah Billings, "Merger of Job Training, Welfare Reform Destroys Political Consensus in Senate," *BNA Daily Labor Report,* September 13, 1995; interview with Tom Lindsley, February 1996.

in the welfare bill. Dole ultimately agreed to take training out of the welfare bill.

Finally, the Republican efforts to eliminate Goals 2000 surprised many of the business managers that had worked for passage of the National Skills Standards Board. President Clinton invited a group of CEOs to the White House in 1995 to discuss the fate of Goals 2000 and began the meeting by asking whether the executives continued to believe in the legislation. When reassured on this point, the president asked those present to speak out on Goals 2000. The Coalition for Workforce Development "took a very strong position on Goals from beginning to end" and organized company letters from the states to members of the Appropriations Committee. The Business Roundtable's only appropriations (as opposed to programmatic) recommendation was that Goals 2000 be funded. Yet some business participants believed that the corporate response was more muted than earlier commitment to the Goals 2000 objectives might have implied, due to the "cultural protests of the far right." As one manager put it, "You can imagine that many business people didn't want to get involved, didn't want to touch it."[76]

Business managers also were active at the state level in meeting with officials to persuade them to participate in the Goals 2000 program. For instance, when Governor Pete Wilson vowed not to accept Goals 2000 funding, the businesses protested loudly until Wilson changed his mind. A NAB officer remembers consulting with a Texas commission to reevaluate Goals 2000: "At the beginning I listened to nutty language for a couple of hours and then educated them about Goals. Over the next six months the group went from highly conservative to endorsing the Goals legislation."[77]

Conclusion

The employment and training domain represents big business at its most proactive. Core supporters adopted the high-performance workplace view of training and struggled to promulgate this view throughout the wider business community. Corporate advocates redefined training as an issue of growth rather than an issue of income maintenance. In part due to the absence of a small-business countermobilization against training, big business was able to generate broad corporate support

---

[76] Interview with industry participants, winter 1996.

[77] Interview with Clinton administration official, July 1996; interview with industry representative, May 6, 1997.

for employment and training policy unheard of in other areas of human capital investment.

This broad support reflected a high degree of corporate policy capacity in the training area. Lyndon Johnson created the National Alliance of Business to develop business support for hiring the hardcore unemployed and in the process established the institutional groundwork for ongoing public-private partnership in training initiatives. Because business and government have cooperated for some time, many of the ideological obstacles have been overcome. In the domain of health care policy, no business group emerged as leader to organize other associations in support of a legislative program. In training policy, however, the National Alliance of Business took charge of the business campaign, helping employers to reach consensus among themselves, conveying corporate concerns to political leaders, bringing business into negotiations over policy at an early stage, and cementing corporate allegiance to the subsequent legislative agenda.

This relatively high degree of corporate organization encouraged bipartisan cooperation on training bills. In spheres where business is relatively better organized, it is much easier for government officials to pursue a politics of consensus. At the same time this bipartisan cooperation made it easier for business to remain focused on broad concerns.

But ultimately policy advocates concluded that this centrist politics of consensus had mixed results. The good news for these advocates was that something actually happened: business and labor, Democrats and Republicans, were able to find common ground and move forward. Setbacks in bills like Goals 2000 largely resulted from opposition by labor rather than by business.[78] Business managers joined with governors to act as peacemakers, to ward off conservative concerns of the Right and to seek common ground between the Right and the Left. Thus as Jennings was to argue, the great irony of Goals 2000 was that a system of national standards for education was effectively established by the center and treated with a fair amount of skepticism by the Left, due, in large part, to intragovernment turf wars.[79] After the 1994 election the political climate changed, and retrenchment and devolution were the operative sentiments in Washington. Business tried to protect the bipartisan gains in employment and training policy and to some extent succeeded. Even in this new highly political climate, employment and training policy was legislated with a greater spirit of bipartisanship than seen in other areas.

---

[78] The U.S. labor movement has historically focused on the needs of those already working over the needs of the unemployed and struggled to protect its own turf in the training legislative debates.

[79] Jennings, *National Issues in Education*.

But it is also important not to overstate business activism in this area. Despite the relative unity among various corporations and the sympathy with which they regarded government initiatives to promote training, most of the large-employer associations and their participating companies did not wage a full-fledged lobbying campaign. Even at its most interventionist, big business lacks the mobilization capacities of small business. Although the National Alliance of Business spent considerable time persuading legislators, other groups such as the Business Roundtable felt more comfortable serving an education function. Rather than supporting specific bills, the Roundtable adopted principles, to which it referred when asked about positions. As one Roundtable insider put it, "The Business Roundtable has other, more important issues. Besides, these companies don't use federal programs, but they do have ideas."

Policy advocates were also frustrated because a politics of bipartisan and business cooperation meant that the comprehensive aspects of the president's training vision were abandoned. The recent acts were limited in scope and resources. Business organization could not eradicate fears of labor power and taxes that permeate corporate consciousness. The considerable business support for training served to delimit the options for training at the same time it pushed forward its broad agenda. Thus an official in the Department of Labor reflected,

> Business support for some of the training activity has been useful, but when you look at the cuts in appropriations, cutting disabled workers [funds] by 30 percent, cutting youth employment [monies], et cetera, business support isn't potent enough to protect these programs. There was a 40 percent cut in the House Appropriations Committee for job training in 1996—all jobs training programs. This is a big cut. Nobody should be taking credit for savings in any of these programs.[80]

---

[80] Interview with Labor Department official, January 4, 1996.

SEVEN

AN AFFAIR TO REMEMBER:

SMALL BUSINESS AND THE REPUBLICAN PARTY

AGAINST FAMILY LEAVE

OUR STORY so far has concentrated on the corporate supporters of human capital investment policies and how organizational limits have diminished their expressed political support for legislative initiatives. Yet the tale of business reaction to these policies is incomplete without attention to the opposition. The organizational weaknesses of large-firm supporters of policies for human capital investment become even more apparent when viewed in contrast to the political strengths of small-business associations, the core opponents of these policies. Although small employers fall across a wide ideological spectrum, the major associations representing them have a definite conservative slant. The members of the small-business lobby (such as the National Federation of Independent Business, the National Association of Wholesaler-Distributors, the National Restaurant Association, and the National Retail Federation) ardently desire to cut back the welfare state and to block new government initiatives.

This chapter has two purposes. First, it completes our case comparisons with a look at business involvement in work-family policy, specifically in the Family and Medical Leave Act (FMLA). The limits to corporate policy capacity that contributed to the demise of large-employer support for health reform were even more pronounced in the Family and Medical Leave Act. There is nearly universal agreement that the health reform plan was deeply flawed, and one can understand managers' misgivings about the product. In comparison, family leave should have been an easier sell to many managers, as it was standard operating procedure in most large firms and backed by over 80 percent of Americans. Yet large employers never made it to the legislative table.

Second, the chapter uses the cases of the FMLA and the Republican's Medicare reform proposal to illustrate the superior lobbying faculty of small business. Major small-business groups have struggled to overcome a least-common-denominator politics with institutional rules to facilitate political action. The most important innovation has been the use of single-issue coalitions, which may include some large companies but are typically organized by one of the small-business associations. These coalitions have fortified commitment to their collective goals with an important decision rule: members must promise to back the entire legislative package and not to lobby against any provisions. For example, the Republican Contract's Thursday Group leadership asked group members to take a "blood oath" to back the contract in its entirety in exchange for action on their concerns.[1]

Small-business political power was deeply influential in keeping the Family and Medical Leave Act off the legislative books for many years. Although Clinton's veto pen stopped Medicare reform, the major small-business groups also gave considerable political support to the Republican Right after the 1994 election. These groups' organizational strength combined with their general aversion to expanded social spending in any form have made it much more difficult for corporate supporters to realize their agenda in human capital investment.

The Family and Medical Leave Act

The Family and Medical Leave Act was signed into law in 1993, but only after enduring seven years of legislative failure and two presidential vetoes. As Senator Christopher Dodd pointed out, the United States joined only South Africa among industrialized nations in failing to mandate unpaid family leave. By 1989, 93 percent of Americans believed that individuals should have a right to take a leave to care for a newborn or sick parent without the threat of losing their jobs.[2] The delay in enactment is rather astounding given the high level of public support and the ubiquitous presence of leaves in the industrialized world; small-business groups may take full credit for the procrastination.

Building on the Private Sector's Legacies

The final law mandated that companies with over fifty workers provide twelve weeks of unpaid leave to new parents and continue to provide health benefits during that period. The employee must have worked at the company for at least twenty-five hours a week for the past year. Initially the bill applied to all firms with over fifteen employees, but stringent opposition from the small-business community pushed up the cut-off

---

[1] Interview with Dirk Van Dongen, September 14, 1995.
[2] "Selected Statements on the Family and Medical Leave Act Delivered February 2, 1989, to the Senate Labor Subcommittee on Children, Family, and Alcoholism," *BNA Daily*

point. Some were alarmed that "reportedly 'universal' standards [were] protecting a shrinking universe of American workers."[3]

The authors of the initiative consciously sought to pattern the public regulation after practices in private firms. Supporters pointed out that the legislation did little to change the status quo because it built on the private sector's programs, ratifying what large firms were already doing and exempting small employers. The Families and Work Institute found that although 14 percent of firms had preexisting policies as extensive as the federal law, only 9 percent found implementing the leave policy to be difficult and only 6 percent cut health benefits in response to the act. In fact working mothers' behaviors changed very little before and after the federal legislation: 78 percent took leaves before enactment, and after 78 percent took leaves after.[4]

Democrats were the major proponents of family leave, in part because the party hoped to use issues like child care and family leave to end the Reagan regime and to erode the Right's claim to speak for traditional family values. In addition, the party sought to draw the issue as an appeal to the middle class, increasingly composed of two-career families.[5]

Republican critics and their small-business allies struggled to reframe the policy as a new entitlement; thus a Chamber of Commerce–led coalition argued, "Although parental and disability leaves are excellent employee benefits, Congress should not dictate benefits. Doing so is contrary to the voluntary, flexible and comprehensive benefits system that the private sector has developed." Michael Rousch at the NFIB worried that the family leave act set a precedent for mandates and promised to be a first step down a slippery slope toward an expanded welfare state.[6] Opponents also feared that the requirement for unpaid leaves would become the proverbial camel's nose under the tent, leading to mandatory paid leaves. Thus the Chamber's Virginia Lamp was to caution, "Mandating unpaid leave is only the first step; clearly, proponents seek to mandate paid leave."[7]

Small business predicted dire economic impacts to companies from the high costs of hiring replacement workers. The Chamber of Commerce originally estimated that employers would spend an extra $16.2 billion a

Labor Report, February 3, 1989, E1; David Anderson, "Survey: Government, Business Should Take on Family Issues," *BC Cycle,* June 20, 1989.

[3] Paul Starobin, "Small Talk," *National Journal,* March 6, 1993, 554.

[4] James Bond et al., *Beyond the Parental Leave Debate* (Watertown, N.Y.: Families and Work Institute, 1991), ii–viii.

[5] Julie Kosterlitz, "Family Fights," *National Journal,* June 2, 1990, 1333.

[6] "Business' Battle over Parental Leave," *Nation's Business,* August 1986, 12; Verespej, "Clinton's First Legislative Child," 57.

[7] William H. Miller, "Employee Benefits," *Industry Week,* January 12, 1987, 48.

year on labor costs should leave be mandated and then revised this figure to $2.6 billion. The General Accounting Office found even this latter calculation inflated, arguing that the Chamber of Commerce overstated the number of individuals who used the leave, the number who would be replaced, and the cost of hiring replacements; the General Accounting Office figured the mandate's cost at $147 million.[8] The $2.6 billion figure prompted David Blackenhorn of the Institute for American Values to tell a House committee that "the Chamber uses a statistic like a drunk uses a lamppost, more for support than illumination."[9]

Small-business opponents also argued that the new benefit would constrict the creation of jobs and hurt female workers by motivating employers to discriminate against women in hiring, replace other goodies in the "employee benefits 'pie,' " and reduce the flexibility with which managers and workers could negotiate compensation packages.[10]

Policy Expertise and Business Organization

Although many large companies have developed work-family policies (see chapter 4), private-sector experts within family-friendly firms had practically no involvement with the national debate on family leave. Private experts in the work-family domain have a much more tenuous position within the firm than health and training experts located in human-resource departments, because they were usually brought in by CEOs and put into newly created special departments. Other human-resource managers were often hostile because they viewed work-family issues as competing claims for scarce resources. Because government affairs representatives had much closer connections to the traditional human-resource departments, these Washington representatives were more likely to engage the issues advocated by these departments. At the same time the work-family issue lacks a policy-level business group in which managers can contemplate public policies.

During the legislative battle over family leave, large employers also feared offending the small-business community. The Women's Legal Defense Fund (WLDF) tried to bring corporate leaders who supported private-sector leave policies into their coalition, but were largely unsuccess-

[8] Statement of William J. Gainer, U.S. General Accounting Office, "Statements on Parental Leave Act (S 249) before Senate Labor Subcommittee on Children, Families, Drugs and Alcoholism," *BNA Daily Labor Report,* April 24, 1987, D1.

[9] He argued that 60 percent of the Chamber's estimated costs came from employment agency fees, while firms normally hire temporary workers in more informal ways. Fern Schumer Chapman, "Health," *Washington Post,* September 22, 1987, Z12.

[10] Testimony by Carol Ball, U.S. Chamber of Commerce, "Selected Statements on the Family and Medical Leave Act Delivered Feb. 2, 1989, to the Senate Labor Subcommittee on Children, Family, and Alcoholism," *BNA Daily Labor Report,* February 3, 1989, E1.

ful. The organization sent letters to the CEOs that headed a *Working Women*'s list of best companies. The overwhelming response to this exercise was, "We agree with you, but we can't alienate our colleagues."[11]

There were a few exceptions to this negative showing. The National Federation of Business and Professional Women's Clubs, not surprisingly, was a strong proponent of the legislation. Early on the National Association of Women Business Owners testified in favor of family leave, but was unable to back the final policy, because the group consisted primarily of small firms that considered twelve-week leaves beyond their capacity. Selected members of the Conference Board, which had done considerable work on company family leave policy, also showed interest in the bill, but the organization did not offer formal support. Toward the end of the policy battle the WLDF organized a small group called the Business Leaders for the FMLA, and the Business for Social Responsibility endorsed the policy as well.[12]

The Small-Business Mobilization against Family Leave

Small business made fighting family leave a cause celebre for seven years, with the U.S. Chamber of Commerce initially leading the attack. This and other "women's" issues such as affirmative action and comparable worth were so central to the Chamber that Virginia Lamp was hired as a lobbyist on the issue, partly on gender grounds. Chamber organized fifty associations and companies to oppose family leave.[13]

But in 1987 others in the antileave coalition began to resent the Chamber's high visibility and believed that it was stealing the spotlight. John Motley of the National Federation of Independent Business complained, "A number of us got frustrated over that type of positioning by the chamber—insisting that their name be attached to every issue and insisting that they have to run the show." Mary Tavenner of the National Association of Wholesaler-Distributors (NAW) added that coalitions "work best when everyone in the group has an equal say. The majority should always rule, like any democracy." Participants also believed that their association with the Chamber could tarnish their ability to influence moderate Democrats. Mary Tavenner remembers visiting Jim Cooper (D-Tenn.) to discuss the family leave bill. Cooper explained that he would not talk to her if she was part of the Chamber group.[14]

---

[11] Interview with Donna Lenhoff, March 31, 1995.

[12] Interview with Donna Lenhoff, March 31, 1995.

[13] Mike Adlin, "Virginia B. Lamp: A Chamber Lobbyist Battles a 'Precedent,' " *National Journal,* August 30, 1986, 2080; Cindy Skrzycki and Frank Swoboda, "Child Care Issue Emerges as Focus of Legislative Efforts," *Washington Post,* February 8, 1988, A1.

[14] Victor, "Step Under My Umbrella," 1063–67; interview with Mary Tavenner, formerly National Association of Wholesaler-Distributors, July 1996.

The discontented, some fifty-eight companies and groups, contributed $175 each to form a new coalition, the Concerned Alliance of Responsible Employers (CARE). Mary Tavenner of the National Association of Wholesaler-Distributors, who had worked on the TRAC coalition, took the lead in organizing CARE after the TRAC model. But Tavenner and others wanted all members to feel a sense of "ownership" to increase their connection to the process; therefore, they tried to avoid domination by any one group by rotating the hosting of meetings. The coalition met on a weekly basis (unlike the Chamber coalition that met when it was summoned) to discuss new information, to tally congressional positions, and to distribute assignments, but its structure was looser than the Chamber's. Each association was expected to organize its own grassroots lobbying.[15]

Both the Chamber coalition and CARE fought to defeat family leave with the usual arsenal of coalition strategies: spin control, Mailgrams, and media events. Faced with formidable public enthusiasm for family leaves, the small employers sought to put a less advantageous spin on the issue. CARE conducted its own public-opinion poll showing that while many Americans supported family leaves, they remained ambivalent about mandating them. In addition, the organization cited a 1989 *Washington Post*/ABC poll that found leave not to be a high-priority issue. Small-business managers also picked up Phyllis Schlafly's (Eagle Forum) refrain that family leave was a "yuppie" issue.[16]

Small-business opponents did a series of massive direct mail campaigns urging members to contact legislators each time the bill seemed to progress. In the fall of 1987 CARE geared up for a major offensive, and the family leave bill lost legislative sponsors. CARE's Mary Tavenner quipped, "We've been all over those guys like a cheap suit." The bill got stuck in the House Education and Labor Committee until the members exempted firms with less than fifty workers; the bill then made it out of committee, but small business continued to oppose the measure.[17]

In August 1988 the Chamber urged members to "blitz" legislators with Mailgrams and phone calls. By October the Senate had killed the family leave bill, with few moderate Republicans defecting from their party's majority. Christopher Dodd (D-Conn.) blamed business lobbying for the

---

[15] Interview with Mary Tavenner, July 1996.

[16] Respondents were asked to choose whether the federal government should mandate fringe benefits or allow employers and employees flexibility in choosing benefits. "American Public Prefers Flexibility to Federal Mandates According to the Society for Human Resource Management," *PR Newswire*, February 28, 1991; "Sen. Cochran Will Lead Opposition to Mandated Parental Leave," *PR Newswire*, July 25, 1988.

[17] Matlack, "Mobilizing a Multitude," 2592.

defeat, angrily adding that "groups that support parental leave or child care don't have any political action committee money."[18]

The 1988 election, however, expanded the contested terrain as George Bush began to play both sides in the leave battle. Worried that Michael Dukakis would seize control of the family issue and capture the female vote, candidate Bush promised to diverge from Reaganomics with a kinder, gentler approach to public policy. At a meeting of Illinois Republican women he even seemed to lean toward mandated leave by stating, "We need to assure that women don't have to worry about getting their jobs back after having a child or caring for a child during a serious illness. That is what I mean when I talk about a gentler nation." This campaign strategy prompted Linda Dorian of the National Federation of Business and Professional Women to comment, "We think the Bush campaign is showing some very good signs. There is room for some productive dialogue on this."[19] Business became skittish about the nominee's buying into the Democratic terms of the debate, and CARE's Mary Tavenner warned, "To keep from being on the defensive, Vice President Bush will have to come up with ammunition to combat Democratic proposals, and the sooner the better."[20]

In May 1990, after both houses had passed the bill, the struggle for the heart and soul of George Bush intensified. Moderate Republicans tried to prevent the president's veto, pointing out that the action was inconsistent with the "family values" theme of the party. Representative Marge Roukema (R-N.J.) went so far as to call the bill "a defining issue for the Republican Party" and "an economic necessity" for a majority of American workers. Representative Bill Green quoted the 1988 Republican Party platform in his defense of family leave.[21]

Meanwhile, enemies of the legislation pumped up the volume. During the Small Business Administration's Small Business Week, employers stormed Washington and the White House to make their case against mandated leave. John Sununu, the White House chief of staff, was sympathetic to their position and promised a presidential veto. Bush himself continued to seem deeply ambivalent. When asked at a press conference

[18] Pamela Brogan and Judy Sarasohn, "Parent's Leave May Hinge on Dukakis," *Legal Times,* August 29, 1988, 8; Joyce Barrett, "Democrats Claim 'Pro-family' Political Victory,' *American Metal Market,* October 12, 1988, 7.

[19] Margaret Wolf Freivogel, "Supporters of Bill on Family Leave Try to Head Off Veto," *St. Louis Post-Dispatch,* June 16, 1990, 1B; "Women's Groups Begin Push for Parental Leave Measure," *New York Times,* September 8, 1988, 22.

[20] Joani Nelson-Horchler, "The Politics of Child Care: What Business Can Expect from Bush, 'Duke,' " *Industry Week,* July 18, 1988, 20.

[21] William Eaton, "Bush Warned by GOP Leave-Bill Backers," *Los Angeles Times,* May 9, 1990, 18.

whether he would veto the bill, the president could not get the answer out, but press secretary Marlin Fitzwater immediately answered in the affirmative.[22]

In the end game the big umbrella associations moved into a position of neutrality. After Clinton's election the Chamber decided to abstain from the Family and Medical Leave Act. The Chamber's chair for labor relations explained that the bill was less threatening than other labor initiatives: "We did not support it, but we decided that because over 70 per cent of our members give [leave] and because there is a Democrat in the White House who will sign it, we could not develop a veto strategy. We also had to realize that as bad as family leave is, it is not going to kill American industry." NAM also abandoned its oppositional stance and concentrated on ensuring that employers and employees together negotiated changes in the work schedule. The neutrality game infuriated critics to the right. Grover Norquist, president of Americans for Tax Reform, colorfully denounced the Chamber's decision to sit out the battle.

> When you don't fight and stake out a position against it, you let the other side have a victory at no cost. It doesn't work for high school girls and it doesn't work for trade associations: You don't get respect by giving in a few times every once in a while. That doesn't make you reasonable; it makes you easy to have, and it makes you had. It doesn't get you invited to the prom. The problem with pragmatism is that it doesn't work.[23]

Family leave was ultimately signed into law, but only after immense effort and only with the arrival of a Democratic president. Even its opponents recognized that their opposition was somewhat overdrawn: at one point Chamber lobbyist remarked, "This is almost an issue whose time has come and gone."[24]

Rewriting Medicare

Small-business group mobilization jumped to new levels after conservative Republicans seized the House leadership in 1994. Giddy from their health reform victory and desiring regulatory transformation on the order of the New Deal, the Republicans promised to pass their Contract with America in the first one hundred days. A strategy to mobilize business

---

[22] Jane Applegate, "Small Businesses Gain New Clout in Washington," *Los Angeles Times,* May 10, 1990, 1; Freivogel, "Supporters of Bill," 1B.

[23] Victor, "Deal Us In," 805.

[24] Karl Vick, "The Principle behind the Family Leave Bill," *St. Petersburg Times,* May 9, 1990, 7A.

was central to the Republican efforts to pass the Contract with America; the small-business groups that delivered tax reform, warded off family leave for many years, and nixed health reform were the House Republicans' core activists. The Monday morning meetings between the House Republicans and small business to defeat Clinton's health plan were moved to Thursday, but otherwise business continued as usual.

The Medicare Reform Proposal

Restructuring Medicare was an important item in the Contract for revenue reasons. Medical insolvency is an old story, but many analysts agreed that the system needed to be restructured.[25] Although as an entitlement Medicare is usually off-limits to deficit reduction, the Republicans proposed to cut $270 billion by reducing Medicare spending by 14 percent in seven years. The Republicans would glean these savings by doubling Medicare premiums from the current rate of $46.10 to $87.60 by 2002 and by moving recipients into managed-care systems. Originally the Republicans had planned to pressure the elderly into managed care with rebates for lower-cost plans, but they switched to offering benefits to managed-care patients that fee-for-service systems do not cover.[26]

Critics believed that behind the Republican desire to "save" Medicare were broad goals to restructure social provision in the area of health care and to reduce the size of government. First, many believed that the Republican proposal was designed less to save Medicare than to reduce overall government spending and to pay for huge tax cuts. The *New York Times* charged that the $270 billion number was chosen because that much was needed to balance the budget by 2002 and to cut taxes by $245 billion after trimming other government programs.[27]

Second, some believed that the Republicans were trying to challenge the social right to health care for elderly and for the poor. Judy Feder argued in the *Washington Post* that the proposed caps on Medicare spending would change the program from one offering a defined benefit (which promises to pay beneficiaries' health care premium every month) to one offering a defined contribution (in which beneficiaries would be given a dollar limit for premiums but would have to come up with the remainder themselves). The obvious advantage of the second approach for govern-

[25] Henry Aaron and Robert Reichauer, "The Medicare Reform Debate," *Health Affairs* 14, no. 4 (1995): 8–30.

[26] Robin Toner and Robert Pear, "Medicare, Turning 30, Won't Be What It Was," *New York Times,* July 23, 1995, A1, 24; "Medicare Plan by G.O.P. Has No H.M.O. Mandate," *New York Times,* September 15, 1995, A32.

[27] David Rosenbaum, "Past All the Talk, Some True Goals," *New York Times,* October 20, 1995, A26.

ment payers is that public funds would no longer have to cover future increases.[28] The Republicans wanted to include Medicaid in a broad block grant to the states, thus ending the entitled right of the poor to medical assistance.

Third, the Republicans wanted to end Medicare as a universal financing scheme for elderly health insurance, by allowing recipients to buy into private HMO and provider service network plans or to set up medical savings accounts (MSAs). Critics charged that medical savings accounts would fracture the pool of Medicare patients, giving healthy patients incentives to opt out and driving up costs for others.[29]

The Congressional Budget Office (CBO) was skeptical about privatization, estimating that only 21 percent of Medicare recipients would be in HMOs by 2002, as opposed to 14 percent currently. It figured that the Republican bill would mainly save money by increasing costs to the beneficiaries (saving $71 billion out of $270) and by decreasing reimbursements to providers (saving $152 billion out of $270). CBO also blasted medical savings accounts, predicting that they would augment total Medicare costs by $2.3 billion over seven years, rather than cutting costs.[30]

Large Employers and Medicare Reform

Large employers were quite concerned about the general thrust of the proposed Medicare changes, but did little to influence the legislative course beyond damage control. Large corporate purchasers' largest objection was to a program (as yet voluntary) for keeping employees in private health plans. As the Business Roundtable put it, the government had an obligation to cover Medicare recipients and should not transfer this responsibility to business. Large employers disliked the proposal to increase the age of Medicare eligibility; to this end the Corporate Health Care Coalition attacked the Republican plan.[31] Some managers also feared that the radical Right would try to slowly phase out the employer-

---

[28] The leadership moved away from an explicit endorsement of a defined contribution system, but Feder and others argued that the cap pushed the program in that direction. Judith Feder, "Double Whammy for the Elderly," *Washington Post*, December 20, 1995, A25.

[29] Sharon McIlrath, "Can MSAs Work for Medicare?" *American Medical News*, August 21, 1995, 1.

[30] Robert Pear, "For Elderly, Bill Promises Entry into a Market of Shifting Forces," *New York Times*, October 20, 1995, A1, 17; Robert Pear, "Senate G.O.P. Plan for Medicare Uses Benefit Cutbacks," *New York Times*, September 28, 1995, A1, B10.

[31] Sharon McIlrath, "GOP Health Plan Blitz," *American Medical News*, October 9, 1995, 1; Robert Pear, "Retirees' Group Attacks G.O.P. Health Plan," *New York Times*, October 6, 1995, A22. The CHCC ultimately grudgingly accepted the plan because it favored the market restructuring aspects.

based system altogether and to turn health care back to individual responsibility. In addition, big-business managers felt threatened by the broad Republican goal of turning policy back to the states, because these efforts might ultimately threaten the ERISA preemption. A representative of a large food products firm explained, "Gingrich is scary to business on many fronts, especially the ERISA issue. We'd hate to be at the mercy of fifty different bodies."[32]

Large employers had been alarmed when the Clinton administration proposed cutting Medicare to pay for expanded access, and they continued to worry that the Republicans wanted Medicare reductions to balance the budget (and pay for the tax cut). Large employers worried that the Medicare cuts would result in greater cost-shifting by hospitals to private payers. Many noted that the Republican plan had no incentives to move beneficiaries into more cost-efficient plans from fee-for-service arrangements. Thus the benefits manager for a large food manufacturing company observed, "The Contract with America's attempts to cut Medicare are cost shifting back to the business community."[33] Business managers also worried that the Republican's proposal to turn Medicaid into a block grant would result in greater cost shifting to private employers, as *Business and Health* warned.

> To the extent that states have been able to control Medicaid spending, they have done so by sharply limiting payments to providers. . . . And guess who makes up the difference? Employers and private insurers. This Medicaid cost shift has been estimated to add between 5 and 10 percent to the cost of health care for private payers. With less money from the federal government under a block grant program, the pressure to ratchet down payments to providers will be even greater. . . . The business community has a strong vested interest in seeing that the Medicaid program gets overhauled carefully. One way or another, it ends up paying the bills.[34]

These concerns about Medicare were consistent with other corporate concerns about the Republican Contract. Many managers worried about the plan to devolve decision making to the states, because multistate employers could encounter a multitude of social and environmental regulations. Business managers were much more interested in reducing the budget deficit than in tax cuts; for instance, a Chamber of Commerce survey found its members ranking tax issues twelfth, fourteenth, and fifteenth out of twenty on a list of priorities.[35] Many large manufac-

---

[32] Interviews with industry representatives, May 10, 1995.
[33] Interviews with company representatives, May 1995.
[34] Steven Findlay, "Block Grants for Sale," *Business and Health* 13, no. 8 (1995): 55.
[35] "Gingrich's Plan Sounds Fishy," 24; Gleckman, Dunham, and Melcher, "GOP's Tax Cuts Falling."

turers wanted to retain Commerce Department programs to encourage exports and subsidies for research and development. Corporate welfare presented another area of conflict between large business and the Republican Right. One manager fretted that "the whole corporate welfare debate showed, first, the power of small business and, second, the lack of fear of big business."[36]

As in the battles over the Health Security Act, large employers' voices were muted. Some business managers blamed the Republicans, complaining that the party was uninterested in their input. A representative of a big midwestern office supplies company remembered working to convince the Republicans that "business wasn't as bad as they thought." Another recalled,

> I was very surprised that big business had no stature or weight with the Democrats, and now I feel that it is equally true with the Republicans. We're not saints, but we have been in the benefits area for years. We were ignored by Clinton and have been ignored by the GOP. The message is not getting through that we have something to offer. It is startling how poor a job we have done in establishing credibility.[37]

To some extent big business did not intervene in the Medicare debate because it was busy on more urgent issues, such as deficit reduction and regulatory relief. The Business Roundtable group Coalition for Change planned to spend $10 million in advertising to support nonpartisan deficit reduction.[38] Large employers were also wooed by the Republican leadership during the period of Medicare proposal development. The Thursday Group pondered how to get large employers on board the Medicare reduction bandwagon. They surmised that if they could shift as many Medicare recipients into HMOs as possible, large employers would be reassured that they would not be subjected to more cost shifting. Early on the leadership moved away from trying to keep retirees in company plans. Gingrich also personally reached out to some of the large corporations that had supported the Clinton efforts in order to convey the message that he was concerned about the big employers' issues on Medicare.[39]

Large employers were also coerced by the Republicans. For instance, the American Insurance Association asked Vin Weber, former Republican Minnesotan legislator, to supplant its Democratic lobbyist, Beryl An-

---

[36] Richard Dunham and Mary Beth Regan, "Let the Wild Rumpus Start!" *Business Week,* January 16, 1995, 28; interview with company representative, May 1995.

[37] Interviews with company representatives, fall 1995.

[38] Peter Stone, "From the K Street Corridor," *National Journal,* August 12, 1995.

[39] Interviews with industry representatives, fall 1995.

thony.[40] Gingrich aide Ed Cutler warned a lobbyist who had worked on the Clinton health plan, "You better be on the right side this year." Although the Republicans denied that they were planning to blackball Democratic lobbyists, some admitted that access to the leadership at least required the correct political credentials.[41] These Republican activities in the Medicare arena reflected a broader party campaign to alter the political representation of big business, by asking them to hire more Republican lobbyists and to remove long-standing employees. Bill Paxton (R-N.Y.) circulated to House Republicans a detailed inventory of contributions from the four hundred largest PACs that "reminds Members who our friends are." The Republicans believed that many in the corporate lobby were Democrats with a pernicious influence within the firm. John Boehner complained, "For years, CEOs have hired liberals for their Washington offices who've kept them in the dark on many things. There's been little change since the election, and that's widened the disconnect between Republicans and the business community."[42] This suddenly made Republican lobbyists a much-sought-after commodity, since they were believed to have more influence with the likes of Newt Gingrich and Phil Gramm. *Industry Week* issued a collective mea culpa, complete with suggestions for correcting the way that corporate America contributed to congressional sins.

> [A]s tempting as it may be to relish "pay-back time" for assorted Congressional sins, one reality still stands out amid the Beltway mess: Corporate America helped create it, and bankroll it. . . . it starts with whom companies choose as their advocates.
>
> "If I were a lobbying czar," states one veteran trade-association president, "I'd get rid of all the people being hired off the Hill and run my offices with operating people on leave or on special assignment for a year or two."[43]

Ultimately, the same organizational weakness that prevented large employers from getting what they wanted from health reform interfered with their exercising a strong political presence in its aftermath. As a manager from a large northeastern manufacturing firm observed, "Corporate

[40] W. John Moore, "Scouting for GOP Talent," *National Journal,* December 10, 1994, 2912.

[41] Interview with industry representative, September 1995; W. John Moore, Richard Cohen, and Peter Stone, "A Loyalty Test for Lobbyists?" *National Journal,* June 3, 1995, 1341–43.

[42] W. John Moore and Richard E. Cohen, "Showing Democrats the Door?" *National Journal,* March 11, 1995, 614; "Big Business vs. the GOP?" *Wall Street Journal,* March 13, 1995, A14.

[43] Charles Day Jr., "It's the Process, Stupid," *Industry Week,* January 23, 1995, 17.

America is preoccupied with short-term issues, and now we don't have short-term health care problems." A manager from a utility reflected, "Business did itself a disservice by not taking a cohesive position on it [Medicare]." An oil company manager explained, "We are not going to put our nose up on Medicare at this point. . . . I don't think that large employers have the clout to rein in the Republican agenda—especially in the House, where many first- and second-termers have no affinity for big business."[44]

National health reform exacerbated the underlying weakness of big business, because some managers did try to engage their peers and failed. The Health Security Act was a critical juncture in the business community, when business mobilization went from the politics of the possible to the far-fetched fantasy of the improbable. Business leaders were reluctant to expose themselves to such glaring defeat again. A Washington lobbyist put it baldly:

> Business got a little embarrassed by its association with Clinton. Old manu-
> facturing industries were quick to jump on a Clinton bandwagon. But it di-
> vided the business community and embarrassed those like the automobile
> industry that were too close to the Clinton process. The ARCO CEO got a
> nasty piece written about him in the *Wall Street Journal*. Other CEOs were
> made to feel like they had knifed business in the back.[45]

Small Business and Health Industry Mobilization

The Republican leadership organized the Coalition to Save Medicare from ninety-nine small-business, insurer, provider, senior, and conservative citizen activist groups. The coalition was cochaired by Pamela Bailey, from the Healthcare Leadership Council, a for-profit hospital group, and Jake Hansen, from the Seniors Coalition, a rightist counterpart to the American Associations of Retired Persons.[46]

Republicans reached out to its diverse coalition with specific provisions designed to curry favor with key interest groups. To assuaged physicians' fears about the huge cuts, Republicans promised that Medicare fees would not be reduced for seven years; indeed, because current law was to have lowered physician reimbursement, this represented an actual savings. The Republicans also appealed to the American Medical Association by allowing physicians to form their own provider groups without an HMO license and to cut out insurance middlemen. The bill would eliminate regulations of medical laboratories and nursing homes, and would

---

[44] Interviews with company representatives, summer 1995.
[45] Interview with industry representative, summer 1995.
[46] William Miller, "Battle Looms," *Industry Week*, September 4, 1995, 82.

require Medicare to reimburse for-profit hospitals for local property taxes.[47] Thus, although the American Medical Association calculated that the biggest savings in the Republican House plan would come from providers (53 percent), it endorsed the measure, drawn to provider networks and tort reform.[48]

For-profit hospitals were with the Republicans from the beginning, drawn to the many special benefits. The American Hospital Association, representing mostly public hospitals, was much more skeptical of the Republican House and Senate plans, feeling that the enormous cuts in Medicare offset any special incentives.[49] But the Republicans made a series of concessions, especially in the Senate, to assuage the concerns of the big teaching hospitals.

Insurers were attracted to the Republican Medicare concept because they liked the party's efforts to move the elderly into the private insurance market. If all seniors traded Medicare for private insurance options, the industry premium revenue would balloon by $1.25 trillion over seven years.[50]

Small-business groups supported the Medicare changes both because they were part of the larger budget package and because they saw the reforms as a way to restrain the rise in payroll taxes. The Chamber of Commerce publication *Nation's Business* suggested that the Medicare Trust Fund was considering raising payroll taxes, from 2.9 percent to 4.23 percent, to pay for Medicare hospital insurance. To make Medicare solvent for seventy-five years, according to the Chamber, the payroll tax would be expanded to 6.42 percent, and 3.2 million jobs would be lost in the process.[51]

The Coalition to Save Medicare and other interests sympathetic to the Republican cause helped the leadership in innumerable ways. First, the various interests generated a seemingly endless source of money. According to Common Cause, from 1985 to 1995 the health insurance industry PACs spent $25.5 million on congressional elections, and doctor PACs contributed another $23.1 million. Although during the past decade

---

[47] This has to do with the dollar conversion factor. Robert Pear, "Doctors' Group Says G.O.P. Agreed to Deal on Medicare," *New York Times,* October 12, 1995, A1; Martin Gottlieb and Robert Pear, "Beneath Surface, New Health Bills Offer Some Boons," *New York Times,* October 15, 1995, A1, 20.

[48] McIlrath, "GOP Health Plan Blitz," 1.

[49] Eric Weissenstein, "Provider Networks Gaining in Senate," *Modern Health Care,* October 2, 1995, 2.

[50] Mary Jane Fisher, "Kennedy Charges Industry with Medicare 'Conspiracy,' " *National Underwriter,* August 14, 1995, 1.

[51] David Warner, "A Medicare Tax Hike's Impact on Business," *Nation's Business,* October 1995, 8.

Democrats and Republicans received equal shares of cash from PACs from the two industries, Republicans surged ahead in the race for cash after capturing Congress. For example health insurance companies gave to Republicans over Democrats by a factor of 3.5 to 1. The groups associated with the Republican legislative agenda spent much more money attacking Clinton's health reform than the Democratic groups devoted to attacking the Republican's Medicare campaign. For example, HIAA spent $15 million on advertising attacking Clinton in 1994; the American Hospital Association spent only $350,000 and AFL-CIO $1 million criticizing Republicans in the first part of 1995.[52]

Second, private-sector allies helped the Republicans to define the Medicare issue in a manner that was appealing to the general public. The Republicans realized that the American public would not sacrifice Medicare for a balanced budget or tax reduction; therefore, the case had to be made that Medicare needed saving in its own right. For instance, political scientist Bob Blendon found 73 percent of his sample favoring reducing the growth in Medicare spending but only 44 percent supporting cuts to balance the budget and 28 percent to finance tax reduction.[53]

During the problem definition stage, the Republicans and their business allies did a full-scale media blitz to convince the public that Medicare was going bankrupt and to establish the legitimacy of the problem. The Republican National Committee started a three-hundred-thousand-dollar television campaign at the beginning of October to saturate the airwaves with positive vibes toward Medicare reform at the critical point of legislation. The Coalition to Save Medicare held a series of "Medicare University" sessions to educate congressional staffers and journalists about the virtues of choice and the dangers of waste, fraud, and abuse in Medicare. The group, working in tandem with coalition whip Paul Coverdell (R-Ga.), persuaded Republican senators to put forth radio commentaries on Medicare reform.[54]

Participants hired political operators to produce ads and polls to present their message to the public, and allies claimed that these campaigns were wildly successful. The Citizens for a Sound Economy's initial focus groups showed a public largely convinced that there was no problem with the Medicare system; follow-up groups a few months later showed a pub-

---

[52] Ruth Marcus, "Health Care PACs Give Freely," *Washington Post,* December 1, 1995, A25; Marilyn Werber Serafini, "Turning Up the Heat," *National Journal,* August 12, 1995.

[53] Serafini, "Turning Up the Heat."

[54] Patrick Jasperse, "Medicare Forces Mobilize to Do Battle over Reforms," *Milwaukee Journal Sentinel,* September 21, 1995, 4; Mary Jane Fisher, "Coalition Holding 'Medicare University' Briefings," *National Underwriter,* September 4, 1995, 36; Peter Stone, "Rallying the Troops," *National Journal,* September 2, 1995, 2152.

lic largely accepting of the Republican line.[55] Later, public opinion shifted against the Republican plan.

Third, business allies worked with the leadership to offer the appearance of overwhelming public support for the Medicare legislation. Shortly before Congress broke for its August recess, the Coalition to Save Medicare held a "Mobilization Event," offering legislators stirring testimonials to take back to the districts. The coalition also offer the occasional grassroots show of force, as when thirty seniors arrived at Congress with one hundred thousand "message-grams." Pamela Bailey described this as a full-scale war.[56]

Fourth, the interest groups allied with the Republicans worked to protect members from marginal districts. The Democratic Congressional Campaign Committee targeted fifty House Republicans in the 1996 election who were narrowly elected and were vulnerable on Medicare. The Republicans tried to protect these members with public-relations materials and "grassroots" interventions. For example, the leaders produced a videotape that members could show in their districts arguing that the alleged Medicare cut in reality constituted increasing spending from $4,800 to $6,700 a year. Groups close to the Republican leadership also set out to give support to members from close districts. Thus the rightist National Council of Senior Citizens explained, "We're having meetings to try to reward those who are sticking with us in the legislative process and to call (the public's) attention in particular areas to those who are part of the problem." The Seniors Coalition spent three to four hundred thousand dollars on a direct mail campaign to marginal members' districts.[57]

The Republican leadership had learned much from the Clinton administration's experiences with health reform. The administration had been criticized for too much secrecy, but the lesson for the Republicans was that too many leaks is a bad thing. The Clinton bill was scrutinized and picked apart for months before legislators had an opportunity to vote on the measure. The Republican rush through the process reminded one of Grant's taking Richmond: The party unveiled its proposal only when it was ready to legislate. Although the administration was slammed in the press for being obsessed with policy over politics, it had made many concessions to special interests. The problem was that these concessions were made without sufficiently firm commitments and at a premature stage in

[55] Interview with industry participant, September 14, 1995.

[56] Mary Jane Fisher, "Both Parties Turning Medicare into Huge Political Football," *National Underwriter*, August 14, 1995, 8; Mary Jane Fisher, "Medicare Reform Is Turning Congress into a Circus," *National Underwriter*, October 9, 1995.

[57] Serafini, "Turning Up the Heat."

the process. The Republicans met secretly through September to make deals with various interest groups and demanded ironclad promises of support in return. The Clinton administration was criticized for being excessively partisan and for shutting Republicans out of the bill-writing process; the GOP pursued this tactic in earnest. By putting Medicare reform in the reconciliation bill, the party could avoid the threat of a filibuster in the Senate. This removed incentives for real bipartisan cooperation: as long as the leadership could keep the Republican ducks in a line, they had little need to cross over to the other side of the aisle. At one point the Democrats held protest hearings on the front lawn of the Capitol in the rain to illustrate their feelings of being shut out.[58] It was not their finest hour.

At first the GOP strategy seemed to pay off. The House Republican members finally introduced the Medicare Preservation Act on Friday, September 29, 1995; by the following Thursday the bill had been marked up by both the Ways and Means, and Energy and Commerce committees. Commerce Committee hearings were initially scheduled for only one day; each member was to be given five minutes to comment on the act. The urgency was emphasized with an electronic clock hanging on the wall, counting down the 197 million seconds until Medicare bankruptcy. Angry with the limited time given to scrutinize the bill and the rushed nature of the proceedings, former chairman John Dingell led the committee Democrats in a walkout. A month after its introduction the Medicare Preservation Act had been passed by both houses. Whether the GOP succeeded in convincing the public that God was on their side, they convinced their own rank and file that the Medicare legislation was a political asset rather than liability. Rather than hiding Medicare in the budget reconciliation, the Republicans choose to stand up and be counted with a vote.[59]

But despite this rapid passage of the bill, Medicare reform was killed by Clinton's sudden willingness to stand up to his political enemies. President Clinton adamantly opposed the huge tax cuts and wanted to reduce Medicare by a much smaller amount than his opponents. Although compromise seemed possible before Thanksgiving when President Clinton accepted the Republican seven-year time frame for balancing the budget, the Republicans refused to move on their tax cut. In early December President Clinton vetoed the reconciliation bill that included Medicare reform, signing with the pen that LBJ had used to make Medicare law in 1965. The

---

[58] Dana Priest, "Cross-Dressing for Success: The Parties Trade Medicare Gowns," *Washington Post*, October 1, 1995, C3; Robin Toner, "Angry Opposition Attacks the Process," *New York Times*, September 22, 1995, A26.

[59] Fisher, "Medicare Reform Turning Congress," 10; Adam Clymer, "Republicans Choose Vote on Medicare Cut," *New York Times*, October 18, 1995, B8.

Republicans argued that this symbolic gesture was a "cheap trick." Richard Armey (R-Tex.) wondered in public if Clinton would authorize troops to be sent to Bosnia with "the same pen that LBJ used to sign the Gulf of Tonkin resolution."[60]

The two branches moved into a politics of brinkmanship reminiscent of Andrew Jackson's battle with the president of the Second Bank of the United States. The impasse caused government shutdowns over Thanksgiving weekend and again in mid-December. During the dark days of government shutdown, Vermeer masterpieces spent lonely hours in the closed National Gallery, a new pernicious classing system separated "essential" federal workers from their "nonessential" peers, and all government employees (with the exception of the culpable legislators) wondered when their next paychecks would arrive. The stalemate continued until the two parties once again passed a temporary spending measure to fill the gap until the official budget passed. But continuing compromise seemed of no avail.[61]

Finally, the Republican game of hardball went too far. The Republicans refused to raise the debt limit and, thereby, threatened to send the federal government into default unless President Clinton agreed to its deficit-reduction measures. This generated anger across the political spectrum, not the least from Wall Street Republicans, who deplored the tactics of their party's radical Right. The chairman of the Federal Reserve went to see Gingrich personally to obtain a promise that the United States would not be the first Western industrialized nation to default on its loans. After this fiasco, Gingrich proposed that the two parties stop negotiations, pass spending and tax cuts agreed on by both, and delay the difficult decisions.[62]

The budget stalemate deeply frustrated the small-business groups who had worked so hard for enactment of the Contract with America. Employers blamed the Republicans for a lack of leadership and focus. Thus one participant remembered, "The leadership was too busy focusing on the numbers, daily sound bites, and on today's polls [to mobilize business]. . . . There was not much clarity of what they [the Republicans] were looking for from them [business]." Another explained, "There was a real loss in momentum because the original game plan didn't work and they didn't know what to do." Many believed that the Republicans tried for too much too soon and set a priority on taking credit for political victories

[60] "Overheard in the House GOP Cloakroom," *Washington Post,* December 13, 1995, A27.

[61] Michael Wines, "Republicans and Clinton Narrow Spending Gap, but Signs of More Compromise Fade," *New York Times,* January 9, 1996, 8.

[62] Michael Wines, "Deficit May Trip G.O.P. as It Rushes for an Exit," *New York Times,* January 26, 1996, A12.

over securing policy goals. A lobbyist for a large small-business group reflected, "Republicans have taken self-destruction to new heights. We all love amateurs; still, some [of the current congressional freshmen] are close to violating their oath of office in trying to shut the government down. They have been overreaching to such a large extent that they are likely to lose everything."[63]

Conclusion

This chapter has investigated the efforts at political mobilization by small business in two legislative initiatives: the Family and Medical Leave Act and the Medicare reform bill. Small-business groups contributed to delaying the FMLA legislation for seven years, even though the bill followed the business practices of most large firms. Small business helped steer rapid passage of the Medicare reform bill, an essential component of the Republican's Contract with America, although the legislation was subsequently vetoed by President Clinton.

These two episodes tell us much about business and the Republican Party. Ideologically in synch, small-business groups and the Republicans have been natural allies in repeated attacks on policies to increase human capital investment. Small employers have limited resources to deal with government regulations, and they detest mandates, Clinton's social vehicle of choice, because these add to the wage rate. Large employers have been much more ambivalent about the Republican agenda. One big-business manager worried that after 1994, "All is driven by the budget deficit. If they [the Republicans] can find a way to gain savings from a program they will. . . . Budgets will drive decisions. Good policies will be driven out."[64]

The Republican Party clearly overreached in its Contract with America, trying for too much too quickly and misunderstanding the institutional limits of American politics. Bill Clinton was quick to grasp the Republican political misjudgment and discovered that taking a stand during the budget battle was a perfect political formula both for defeating his opponents and for improving his character ratings in the polls.

But although the Republican Contract failed to achieve its entire radical agenda, it defined the public debate in new terms, not the least of which was getting Bill Clinton to endorse a seven-year balanced budget. If not for Clinton's presidential show of force, the Republicans and their small-business allies could have profoundly changed the nation's health system.

[63] Interview with industry lobbyist, February 23, 1996.
[64] Interview with company representative, May 1996.

Clinton's victory in 1996 was due, in part, to his absorbing many Republican positions. The alliance between small business and the Republicans undoubtedly will continue to have an important impact on initiatives to promote human capital investment.

Large employers' interests may be at risk in the long term, not because liberal Democrats add to their regulatory burden but because conservative Republicans seek to alter the policy landscape. The balance of power within the business community is shifting: what members of the major small-business groups lack in size, they make up for in organization. Large employers with very different stakes in human capital investment initiatives are likely to be underrepresented in the political arena unless these managers address their political incapacities.

EIGHT

IMPLICATIONS FOR OUR

ECONOMIC FUTURE

THE FUTURE of economic growth and social renewal is fraught with seemingly intractable trade-offs. Heightened world competition, rapid technological growth, and changing forms of manufacturing may set new parameters for economic and social well-being in the postindustrial age. At one level, these trade-offs represent dilemmas for all industrialized countries. The bird's-eye view shows nations struggling with a similar problem: to satisfy the needs of the workforce that are generated by new forms of competition and production, while preserving employment and quality of life.

But national responses to these trade-offs vary enormously, so much so that scholars now suggest that different varieties of capitalism distinguish advanced industrialized states. Legal and regulatory institutions, including broad patterns of social provision, set limits on the competitive strategies available to firms and generate national models of production.[1]

This book investigates how patterns of corporate deliberation contribute to the regimes of social policy that shape capitalist development. As the case studies document, big American firms have been largely unable to secure their expressed interests in the realm of social policy. Although opinion polls reveal that many managers favor policies for human capital investment, large employers have only rarely joined political coalitions to enact this legislation. Business associations have been insufficiently strong to organize managers in support of their expressed social concerns. The limits to collective political action among potential business supporters may partially explain why policies to expand human capital investment have not enjoyed greater legislative success. The political weakness of big business detracts from the political viability of legislation to promote human capital investment, and the policy landscape is shifting to favor the interests of small companies, low-wage employers, and the service sector.

The political incapacities of big business may also be affecting the private provision of benefits. Many managers have viewed government social initiatives as a last-ditch effort to save the private employee benefits sys-

---

[1] See Kitchelt et al., *Continuity and Change in Contemporary Capitalism*; Manow, "Welfare State Building and Coordinated Capitalism.".

tem. If public policy fails to bring health costs under control and to end cost shifting, firms are likely to continue to cut back their benefits. The raiding of company-trained talent gives large paternalistic companies added incentives to divest benefits and services. Downsizing and outsourcing may be the logical directions for once-paternalistic firms that must cope with the new competitive climate and receive limited help from government in doing so. Thus the downsizing phenomenon could be related to the big-business failure to secure policies favorable to human capital investment.

This chapter asks what the pattern of business political representation portends for the future of the political economy. The institutional balance of political power within the business community is bound to have consequences, yet the meaning of the institutional profile of corporate power for our economic future depends on one's view of policy interventions. Competing views of the role of government in economic growth project different economic consequences.

Laissez-faire economists celebrate the limits to the expansion of national social policy, believing that government intervention only disrupts the elegant counterpoint of market supply and demand.[2] Today's entrepreneurial winners are downsized, flexible, and lean and mean. Manufacturing demands for human capital will be provided for by the market. Laissez-faire followers are partially joined in their optimism by those who believe that policies to promote human capital investment must be tied to regional economies and that national interventions can never solve local needs. Thus the current stalemate over policy may hold the potential for a needed transformation of the existing landscape and a fundamentally redefined role for government in the economy.[3]

High-performance workplace advocates believe that the limits to national policy are cause for pessimism. If big-business managers are unable to back policies to promote human capital investment, we may continue to see a domestic undersupply of training. If corporate providers cannot organize themselves to give political support to an overhaul of the health financing system, we may find it impossible to rationalize health care. The political shortcomings of big business may shape future economic development: large employers' failure to satisfy political interests could ultimately take them down an economic path very different from the high-

---

[2] Chiaki Nishiyama and Kurt Leube, eds., *The Essence of Hayek* (Stanford, Calif.: Hoover Institution Press, 1984). For recent economic summaries of the empirical work investigating sources of long-term growth see Jeffrey Sachs and Andrew Warner, "Fundamental Sources of Long-Run Growth," *American Economic Review* 87, no. 2 (1997): 184–88; Xavier X. Sala-I-Martin, "I Just Ran Two Million Regressions," *American Economic Review* 87, no. 2 (1997): 178–83.

[3] Piore and Sabel, *The Second Industrial Divide.*

performance workplace.[4] An undersupply of investment in human resources could make it more difficult for U.S. firms to compete in manufacturing sectors that require highly skilled labor, unless, of course, they
move production offshore in search of skilled labor. Thus, America's inability to rationalize its systems of social provision and to prepare its
workforce adequately has two potentially pernicious ramifications: to accelerate the flight of companies overseas (ironically in search of skilled
rather than cheap labor) and to hurt the competitive position of those
willing to maintain domestic operations.

Business Preferences, Public Policy, and the Political Economy

Advanced industrialized nations everywhere are struggling to satisfy
somewhat contradictory goals of increasing the skills of the workforce to
satisfy knowledge-intensive production needs and of preserving employment under conditions of heightened international competition. But national solutions to these trade-offs vary, and how countries solve these
dilemmas may influence their economic prospects.[5] Economic choices
may be influenced by labor-management, financing, social welfare, and
national political institutions.[6] Firms can derive economic advantage from
cooperation and coordination, as well as from low wages, and certain
social or labor-market policies may enhance coordination, productivity,
and skills. This cooperation may enable firms to move into market niches
not otherwise available to them. Individual firm's strategies (shaped as
they are by national systems of regulation) add up to national models of
production.[7]

But within national models of production is much diversity. Both sectors and firms within sectors diverge in competitive strategies: some rely
greatly on a skilled and productive workforce, while others look to low

---

[4] See, for example, Freeman, *Working under Different Rules.*

[5] Suzanne Berger and Ronald Dore, eds., *National Adversity and Global Capitalism* (Ithaca, N.Y.: Cornell University Press, 1966).

[6] Dore, *British Factory, Japanese Factory;* Soskice, "Wage Determination"; Maurice, Sellier, and Silvestre, *Social Foundations;* James Womack, Daniel Jones, and Daniel Roos, *The
Machine That Changed the World* (New York: Macmillan, 1990); Stewart Wood, "Employer Preferences and Public Policy," paper presented at the APSA Annual Conference,
Washington, D.C., August 28–31, 1997; Duane Swank, *Diminished Democracy?* forthcoming; Evelyne Huber, Charles Ragin, and John Stephens, "Social Democracy, Christian Democracy, Constitutional Structure, and the Welfare State," *American Journal of Sociology*
99 (1993): 711–49; Pierson, *Dismantling the Welfare State.*

[7] Hall, "Political Economy of Adjustment," 297–98; Manow, "Welfare State Building."

factor costs for competitive advantage. Business factions struggle for the enactment of policies best suited to their interests; thus one needs to understand how the political struggles over social policies are resolved.

In the United States the features of business representation work against corporate support for policies to expand human capital investment. Despite important subnational variations, the general institutional profile of American business is one of fragmentation, making it difficult for employers to generate collective positions on social issues. Thus, even when policy affecting human capital investment enjoys considerable support among managers, it is difficult for employers to express a preference for it in the political arena. Competition for members makes the major groups afraid to alienate any constituency and, consequently, hesitant to articulate substantive positions on controversial issues. Of course these constraints do not affect corporate action toward most industry- or firm-specific concerns; when a few large firms or sectors have direct economic interests, producers tend to dominate the policy process.[8] But when a wide spectrum of companies shares a broad collective goal, such as a skilled workforce, employers are hard pressed to find common ground.

In addition, the relative organizational strength of the major small-business associations diminishes support for social policies. Taking advantage of their large and varied membership, small-business groups have developed extensive grassroots lobbying strategies. Seeking to unify their multitude of voices, these groups have formed highly successful, single-issue coalitions with decision rules to keep participants committed to the key objectives.

The legacies of private provision also limit big-business managers' ability to articulate collective political positions, because firms with extensive private plans have very different interests from those without. Managers may desire public-policy solutions but may fear any erosion of their current market positions. Many large employers were willing to support employer mandates and comprehensive reform of the health system, but only so long as the government's solution did not harm their own market power vis-a-vis health providers. Thus features of large employers' political representation may be helping to restrict the development of national policies to expand human capital investment.

The question, of course, is what difference it makes that government has not intervened more in the area of human capital investment. Does this have an impact on productivity, competitiveness, or equality? There is little consensus about this impact, because the various beliefs about the nature of economic growth project different scenarios.

[8] Wilson, *The Politics of Regulation.*

The Laissez-Faire View

For laissez-faire advocates the limits to national social policy are a cause for celebration, because government regulation only interferes with market allocations. Government efforts to compensate for market failures are invariably distorted by the demands of special interests; therefore, political solutions have pernicious, unintended consequences, and policies that interrupt the natural course of entrepreneurship hurt the economy in the long run.[9] Mechanisms for the development of skills will emerge if the market demands them. Some believe that capital accumulation measured properly explains most growth in productivity and that reducing constraints against capital investment is the proper course of action.[10]

In this view, the flexibility of firms is a critical factor, and here U.S. firms have a distinct advantage over companies in many advanced industrial countries. Trends such as downsizing and outsourcing only increase flexibility and are, therefore, viewed with enthusiasm. There is considerable worry in West European countries that expansive social benefits detract from employment and economic growth. High wages for unskilled labor (due to aggressive labor negotiations) have suppressed employment, especially in the service sectors, and have bloated the prices of products. The European Community had unemployment rates of 11 percent in the early 1990s, compared with 7 percent in the United States[11]

Laissez-faire advocates believe that recent events in health care illustrate the advantages of market solutions and the irrelevance of government intervention, because the growth in company health costs seems to have dropped off since the failure of health reform. Total spending on health grew by only 7.8 percent from 1992 to 1993, the lowest rate since 1987; much of this growth was concentrated in the public sector. A Foster Higgins study found health costs in 1994 actually declining, by 1.1 percent, for the first time in a decade.[12] A large-employer study of employees'

[9] Dwight Lee and Richard McKenzie, *Failure and Progress* (Washington, D.C.: Cato Institute, 1993), xi, 13; James Buchanan, *The Limits of Liberty* (Chicago: University of Chicago Press, 1975).

[10] Jeffrey Fuhrer, "Technology and Growth: An Overview," *New England Economic Review,* November 21, 1996, 3.

[11] Commission of the European Communities, *Growth, Competitiveness, Employment,* 11, 40.

[12] Katharine Levit, Cathy Cowan, Helen Lazenby, Patricia McDonnell, Arthur Sensenig, Jean Stiller, and Darleen Won, "National Health Spending Trends, 1960—1993," *Health Affairs* 13, no. 5 (1994): 14—31; Milt Freudenheim, "Business May Pay More for Health as Congress Cuts," *New York Times,* November 4, 1995, 49.

attitudes about health plans found the greatest proportion (86 percent) pleased with HMOs.[13]

To bolster their claim that government social interventions are harmful to economic prosperity, followers of laissez-faire point to U.S. improvements in competitive position and in the rate of growth of productivity.[14] OECD data suggest that the United States remains firmly ahead of Japan and Germany in both productivity and in GDP per capita.[15] In meeting the challenges of global competition and changing technologies U.S. companies have made enormous gains in productivity. Low unemployment, low inflation, high profits, and sustained expansion inspired *Business Week* to editorialize about a new "wonder economy."[16] Many now considered the United States a model for the rest of the world, as is reflected in recent remarks by the Federal Reserve's Alan Greenspan: "The flexibility of our market system and the vibrancy of our private sector remain examples for the whole world to emulate."[17] (Not all share this exuberance: some writing in the laissez-faire mode, especially supply-side economists, believe that the United States has still not achieved its full growth capacity due to the fetters of government regulation.[18] They ridicule Clinton's claims about leading the country to economic renewal, arguing that the nation could be enjoying a much higher GDP growth rate than the current 2.5 percent.)[19]

The Regional Economic View

Another group of scholars, advocating flexible specialization and regional economic-development strategies, concur that the limits to national policies for human capital investment are appropriate, because they view national policies as outmoded and ill suited to regional differences. These scholars believe that public policy might play a role in channeling investment into human resources, but believe that political decisions should be

[13] David Jones, "Firms Surprised at Managed Care Study Results," *National Underwriter Property and Casualty-Risk and Benefits Management,* July 24, 1995, 33.

[14] Mike McNamee, "An Economy on Steroids?" *Business Week,* July 7, 1997, 126.

[15] McKinsey Global Institute, *Service Sector Productivity* (Washington, D.C.: McKinsey, October 1992), 1–9.

[16] "New Thinking about the New Economy," *Business Week,* May 19, 1997, 150.

[17] Alan Greenspan, "Inflation and Money Supply: The Exuberant Stock Market," *Vital Speeches,* March 15, 1997, 347.

[18] Paul Craig Roberts, "Why Is the U.S. Settling for Stunted Growth?" *Business Week,* January 8, 1996, 22.

[19] Stephen Moore, "The Lean Years," *National Review,* July 1, 1996, 38.

made at the local level. Thus, Regini argues that training programs must be connected to the production strategies of the companies and the composition of the workforce in the region. There is no single appropriate model for improving the skills of the workforce; rather, interventions should be geared to local needs.[20] In addition, some authors doubt that training programs to develop skills, a "supply push" approach, will be successful unless companies make a commitment to expanding the skills necessary to their production processes. Training must be accompanied by policies that restore wage growth among less-skilled workers, and that address the growing polarization of wages.[21]

The flexible-specialization camp suggests that small firms are more entrepreneurial and innovative and welcome the breakup of industrial behemoths. For example, economist David Birch attacks John Kenneth Galbraith's argument that large corporations are the crux of the American economy; rather, "the bubbly, yeasty, creative segment" is the small-business sector.[22] It is also in the world of small enterprise that most new companies and new jobs are located: the smallest companies (employing less than twenty workers) created 88 percent of the new jobs in 1981–85.[23] Piore and Sabel suggest that the breakup of firms into smaller units has often been accompanied by networks between companies that increase cooperation, local control, and more equal relations between firms.[24] (Harrison disputes the claim that networks increase equality and cooperation among firms and between labor and management; rather, the breakup of large companies is reducing corporate benefits. Networks have not produced a resurgence of localism, but require a global reach, producing a system of concentration without centralization.)[25]

These scholars see small firms as the creative sector of the economy and are not worried about limits to policies for human capital investment. Big firms have wielded their political power in the social sphere largely to benefit their own workers. For too long the distinctly American mix of private and public social provision has disproportionately benefited large

---

[20] Marino Regini, "Firms and Institutions: The Demand for Skills and Their Social Production in Europe," *European Journal of Industrial Relations* 1, no. 2 (1995): 191–202.

[21] Mishel and Teixeira, *Myth of Labor Shortage,* 2–3; David Howell and Edward Wolff, "Trends in the Growth and Distribution of Skills in the U.S. Workplace, 1960–1985," *Industrial and Labor Relations Review* 44, no. 3 (1991): 486–502.

[22] David Birch, *Job Creation in America* (New York: Free Press, 1987), 9, 15, 29–31; Richard Nelson and Sidney Winter, *An Evolutionary Theory of Economic Change* (Cambridge: Harvard University Press, 1982).

[23] Birch, *Job Creation in America,* 15–16.

[24] Piore and Sabel, *The Second Industrial Divide.*

[25] Bennett Harrison, *Lean and Mean* (New York: Basic Books, 1994), 8–12.

manufacturers and reinforced inequalities between the core and the periphery. Reductions in the private sector's provision might ultimately help those left out of its largesse and move the country to a more universal system.[26]

The High-Performance Workplace View

High-performance workplace advocates believe that the lack of national policy means that the United States will fail to invest adequately in human capital. Confronted with declining manufacturing jobs and rising unemployment, most industrialized nations much decide whether to allocate resources to training skilled workers or to providing (often unskilled) jobs. The United States seems to favor policies designed to prop up employment but to do little for skills; thus, Appelbaum and Schettkat show that production of jobs in the United States (increasing by 15.2 percent between 1979 and 1987) has been concentrated in the service sector. The authors' point of comparison, West Germany, saw much more industrial restructuring and much more possibility for high-skilled growth.[27]

High-performance workplace advocates believe that the lack of a legislative framework for training will also lead to a diminishing supply of benefits by firms. Business incapacities for providing adequate training (or for securing this training through public policy) are leading to an undersupply of skilled workers. Because decisions about training are almost entirely made at the level of the individual worker or firm, there is practically no systematic effort to tie training to future skill needs. U.S. firms spend only 1.2 to 1.8 percent of total employee compensation on training. Company training budgets actually declined in 1991, and growth rates have barely kept up with inflation since.[28] U.S. companies also spend less on the basics and on nonmanagement workers than do companies elsewhere. Less than 10 percent of all companies do most of the spending of the $30 billion a year on training, and, according to some, most of this $30 billion is spent on executives and managers. In one study 80 percent of the sampled firms complained about employees' writing skills, but only 24 percent offered remedial writing programs. Over half of this group relied instead on improved screening processes for employee hires. In another group one-third of the sampled firms tested for basic skills when

---

[26] Piore and Sabel, *The Second Industrial Divide.*

[27] Appelbaum and Schettkat, "Employment and Industrial Restructuring," 137.

[28] Office of Technology Assessment, *Worker Training,* 13, 15; "Industry Report," *Training,* October 1994, 37.

hiring, and 89 percent of the testers simply refused to hire applicants who lacked basic skills.[29]

In similar fashion high-performance workplace advocates believe that the failure of comprehensive health reform will ultimately mean a reduction in the private sector's health benefits, because these benefits are becoming too costly or because firms will have few constraints against free-riding. For example, despite the seeming success of managed-care plans in restraining prices, a recent survey found 80 percent of executives continuing to worry about escalating health costs. Huskamp and Newhouse have cast doubt on the aggregate figures on health spending. Using National Income and Product Accounts data instead of Health Care Financing Administration data, and employing a different deflator for inflation adjustment, the authors concluded that the health care spending slowdown "is modest at best."[30]

Many employers fear that costs were artificially restrained during the health reform political cycle (in an effort by providers to demonstrate that national legislation was not necessary to curb increases) and are again on the rise. Foster Higgins found a 2.1 percent increase in 1995, although the increase was concentrated in traditional indemnity plans. Towers Perrin found health costs for employers up 4 percent in 1996, a modest growth rate but still above the 1995 figures.[31] Some analysts believe that the declining growth rate simply reflects a movement out of fee-for-service plans: when this process is completed, health costs will continue to rise. In addition, business managers fear that the initial savings from moving into managed care will not be sustained over time. An early innovator in point-of-service plans reported that after the first few years the plans began to engage in shadow pricing: the POS plan prices rose at the same rate as the traditional indemnity plans, albeit rising from a slightly lower baseline. Administrative costs for point-of-service plans also seem to be higher than those for traditional indemnity plans. There is also the problem of adverse selection—only the healthiest may be willing to join managed care.[32]

[29] Stanfield, "Quest for Quality," 1832; "Whining about the Skill Gap," *Training Today* 31, no. 1 (1994): 14; Ellen Sherman, "Back to Basics to Improve Skills," *Personnel,* July 1989, 22–26.

[30] Bruce Japsen, "Healthcare Costs Are Still Near Top of Executives' Worry List," *Modern Healthcare,* September 4, 1995, 52; Haiden Huskamp and Joseph Newhouse, "Is Health Spending Slowing Down?" *Health Affairs* 13, no. 5 (1994): 32–38.

[31] Milt Freudenheim, "Survey Finds Health Costs Rose in '95," *New York Times,* January 30, 1995, D1; Towers Perrin, "1996 Health Care Cost Survey," Towers Perrin Employee Benefit Information Center, March 1996.

[32] J. P. Donlon and Barbara Benson, "The New Anatomy of Health Care," *Chief Executive,* January 1996, 52; Nancy Bell, "Pros and Cons of Point-of-Service Plans," *Business and Health* 10, no. 1 (1992): 34.

Fears about the future of managed-care price restraints have been exacerbated by the current wave of mergers and acquisitions within this field. The managed-care industry had eleven hundred mergers and acquisitions in 1994, totaling $60 billion. Reducing the number of competitors may eventually allow premium prices to rise. Profits in the for-profit HMO sector increased by 40 percent from 1992 to 1994.[33] Big-business managers are also concerned about the "any willing provider" legislation now being considered in many states in response to aggressive lobbying by the medical profession. These laws could stop employers from having exclusive contracts. As one employer humorously put it, the "any billing provider" legislation could effectively prevent firms from controlling costs at the state level.

Some high-performance workplace advocates also worry about the increasing advantage accorded by public policy to small business. Big multinational manufacturers, once the cutting edge of American industry, used to enjoy an exorbitant privilege at home as well as abroad. Large employers received powerful tax incentives for capital-intensive investment, favorable trade laws designed to maintain American hegemony, and many fiscal incentives to maintain their expensive employee benefit system. But the rise of small business as a political force is gradually transforming the regulatory system, giving many concessions to small employers. Family leave and the proposed health reform were examples of policy concessions to small business described in this book. Environmental, health, and safety regulations are enforced less stringently in small companies; indeed, the Regulatory Flexibility Act of 1980 explicitly encouraged bureaucrats to scale down regulations so that small firms were not unduly burdened. Yet this unburdening of companies contributes to less protection for workers in smaller enterprises. By exempting companies with less than one hundred employees, a third of American workers lose social, environmental, and safety protections.[34] Certainly small firms do have fewer accounting and management resources to cope with the manifold regulations governing business operations. Nonetheless, we are creating a dualistic regulatory framework that benefits small business over big business, domestic-oriented producers over export-oriented ones.

The two-tiered rules for large and small companies further encourage a human-resource divestment strategy, because large companies are increasingly frustrated with cost shifting from small firms. If public policy

---

[33] Donlon and Benson, "New Anatomy"; Karen Davis, Scott Collins, and Cynthia Morris, "Managed Care: Promise and Concerns," *Health Affairs* 13, no. 4(1994): 178—85; Findlay, "Block Grants for Sale," 55.

[34] Brown, Hamilton, and Medoff, *Employers Large and Small*, 82–84, 90; Anya Bernstein, "Inside or Outside?" *Policy Studies Journal* 25, no. 1 (1987): 87–99.

continues to evolve in ways that are contrary to big-business interests, large enterprises may have no alternative but to reduce employee benefits. Thus after health reform's demise companies are shifting costs onto their employees; indeed 78 percent of a recent *Business and Health* survey found firms (often regretfully) anticipating this course of action. In 1991 only 48 percent believed that cost shifting was an effective way to curb costs.[35]

We might deem policies to benefit small business appropriate if they protected jobs and American workers; indeed, job creation provides much of the rationale for awarding special benefits to small employees. But some analysts believe that the small-business sector is less critical to new employment than their Washington representatives maintain. Although small companies create more jobs, they also destroy more, so that the net gain is no different from larger firms. Policies to promote high skills and flexibility are preferable to ones rewarding size, especially as the majority of "good" manufacturing jobs are created by large firms rather than small ones. Employees of large companies receive 30 percent higher wages than those at small firms. Birch's original calculations were flawed because he ignored job destruction, the decrease in the small-firm share of economic activity, and situations where small establishments were actually part of larger companies.[36]

The inability to rationalize social provision may also contribute to downsizing and outsourcing. *Institutional Investor* found that 70 percent of its sampled companies downsized in 1994. The American Management Association (AMA) believes downsizing to be a permanent fixture of corporate life: 63 percent of the companies that cut workers in one year slash again in the next.[37] The downsizing trend is somewhat overstated because as firms are downsizing in one corner they are hiring in the other. Nonetheless, even when new employees are hired, downsizing alters the expectation of life-time employment. As Regini points out, a great irony is that at the same time as companies are emphasizing increased teamwork, they are outsourcing to reduce labor costs.[38] In addition many companies have solved the problem of high domestic labor costs by simply relocating to

[35] Wayne J. Guglielmo, "Business Has a Mixed Message for Doctors," *Medical Economics,* January 15, 1996, 180; Business and Health, *National Executive Opinion Poll,* 1993.

[36] Brown, Hamilton, and Medoff, *Employers Large and Small,* 29; Steven Davis, John Haltiwanger, and Scott Schuh, *Job Creation and Destruction* (Cambridge: MIT Press, 1996), 154, 169; Zoltan Acs and David Audretsch, "Has the Role of Small Firms Changed in the United States?" in *Small Firms and Entrepreneurship* (Cambridge: Cambridge University Press, 1993), 55–57.

[37] "Downsizing Downsized," *Institutional Investor,* December 1995, 28; "Upswing in Downsizings to Continue," *Management Review,* February 1993, 5; Gene Koretz, "Downsizing Isn't Down Enough," *Business Week,* December 4, 1995, 24.

[38] Marino Regini, *Uncertain Boundaries* (New York: Cambridge University Press, 1995).

third-world countries, leaving American workers scrambling for fast-food employment at half their former wages. Thus transformations in the firm such as downsizing and outsourcing may be partially viewed as a failure of politics—an organizational embodiment of the limits to big-business political action.

Downsizing has further reduced human-resource investments, as firms have eliminated permanent workers and hired contingent independent contractors who lack benefits (even though they perform the same tasks as permanent workers and were often formerly part of the core workforce). Downsizing also can erode the political commitment within the firm to invest in human capital because it has often been concentrated in those parts of the firm where concern about such investment is the strongest; thus, the decline in human-resource departments due to downsizing has produced a decline of in-house skill training.[39]

Its detractors believe that downsizing may have negative long-term effects on the quality of management, because managers become so preoccupied with transformational roles such as innovating and brokering that they pay less attention to monitoring. Companies have become so anxious to downsize, in no small part to improve their attraction to Wall Street, that they sacrifice long-term strategy for short-term containment of costs.[40] Even in large firms where downsizing is more likely to be related to strategic considerations than to a change in business climate, only 45 percent of an American Management Association (AMA) sample saw its profits rise. In another study less than half of the firms realized cost reductions, less than a quarter achieved gains in productivity, and only 12 percent gained market share.[41] The (AMA) found that downsizing was much more likely to enhance workers' productivity when training budgets were also expanded: only 28 percent of companies that cut both workers and training saw growth in productivity, as opposed to nearly half of those who increased training budgets while downsizing. Downsizing is presumably moving workers out of good jobs into worse ones, limiting demand, and spurring additional downsizing.[42]

[39] Kathleen Christiansen, "The Two-Tiered Workforce in U.S. Corporations," in *Turbulence in the American Workplace,* ed. Peter Doeringer (New York: Oxford University Press, 1991), 140–55: Thierry Noyelle, ed., *Skills, Wages, and Productivity in the Service Sector* (Boulder, Colo.: Westview Press, 1990).

[40] Alan Belasen, Meg Benke, Laurie DiPadova, and Michael Fortunato, "Downsizing and the Hyper-Effective Manager," *Human Resource Management* 35, no. 1 (1996): 87–117; Alan Downs, "The Truth about Layoffs," *Management Review,* October 1995, 57.

[41] "Downsizing Trends," *Small Business Reports,* November 1994, 62–63; Michael Hitt, Barbara Keats, Herbert Harback, and Robert Nixon, "Rightsizing," *Organizational Dynamics* 23, no. 2 (1994): 18.

[42] "Training Investments Pay Off for Downsized Companies," *HR Focus* 72, no. 2 (1995): 20; Louis Uchitelle, "We're Leaner, Meaner, and Going Nowhere Faster," *New York Times,* May 12, 1996, E1.

Some believe that firm downsizing has failed to produce the expected gains in productivity. Companies that expanded both employment and productivity were as critical to growth in productivity in the 1980s as those that increased productivity by cutting employment. Smaller manufacturers have lower rates of productivity because of their limited economies of scale, lower rates of capital investment, lesser managerial capacities, and more limited human resources.[43] The American Management Association reported considerable downsizing in 1994 but limited evidence of gains in productivity: only one-third of the sampled companies experienced productivity growth, but for another third productivity actually dropped with downsizing. Only half of the companies' profits went up with downsizing, and employee morale dropped in 83 percent of the cases.[44]

High-performance workplace advocates worry that neglecting human-resource investment will dampen productivity. Although the United States continues to lead in productivity growth, Japan has higher productivity than the United States in key export sectors such as machinery, electrical engineering, and transport equipment. The U.S. lead is least impressive in advanced manufacturing sectors such as steel, autos, consumer electronics, auto parts, and metalworking; thus, aggregate figures may mask threats to the United States in key sectors.[45] Some charge that the rate of growth in productivity in the 1990s actually remains comparable to the languid performance of the prior two decades. The Council on Competitiveness reported that inadequate training programs were partially responsible for low growth in productivity.[46] Although the United States still has a higher GDP per capita than other advanced nations, Freeman argues that its advantage narrows when evaluated per worker and declines even more when one factors in that Americans work more hours. Hourly productivity is actually fairly constant across advanced industrialized nations, and a slower hourly productivity growth will eventually make the United States fall behind.[47]

[43] Martin Bailey, John Haltiwanger, and Eric Bartelsman, "Downsizing and Productivity Growth: Myth or Reality?" Working Paper No. 4741 (Cambridge: National Bureau of Economic Research, May 1994); Eric Oldsman, "Does Manufacturing Extension Matter?" *Research Policy* 25 (1996): 215–32; Daniel Luria, "Toward Lean or Rich?" paper produced for the conference "Manufacturing Modernization," Atlanta, September 11–12, 1996.

[44] The Editor, "Corporate Surveys Can't Find a Productivity Revolution, Either," *Challenge* 38, no. 6 (1995): 31–32.

[45] McKinsey Global Institute, *Service Sector Productivity*, 1–9; McKinsey Global Institute, *Manufacturing Productivity*, 1–6.

[46] Council on Competitiveness, "Analysis of US Competitiveness Problems," in *America's Competitive Crisis* (Washington, D.C.: Council on Competitiveness, April 1987); Oliner and Wascher, "Productivity Revolution," 18–30.

[47] Richard Freeman, "How Labor Fares in Advanced Economies," in *Working under Different Rules*, 9–10.

In addition, it is not clear that laissez-faire policies have contributed to an improved economy in other countries; for example, the European easing of restrictions on layoffs has had few ramifications and did not prevent recession in the early 1990s. Relaxing severance laws did not shorten the period before individuals were reemployed, one measure of flexibility. Nor do severance requirements seem to affect firms' adjustments to changing market conditions; many European countries use a reduction in hours instead of a cut in workers to adjust to less market demand.[48] Reduced social spending has had a similarly disappointing effect on flexibility: although income maintenance programs may create disincentives for the acquisition of skills, spending on active labor market policies is positively correlated with both improved skills and employment.[49] Glyn and Miliband's empirical examination of the gains of the laissez-faire 1980s suggests that the popular notion of a trade-off between equality and efficiency is wrongheaded and that equality may be more efficient than inequality.[50]

There seem to be trade-offs with both the European and U.S. models. The United States has been successful in preventing "Eurosclerosis," the high rates of unemployment that have plagued European countries. But Eurosclerosis is only one kind of problem; the choices made in the United States have produced an abundance of jobs (but too many of the low-paying variant), no increases in real wages, and waste and confusion in systems of social provision.[51] In addition, the deficit in human capital may inhibit our ability to move into manufacturing sectors requiring highly skilled workers.[52] An undersupply of skilled workers and downsizing can curb industrial restructuring, which in turn checks further job creation. Old semiskilled manufacturing jobs are in decline: once constituting almost a third of total jobs in America, their portion fell to only 15 percent by the 1990s. Few new jobs today (only 11 percent in 1988–93) are in industries with above-average earnings.[53]

[48] Blank, "Larger Social Safety Net," 162; Katharine Abrahm and Susan Houseman, "Does Employment Protection Inhibit Labor Market Flexibility?" in *Social Protection versus Economic Flexibility,* ed. Rebecca Blank (Chicago: University of Chicago Press, 1994), 68, 88.

[49] Egon Matzner, "Policies, Institutions, and Employment Performance," in Matzner and Streeck, *Beyond Keynesianism,* 242–43.

[50] Andrew Glyn and David Miliband, *Paying for Inequality* (London: IPPR/Rivers Oram Press, 1994), 2, 8; Baily, Burtless, and Litan, *Growth with Equity.*

[51] Roy B. Helfgott, "Labor Market Models in Europe and America—and Unhappiness with Both Labor Market Characteristics and Some Possible Solutions," *Business Horizons,* March 1996, 77.

[52] Michael Hitt and Robert Hoskisson, "Human Capital and Strategic Competitiveness in the 1990s," *Journal of Management Development* 13, no. 1 (1994): 35–46.

[53] Carnevale, "American Workers and Economic Change," 7.

Another downside of American public policy may be its impact on social peace: flexibility heightens workers' insecurity and discontent. Wages have been essentially flat for the past few decades. The economy today offers a growing premium on skills, or monetary reward to workers for certain kinds of competencies, that is widening the wage gap between well-compensated and poorly paid workers. Inadequate training institutions contribute to discontent by limiting growth in workers' compensation.[54] Nonwage components of total compensation such as health care have claimed an ever larger proportion of total pay and have eaten away at purchasing power. Downsizing and outsourcing contribute to social instability by changing the pattern of social provision for the middle class. Middle-class jobs are disappearing, and the vacuum at the center is good neither for political stability nor economic well-being.[55] Where gross domestic product (adjusted for inflation) grew at 4 percent in the 1950s and 4.4 percent in the 1960s, it dropped to 2.8 percent by the 1980s. The index of social health, a measure of sixteen different social problems, dipped to its fourth lowest point in the past quarter century in 1993.[56] Few are safe from economic anxiety in America today.[57]

The worsening condition of the working person fuels concerns about political stability. As the meteoric rise of Pat Buchanan suggests, if the revolution comes, it may come from the trailer parks and pickup trucks of the Ross Perot voters—the semiskilled workers who have lost big time in the global fight and flight. Regardless of what one thinks of Perot, his "giant sucking sound" aphorism struck a respondent cord in the hearts of many Americans.

Conclusion

At least some business managers believe that America's survival as a nation in the evolving postindustrial economy may depend on radically dif-

[54] A decline in the real earnings of workers has occurred only in the United States and reflected the inability of U.S. workers to meet the increasing demand for skills. Richard Freeman and Lawrence Katz, "Rising Wage Inequality," in Freeman, *Working under Different Rules,* 30–31; Lawrence Katz and Kevin Murphy, "Changes in Relative Wages, 1963–1987," *Quarterly Journal of Economics* 107, no. 1 (1992): 35–78; Sheldon Danziger and Peter Gottschalk, *Uneven Tides* (New York: Russell Sage Foundation, 1993), 11–12. For a critique of this argument see David Howell, "The Skills Myth," *American Prospect,* summer 1994, 81–90.

[55] Maury Gittleman and David Howell; "Salaried Workers Are Targets of Corporate Downsizing," *HR Focus* 71, no. 6 (1994): 21.

[56] Louis Uchitelle, "It's a Slow-Growth Economy, Stupid," *New York Times,* March 17, 1996, E5; "W.S. Social-Health Index Dips, Scientists Say," *New York Times,* October 15, 1995, 34.

[57] Katherine Newman, *Declining Futures* (New York: Russell Sage Foundation, 1993).

ferent human capital investment policies. These managers believe in rationalizing, targeting, and often expanding social spending by governments and/or firms in order to develop the competent, productive workforce necessary to knowledge-intensive, high-tech production. Yet their system of political representation makes it difficult for large employers to take action toward realizing their interests.

Those who believe that government intervention only disrupts the natural workings of the market are delighted with these limits to the expansion of policy. The American model is enjoying a popularity reminiscent of its heyday in the 1960s. The Japanese miracle was revealed as mirage when the Asian stock market collapsed as dramatically as the Berlin Wall. Welfare states are under attack in European strongholds of social democracy.

High-performance workplace advocates are more gloomy about our economic prospects. In their view sustained growth depends on government policy to ensure long-term investments in human capital. A decade ago, business scholars began to worry about companies' short-term perspective in economic investment.[58] Many believe that a similar short-term perspective may constrain business managers' perceptions of where their true interests lie in the area of human capital investment.[59] The economic debate is one that cannot be settled here, but it is my hope that the description of the political processes at play in these conflicts over policies to promote human capital investment will educate participants on both sides.

This book is not a plea for a more centrist politics; indeed, from a policymaker's point of view, cultivating business might be seen as something of a trap. Cultivating corporate allies has high costs for reformers and represents something of a Hobson's choice: policy arrived at through the mobilization of business acquires conservative hues. Large employers refuse even to consider certain types of solutions and do little to push for the measures that they favor. A range of alternatives are simply left off the table, and when politicians fix themselves squarely in the center expecting corporate aid, managers are nowhere to be found. A strategy to mobilize business works within the constraints of class, money, and power distributions and gives a decidedly conservative tinge to policy outcomes. There is also a fundamental conflict between two goals, addressing the needs of the truly poor and intervening to help the lower working class. Social interventions designed to further economic growth may have little to offer those outside of the mainstream market economy or to

[58] Steven Wheelwright and Robert Hayes, "Competing through Manufacturing," *Harvard Business Review* 63, no. 1 (1885): 99–109.
[59] Interviews with industry respondents, 1992–97.

contribute to the goals of distributional equity that command much interest in the welfare state.[60]

But the book is also not a condemnation of business managers who are struggling to contribute to public policy on both sides of the debates. They deserve to be viewed as social actors with more complicated motivations than they are often credited with having. Indeed, these pages have tried to solve a paradox—why policymakers keep searching out business allies, why managers keep struggling to contribute, and how political structures thwart everyone's best intentions. That many business managers are ideologically open to broader national frameworks for investment in human capital, but organizationally incapable of doing much to advance national policy, explains why government actors work so hard at getting business approval and why they are frequently disappointed in the outcome. The U.S. policy process tends to solicit considerable corporate input without much commitment.

For those managers who seek to advance ideas of the high-performance workplace, political rejuvenation may depend on the revamping of the organizations that represent their interests. Much is made about divided government, but a similar fragmentation shapes corporate action. We live in a society with little space between left and right, but enormous institutional conflict in the private, as well as the public, sphere. Managers may decide that they must overcome this fragmentation in order to get what they want from government.

---

[60] Policies tied to economic adjustment often neglect society's have-nots. There is a tension between two equities—helping the very poor and helping the urban working class. Joan Nelson, "Poverty, Equity, and the Politics of Adjustment," in *The Politics of Economic Adjustment,* ed. Stephan Haggard and Robert Kaufman (Princeton: Princeton University Press, 1992), 221.

INDEX